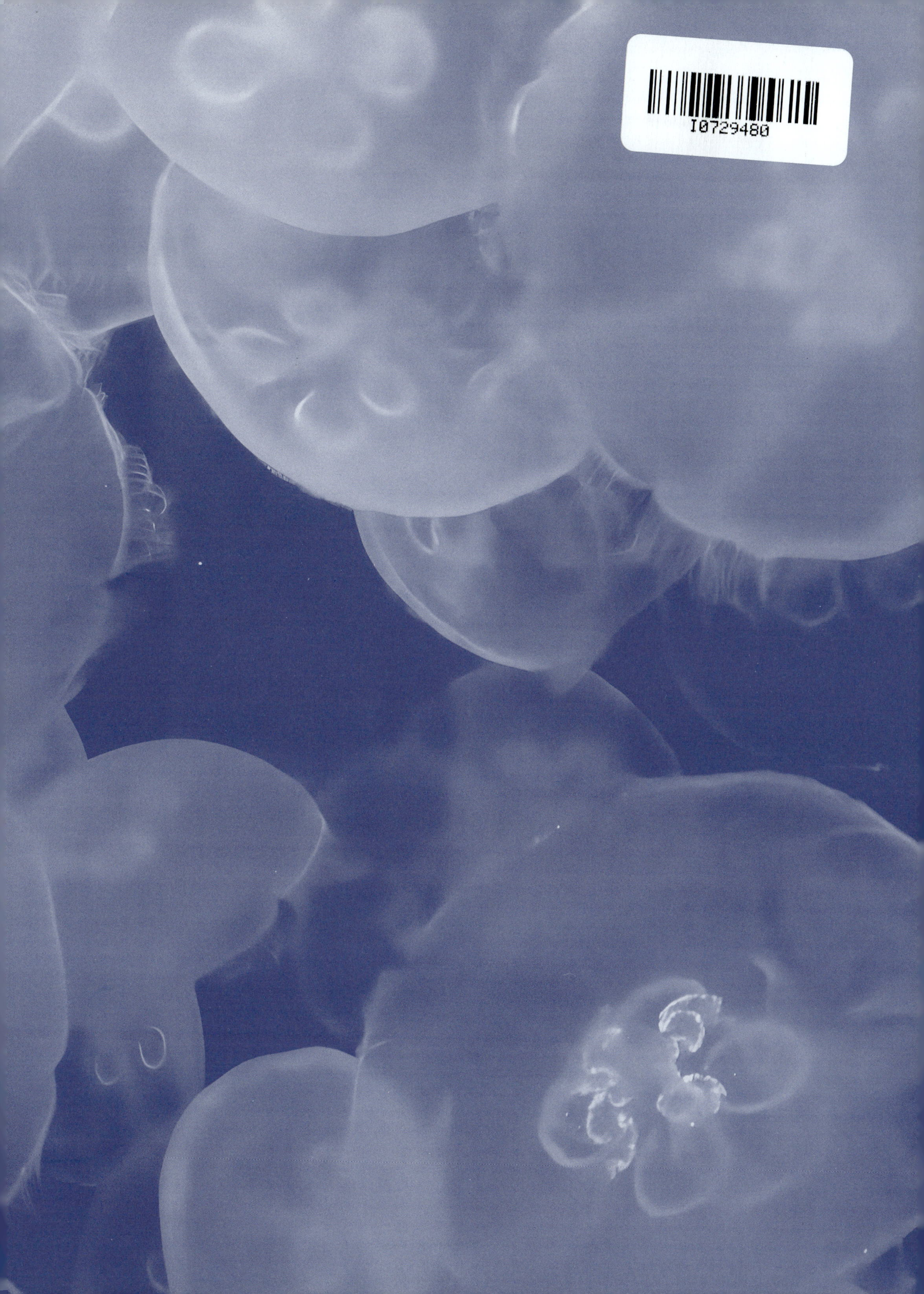

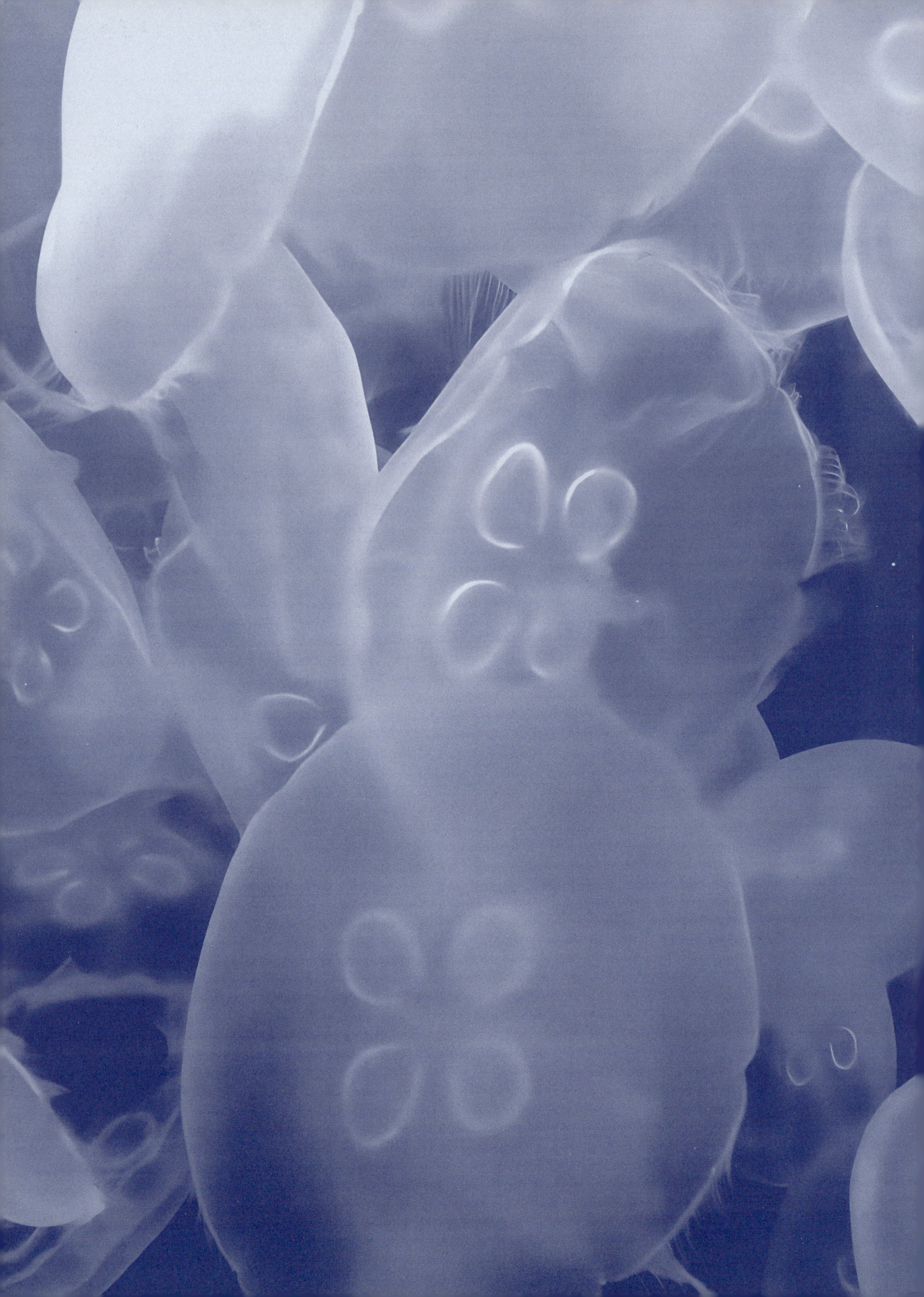

Shapeshifters

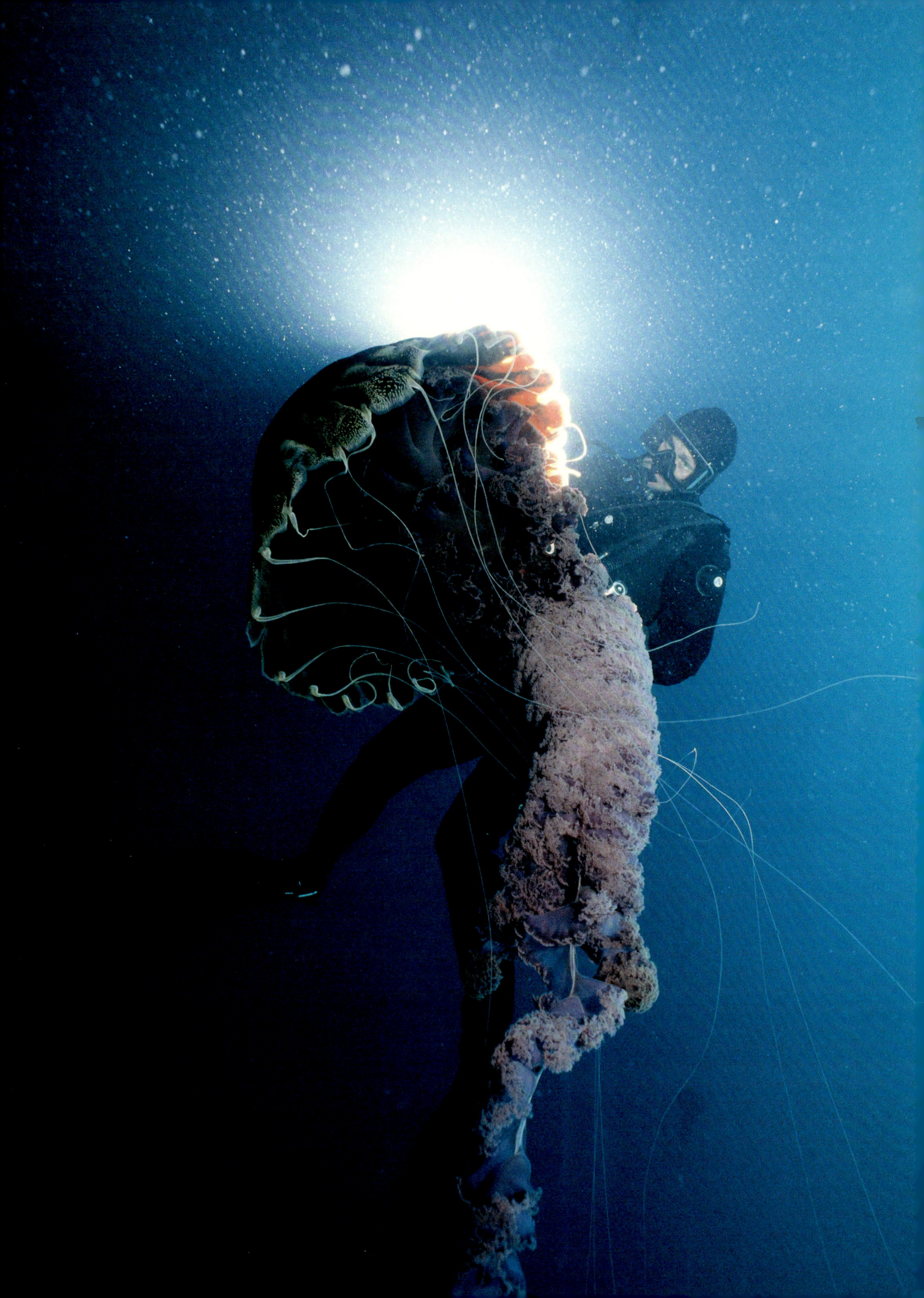

Shapeshifters

THE WONDROUS WORLD OF JELLYFISH

LISA-ANN GERSHWIN

ABRAMS, NEW YORK

Contents

Thriving Living Fossils

Jellyfish, jellies, medusae, quallen, and agua mala—regardless of what you call them, they instill fear and wonder in humans. They are slimy, cold, wet, and jiggly, lacking a brain or a heart or any sort of remorse when they sting us. Indeed, the world's most venomous animal is a jellyfish—this creature doesn't just sting; it kills its victims in as little as two minutes. The pain can be so intense that some say death would come as a relief.

Jellyfish, however, are as beguiling as they are dangerous. They are found in a dazzling array of colors, shapes, and sizes. They are distributed from the North Pole to the South Pole, from the surface to the deepest of the deep seas, and even in freshwater. Some are so delicate they shatter with the smallest disturbance to the water, while others are so appallingly tenacious they can withstand almost any temperature or salinity, starvation, or even being chopped into bits. Some are biologically immortal.

Academic and amateur study of natural history has been dominated by charismatic megafauna, that is, creatures with fur and feathers, plus frogs. Jellyfish have been virtually ignored for hundreds of years. However, they are now enjoying something of a renaissance. This, one might argue, is because jellyfish have become so bothersome that they are demanding our attention.

Increasingly, many people are noticing larger blooms of jellyfish in areas impacted by humans. Overfishing, pollution, climate change, and many other types of disturbance to coastal habitats are stimulating some species of jellyfish to bloom into superabundances, where they wreak unimaginable havoc. Industries from aquaculture to

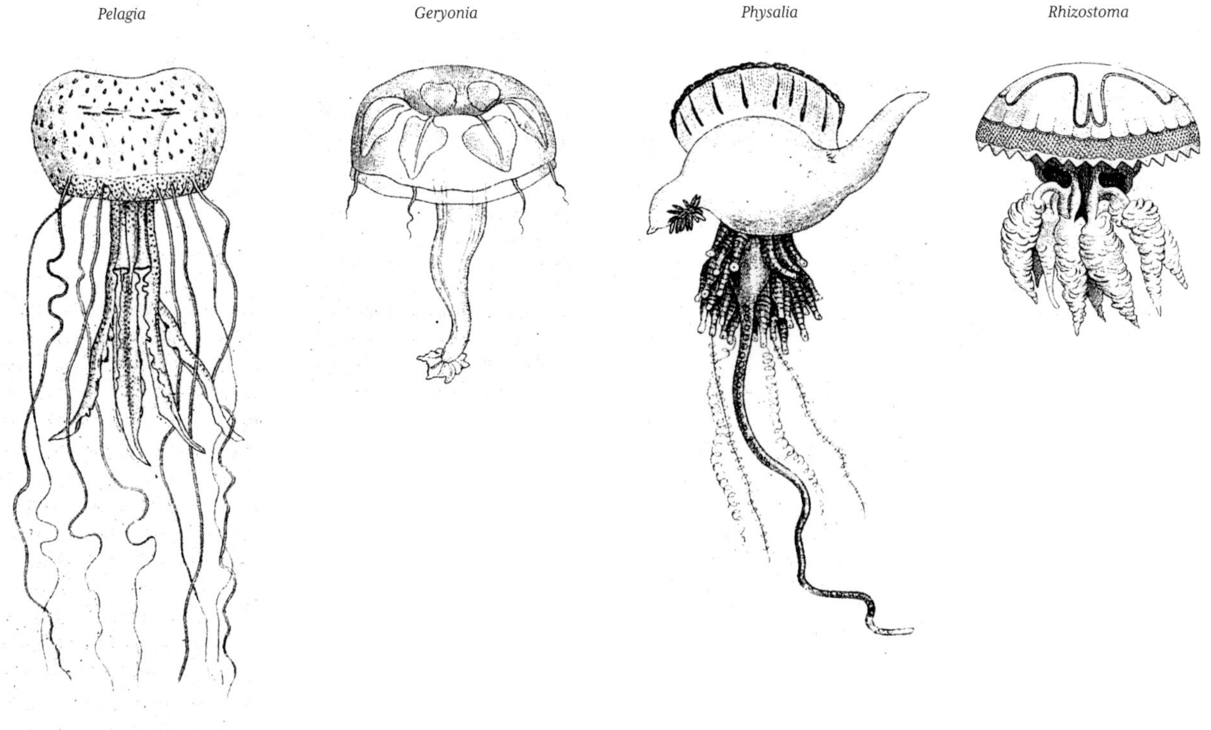

power plants, from shipping, to tourism the world over are cursing the losses they incur because of jellyfish.

But while some are shaking their fists in anger, others are smiling all the way to the bank. Jellyfish are now being commercially harvested and used in a range of products, including thickeners for caramel candies, fat-free substitutes in baked goods, potato-chip-like snacks, a super-growth fertilizer for rice, super-absorbent paper towels and sanitary products, and as a delicacy in many Asian cuisines.

With this attention on jellyfish problems and opportunities, their fascinating biology and ecology are receiving more interest too. People want to understand these mysterious alien beings. One of their least-told secrets is how these living fossils have survived more than half a billion years of Earth's ever-changing history. Millions of other species have evolved and become extinct, some have grown legs or bones or feathers, or walked on land or learned to fly, but jellyfish haven't changed. They haven't needed to. What they do, and how they do it, works. They are so adaptable and so perfectly suited to changing environments they have outlived 99 percent of the species that have ever existed. And still they thrive.

In the pages that follow, we take a deep dive into the wondrous world of jellyfish, to explore these timeless organisms that are beautiful and deadly in equal measure. Some splendid, some strange, some poisonous, some with surprising secrets, and some barely known, but all amazing in their own way.

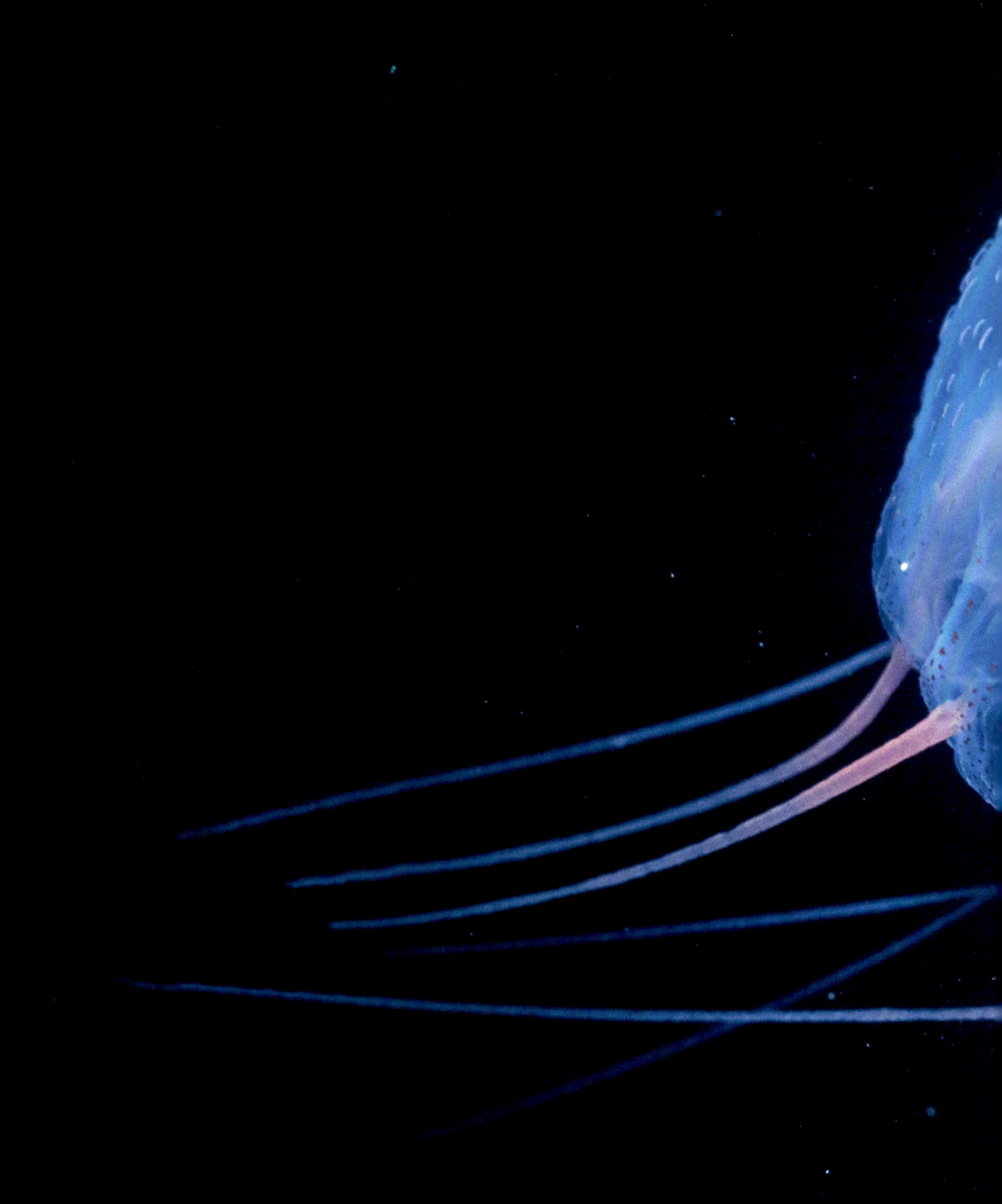

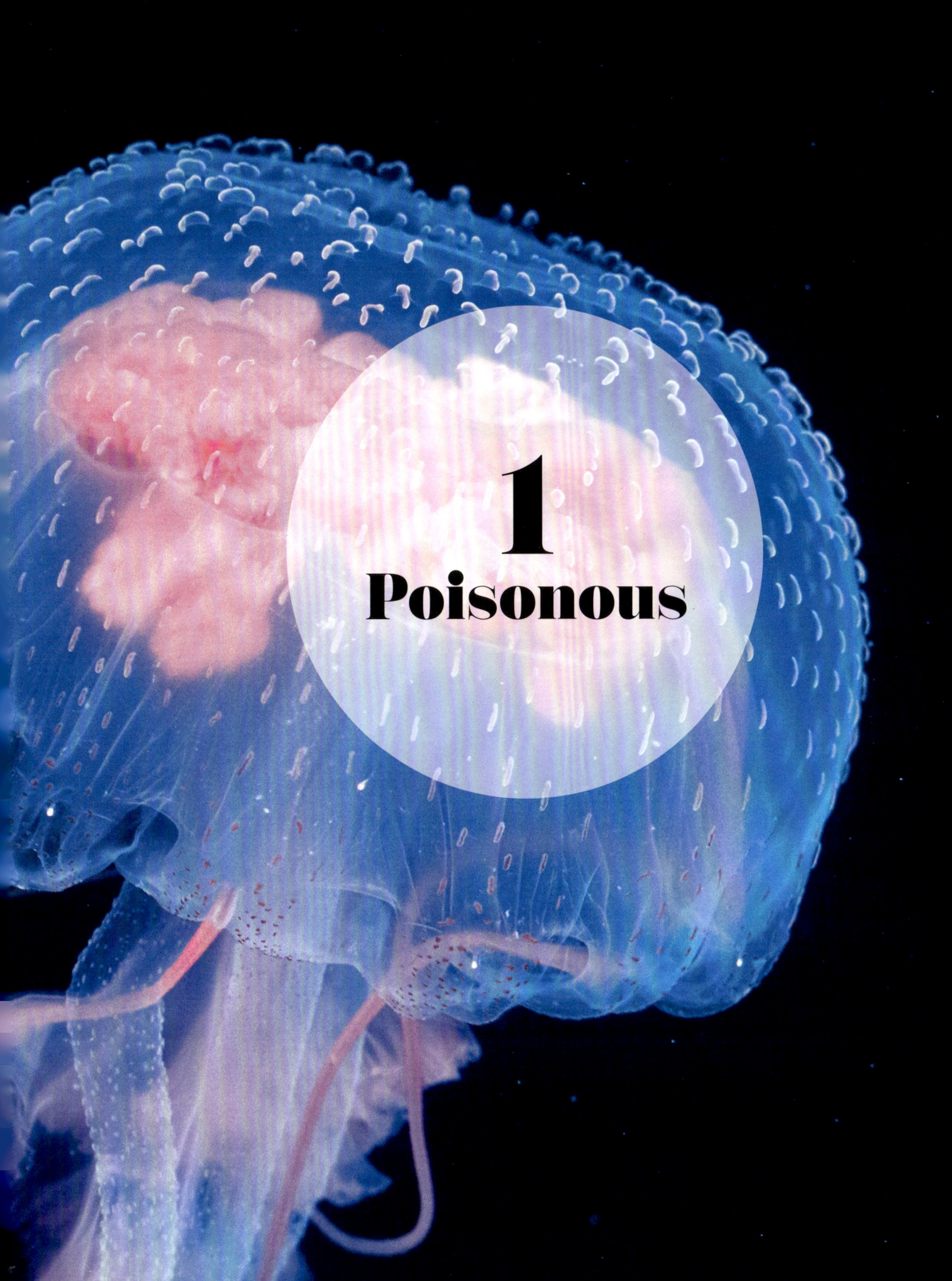

1
Poisonous

The cinematic theme of beauty and beast has played out in many fables. Typically, the fair maiden is repulsed by the monster, but eventually comes to see its gentler side. Jellyfish embody both sides of this duality, being simultaneously fair maiden and monster, mesmerizingly beautiful and yet frighteningly dangerous.

When most people think of jellyfish, they associate these creatures with pain and poison. For those who look past their monstrous side, however, jellyfish present a never-ending supply of delight and amazement.

In this chapter, we look at some of the world's most venomous animals. In some cases, this provides fodder for our darkest nightmares. And, as we will see in the next chapter, this isn't the only monstrous effect of jellyfish. All jellyfish, like their brethren the corals, sea anemones, and sea fans, deliver their sting through minute hollow harpoons. It's like being jabbed with thousands of tiny, venom-filled hypodermic needles all at once.

Nematocysts, or stinging cells, are wondrous weapons. They consist of a very long thread and barb coiled up inside a microscopic capsule that has a hair trigger (known as a cnidocil) at one end. Nematocysts are arranged along the tentacles and body of the jellyfish with the hair trigger pointing outward. So, if you brush against a jellyfish, then, wham!—the sting is automatic and instant. It fires at a force of

40,000 Gs—that's 40,000 times the force of gravity, or about half the acceleration force of a bullet fired from a gun—making it the fastest process known in the animal kingdom.

The venom of some jellyfish species enters the body through the tip of the harpoon, while in others it may flood through many pores along the thread. Regardless, the nematocyst has but one purpose: to poison and repulse predators, prey, and threats of any kind.

Intriguingly, all jellyfish sting . . . except one, the lagoon jellyfish (*Mastigias papua*, see page 74). This jellyfish is believed to have lost the ability to sting because of its unique predator-less and prey-less lifestyle. The stings of other species of jellyfish do not cause pain because either the venom is too weak, or the threads are too short to penetrate deep into the skin. Many species, however, cause painful welts or itchy rashes. Some, most notably the box jelly, Irukandji, and Portuguese man-of-war, have proven lethal. Scientists ponder why these are so venomous. Certainly, soft-bodied jellyfish need to quickly neutralize their thrashing, hard-bodied fishy or crabby prey. But in many cases, this is overkill. Most curious of all are the Irukandji, the sting of which produces a delayed "constellation" of debilitating symptoms. This delay appears to make no sense ecologically; it's just one of the many mysteries surrounding jellyfish.

Deadly Box Jellyfish

Chironex fleckeri

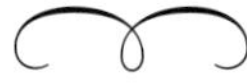

Imagine taking a cooling dip on a tropical summer's day.
And then the unthinkable happens—you are searingly
stung by the world's most venomous animal. Meet
Chironex fleckeri, the Australian deadly box jellyfish.
Those who are lucky will scar for life. The unluckier
ones will succumb to the venom and die within two
to four minutes as their heart locks in a contracted
state. *Chironex fleckeri* is an adept swimmer, capable
of sustaining four knots and skillfully navigating
mangroves and rocks in its normal habitat . . .
surprisingly, with well-developed eyes but without
a brain! It is common throughout tropical Australia in
the warmer months, while closely related (and equally
venomous!) species are found along shallow
coastlines throughout the Indo-Pacific.

SIZE: Bell diameter to 12 inches (30 cm)

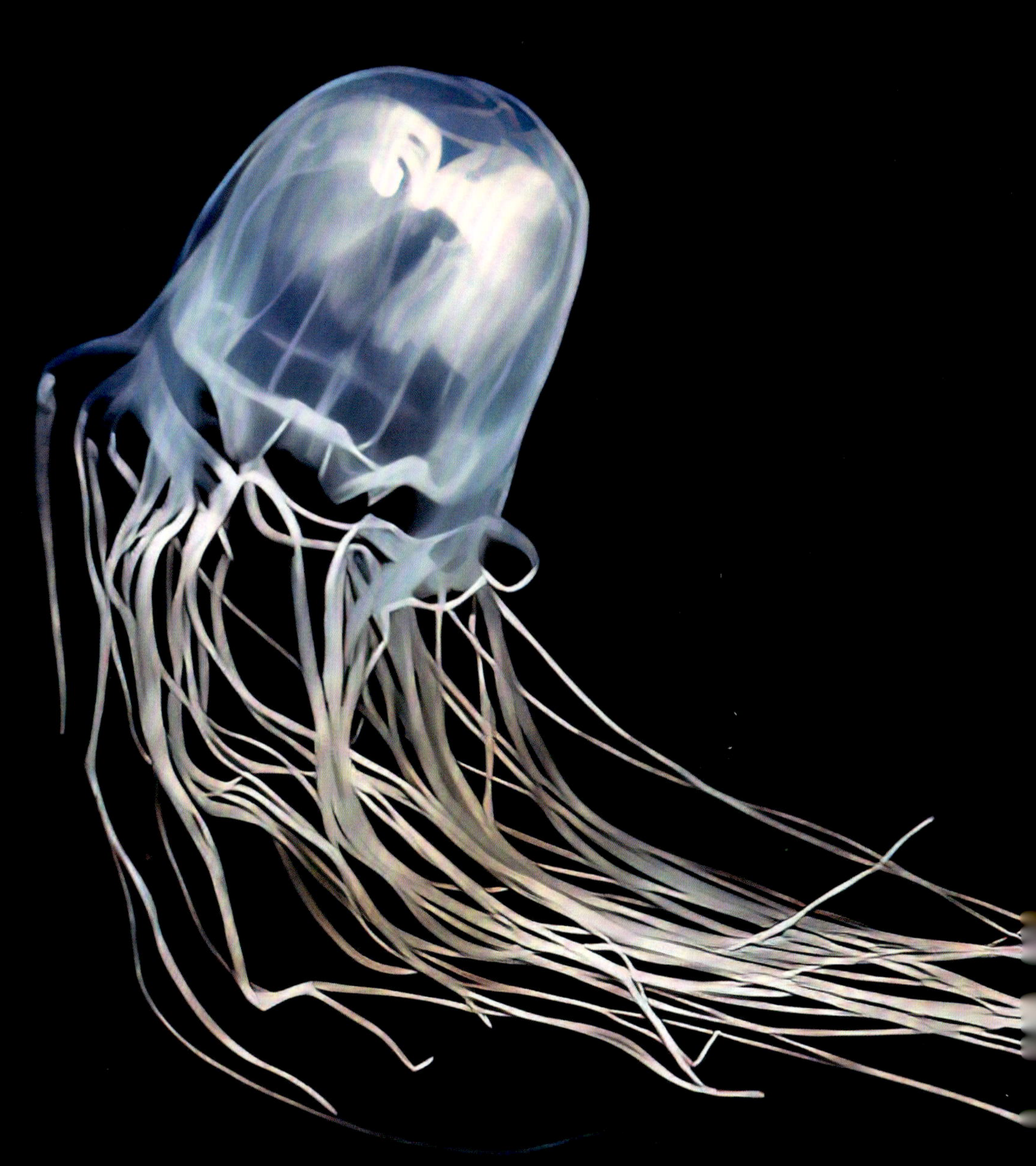

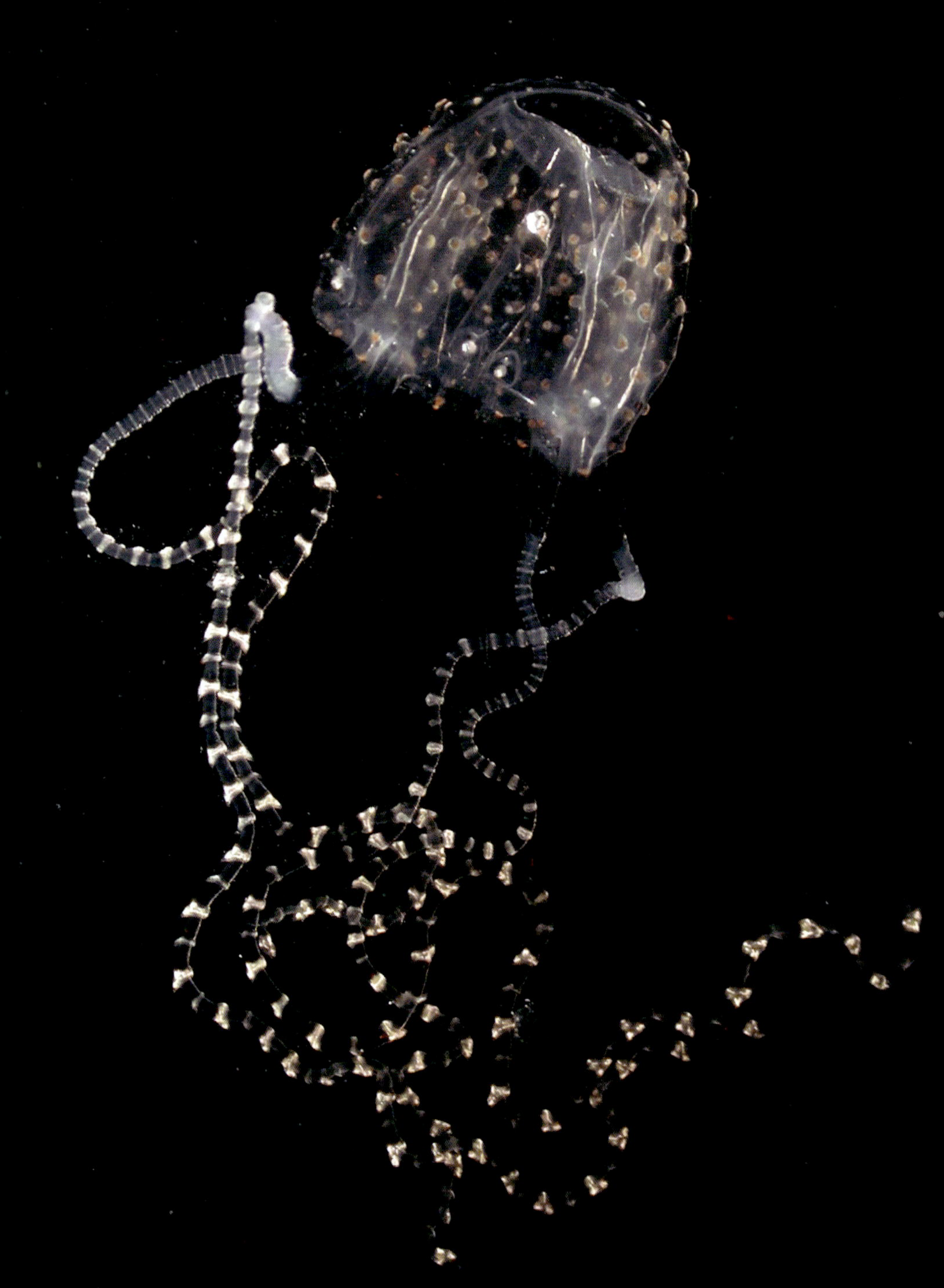

Irukandji

Carukia barnesi

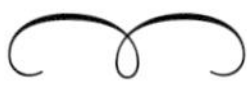

Once blamed on "invisible sea snakes," the illness caused by an Irukandji jellyfish sting is scarier than any Hollywood thriller . . . but it's real. Nausea. Vomiting. Difficulty breathing. Sweating. Heart failure. Brain hemorrhage. The most common Irukandji species, *Carukia barnesi*, is just a centimeter tall with four tentacles that are a hundred times its body length and as fine as cobwebs. Each tentacle is studded with peculiar neckerchief-shaped bands of stinging cells. Together, the sixteen known jellyfish species that cause Irukandji syndrome are found from Cape Cod in the United States and north Wales in the United Kingdom to Victoria and New South Wales in Australia, and are most common in tropical places such as Hawaii, Thailand, the Caribbean, and the Great Barrier Reef.

SIZE: Bell height to ⅜ inch (10 mm)

Portuguese Man-of-War

Physalia physalis

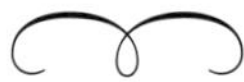

The Portuguese man-of-war, *Physalia physalis*, may
be the "Terror of the Atlantic," but it is also a most
intriguing paradox. Debate has raged among scientists
for more than a hundred years as to whether the man-of-
war is a colony (repeating groups of functionally distinct
zooids, or living units), or an individual—it has elements
of both and yet is not really either. Its body parts are
specialized to function separately, like a colony, and yet
they cannot function apart, like an individual. Each of
these parts, which are called "persons," cooperate for the
benefit of all. If you peer closely at a specimen to make up
your own mind, be careful: Its tentacles, said to reach
100 feet (30 m) in length, pack a lethal punch to
its prey . . . and sometimes to people too.

SIZE: Air bladder to 12 inches (30 cm) long

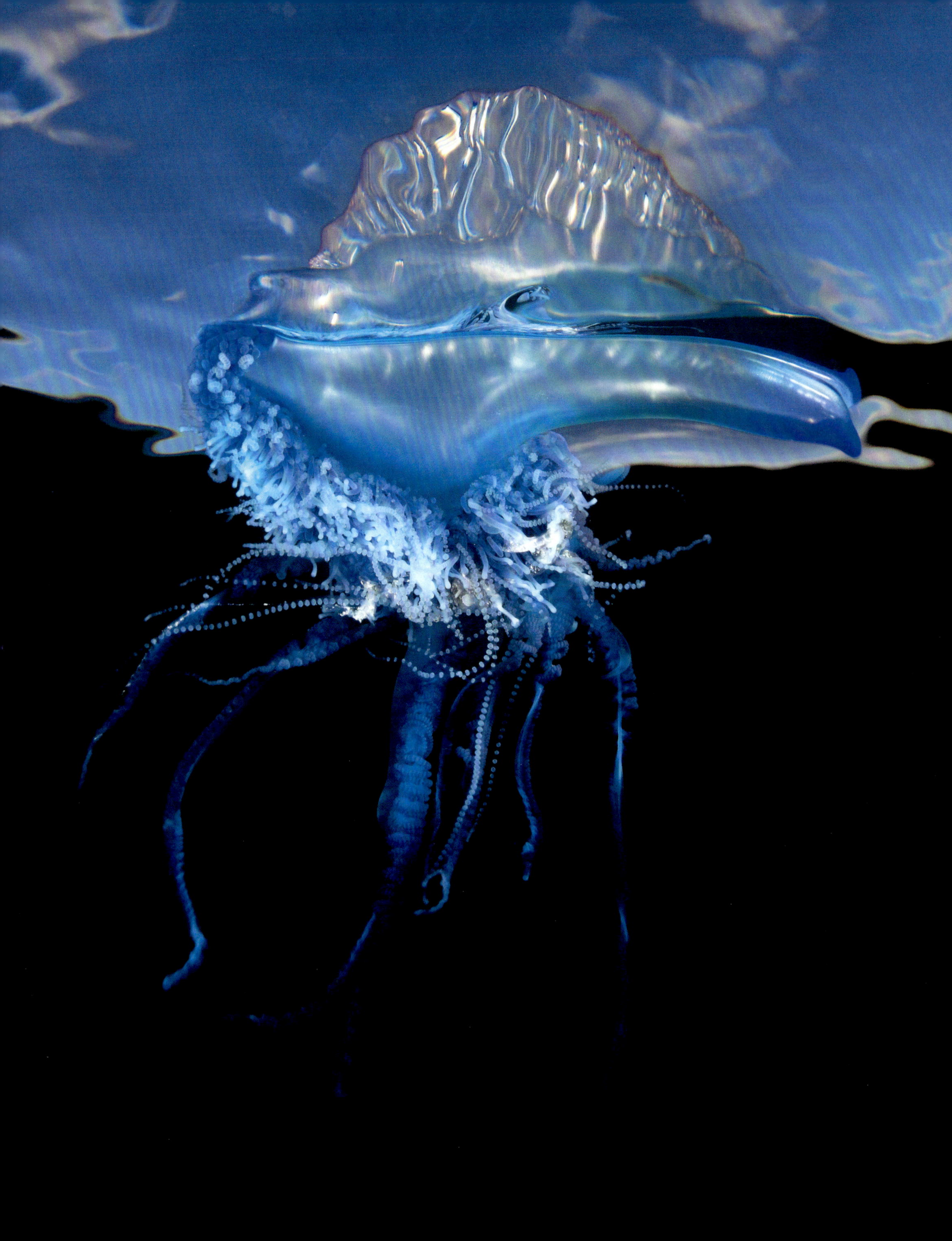

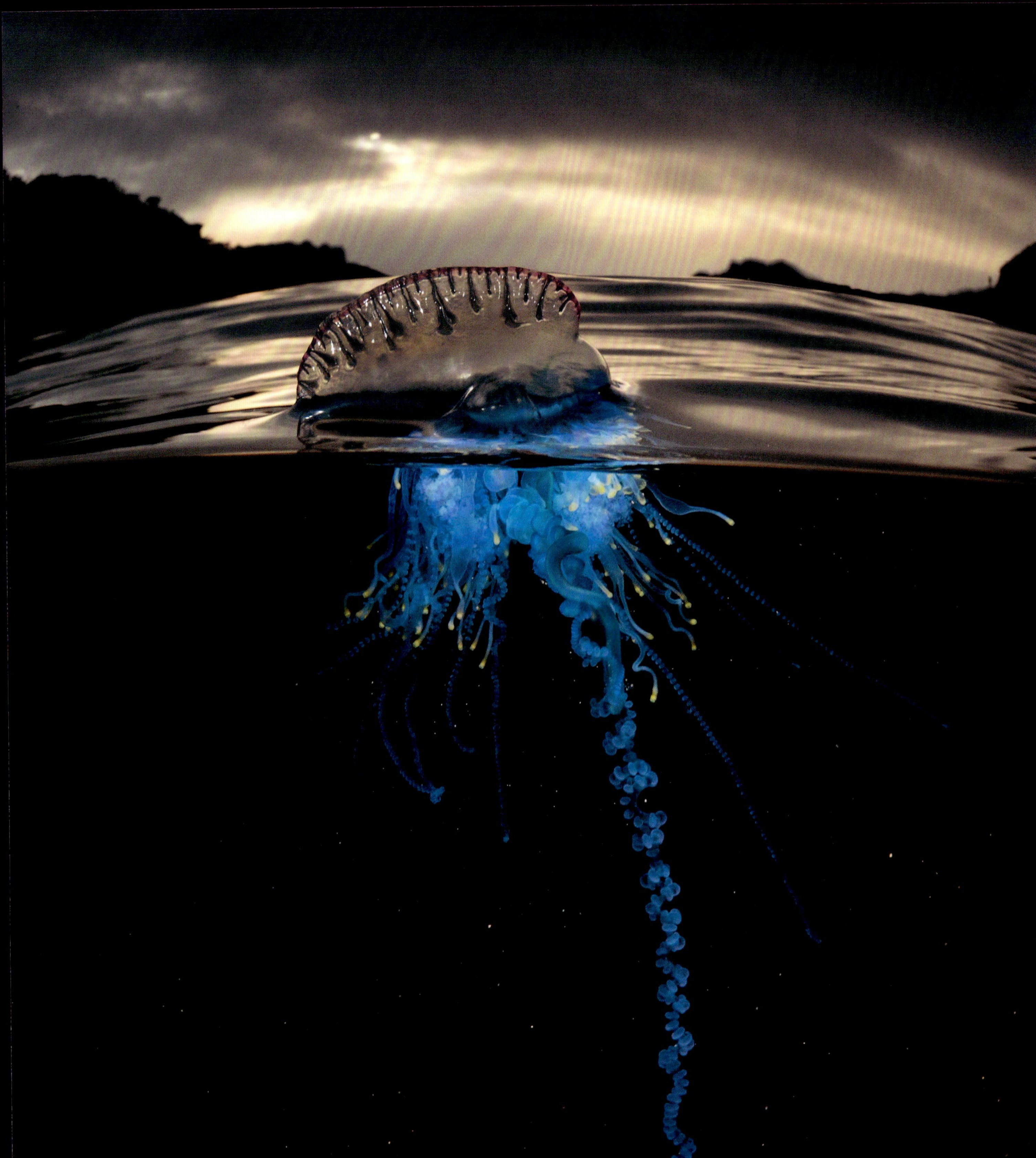

Bluebottle

Physalia utriculus

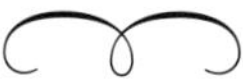

Diminutive compared to its Atlantic cousin
the Portuguese man-of-war, the Indo-Pacific bluebottle is
nonetheless a fearsome stinger. In Australia alone, they
can sting more than 40,000 people each year when vast
armadas of these passive drifters blow ashore. In some
cases, bluebottles can cause systemic illness similar to
Irukandji syndrome (see page 15). *Physalia utriculus* is easy
to avoid, being bright blue, but in doing so, most people
overlook some of the most marvelous organisms in the
ocean that travel with them, the pleuston. The pleuston
refers to a community of creatures that live at the air-
water interface, including the sea lizard (see *Glaucus
atlanticus*, page 190), the purple bubble snail, and
chondrophores (see *Porpita porpita* and
Velella velella, page 71 and 108, respectively).

SIZE: Air bladder to 3 inches (8 cm) long

Clinging Jellyfish

Gonionemus vertens

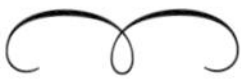

One of nature's most surprising venomous animals
is the clinging jellyfish, which is common in quiet
bays of the northern Pacific and Atlantic Oceans. This
demure, orange, lace-like jelly mostly whiles away its
time clinging to blades of algae and stalks of seagrass,
utterly harmless to humans. But in some populations,
such as in the northeastern United States and the east
coast of Russia, it packs an unexpected punch to the
unsuspecting and curious alike. A seemingly minor
contact with the tentacles—a touch to the finger or a mere
brush against the arm—can land a person in hospital
with severe muscle cramps and difficulty breathing.
The reason for these differences remains a mystery.

SIZE: Bell diameter to 1¼ inches (3 cm)

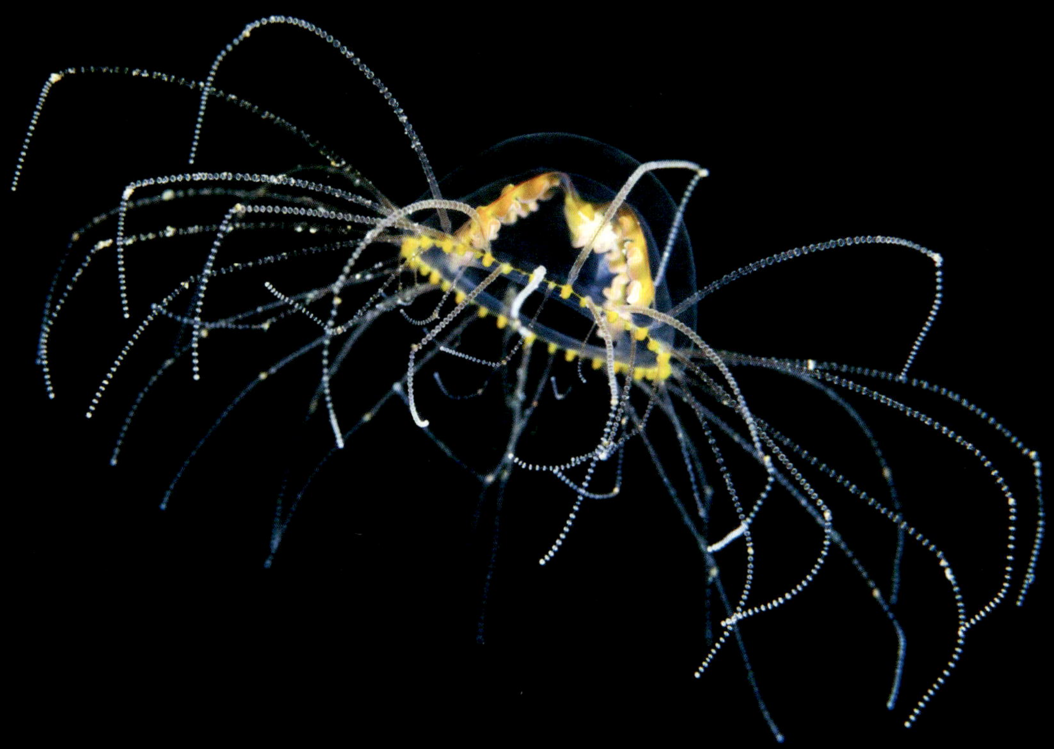

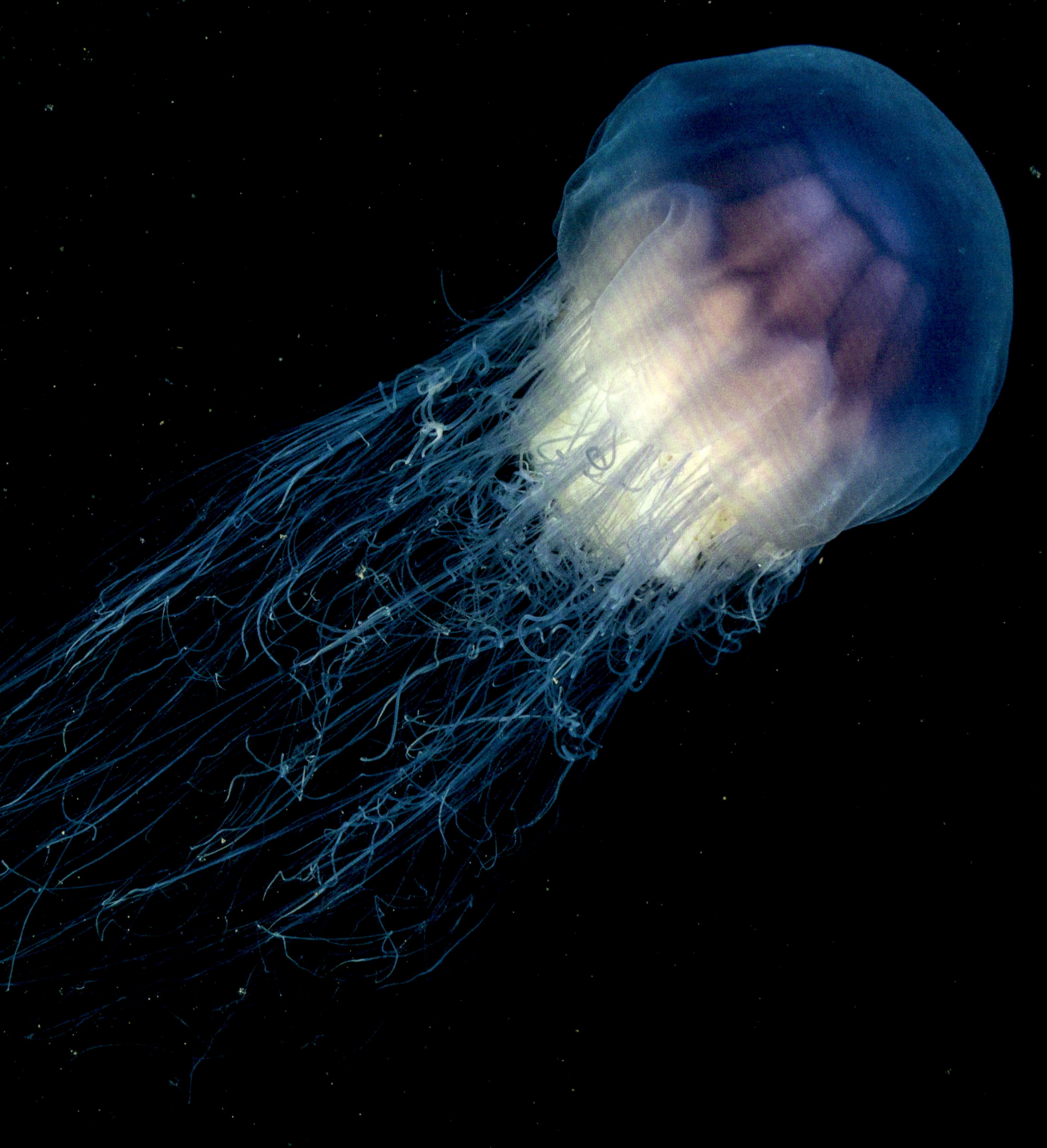

Bluefire Jelly

Cyanea lamarckii

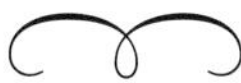

People with a fascination for murder mysteries may
wonder if these menacingly blue, wild-looking jellyfish
can be used as a weapon. Indeed, the legendary sleuth
Sherlock Holmes alluded to this question in the short
story "Adventure of the Lion's Mane." But literary license
aside, perhaps. All lion's mane jellies can sting.
And a closely related—and freakishly venomous—type
found in the Irish Sea delivers a sting that may be life
threatening, since victims may experience nausea,
cramps, and difficulty breathing. This raises the
question: what might it take, such as warmer waters
or a different food source, for other lion's manes,
such as the common bluefire jelly, to kill?

SIZE: Bell diameter to 12 inches (30 cm)

Long Stingy Stringy Thingy
Rhizophysa filiformis

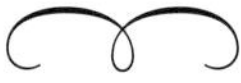

The long stingy stringy thingy may be one of
the most descriptive, accurate, and amusing common
names ever given to an animal. And this animal is one of
the most bizarre of all species in the ocean. It is a colony,
comprising a spherical or oval float atop a muscular stalk,
with many threads and baubles hanging from it, rather
like a cross between a Christmas tree and a mishmash of
spaghetti. It is common in the deep sea of all the world's
oceans, but sometimes drifts into shallower waters
like bays and harbors where it may be observed.
But you wouldn't want to touch this jelly,
for it packs a sharply painful sting.

SIZE: Colony length to at least 12 inches (30 cm)

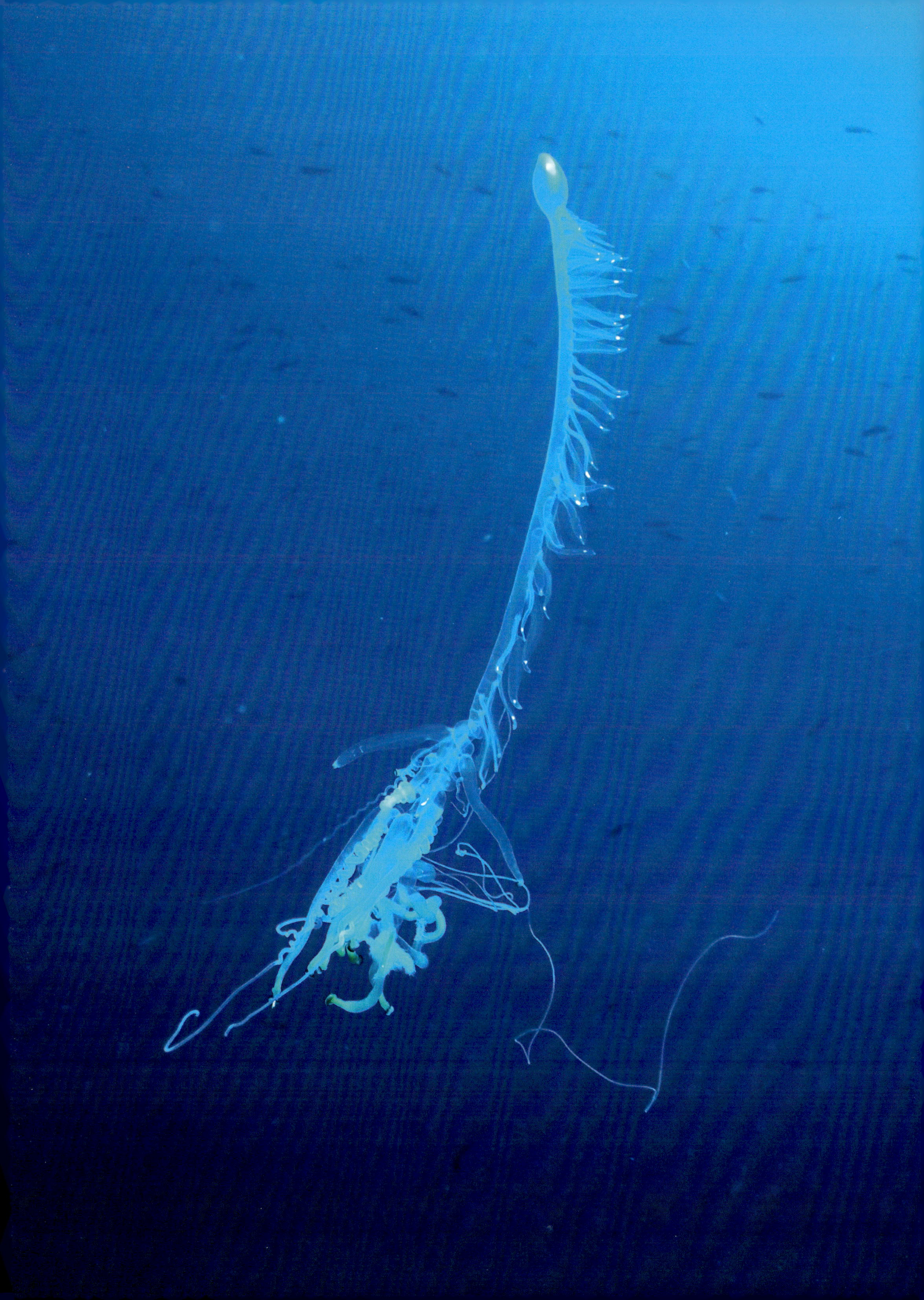

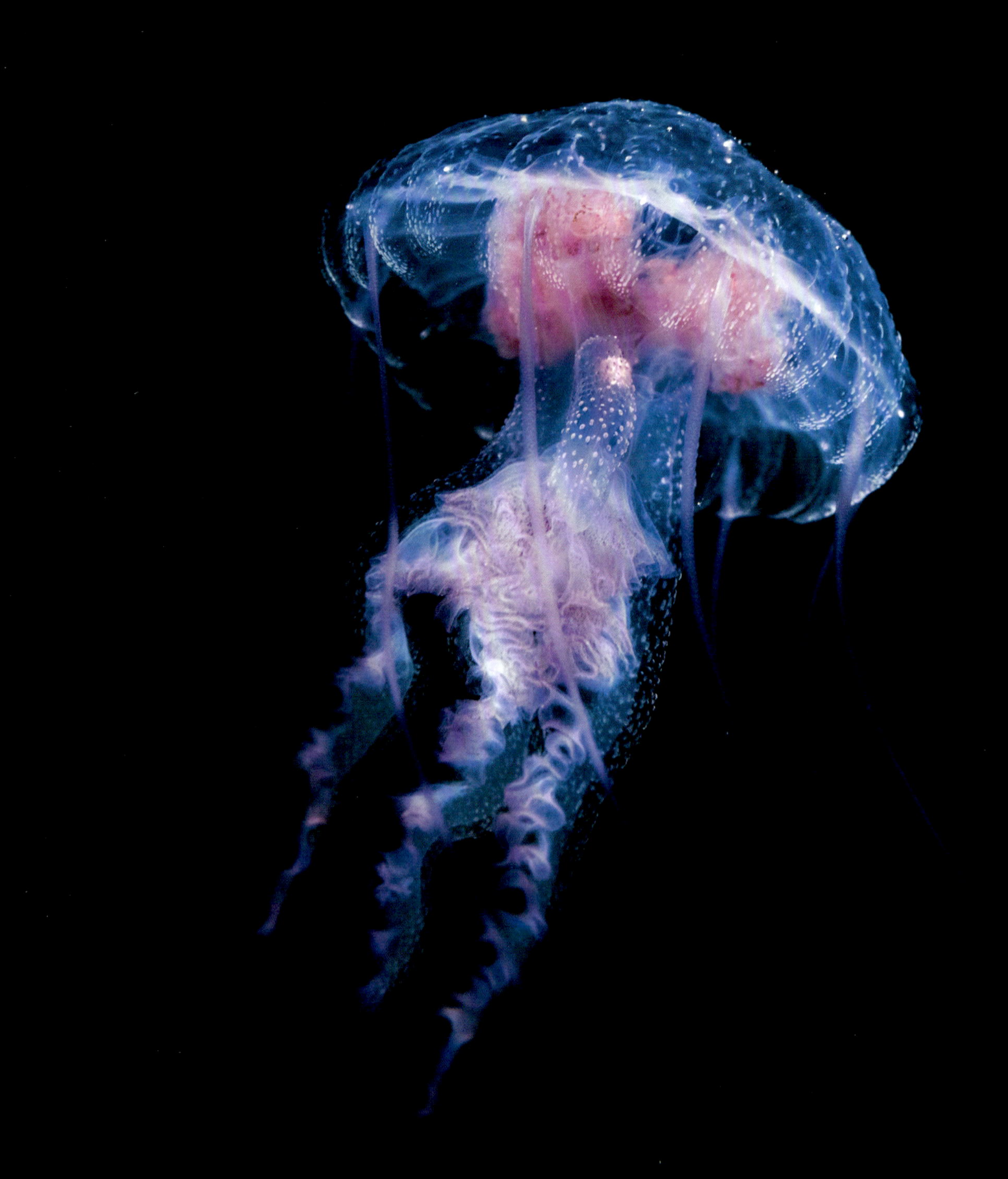

Purple People Eater

Pelagia noctiluca

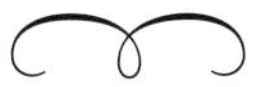

Boldly embodying the fascinating beautiful-but-deadly
duality of jellyfish, *Pelagia noctiluca* is often called the
mauve stinger. It is indeed purple, or mauve, and also a
stinger (but it doesn't eat people!). Watching its classic,
jellyfish-shaped, pulsating bell and flowing tentacles is
a mesmerizingly perfect antidote to stress. But don't be
fooled—this beautiful creature is dangerous. The sting
is sharply painful and in a few notable cases has caused
anaphylactic shock, which can prove fatal. It occurs in
vast blooms, which too frequently require the closure
of beaches along the French Riviera and in Spain's
Costa del Sol region, and it has killed millions of
farmed salmon in Ireland and Scotland.

SIZE: Bell diameter to 4¾ inches (12 cm)

Ballerina Stinger

Physophora hydrostatica

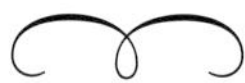

As the name suggests, this delightful species resembles a ballerina, with its upright body, skirt of pearlescent pink batons, and graceful tentacles hanging down. But beware—the pink batons pack a painful punch. The "body" of the colony is composed of several rows of swimming bells, or nectophores, which give it significant power of locomotion, plus a gas bubble, or pneumatophore, which holds the colony upright by floatation. This jellyfish dances an exquisite ballet of lunges and twirls as it swims. *Physophora hydrostatica* is common in all the world's open oceans, in shallow or deep water, and occasionally drifts into coastal locations where we may marvel at its strangeness and beauty, or cry in agony if we get too close.

SIZE: Colony length to 4¾ inches (12 cm)

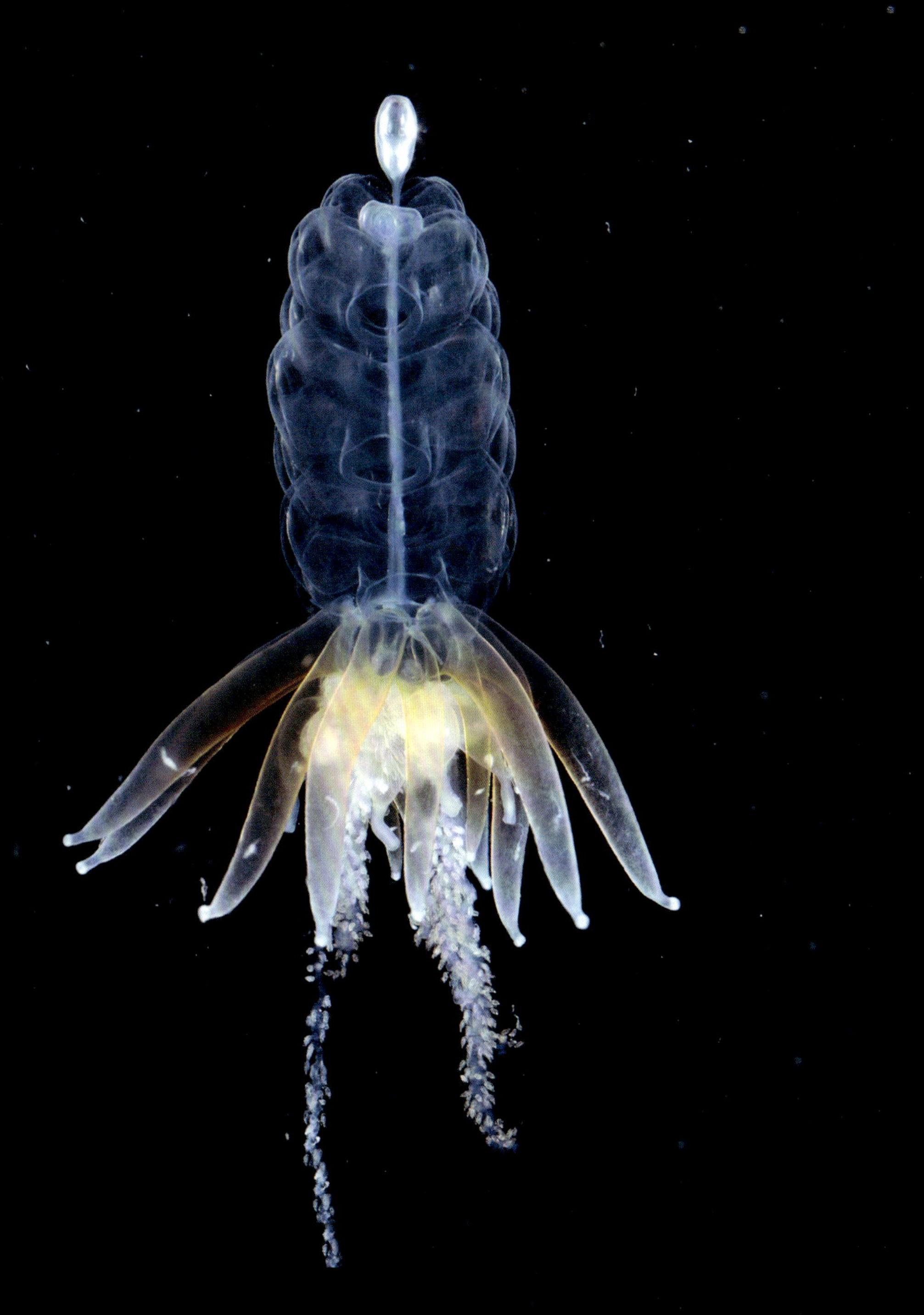

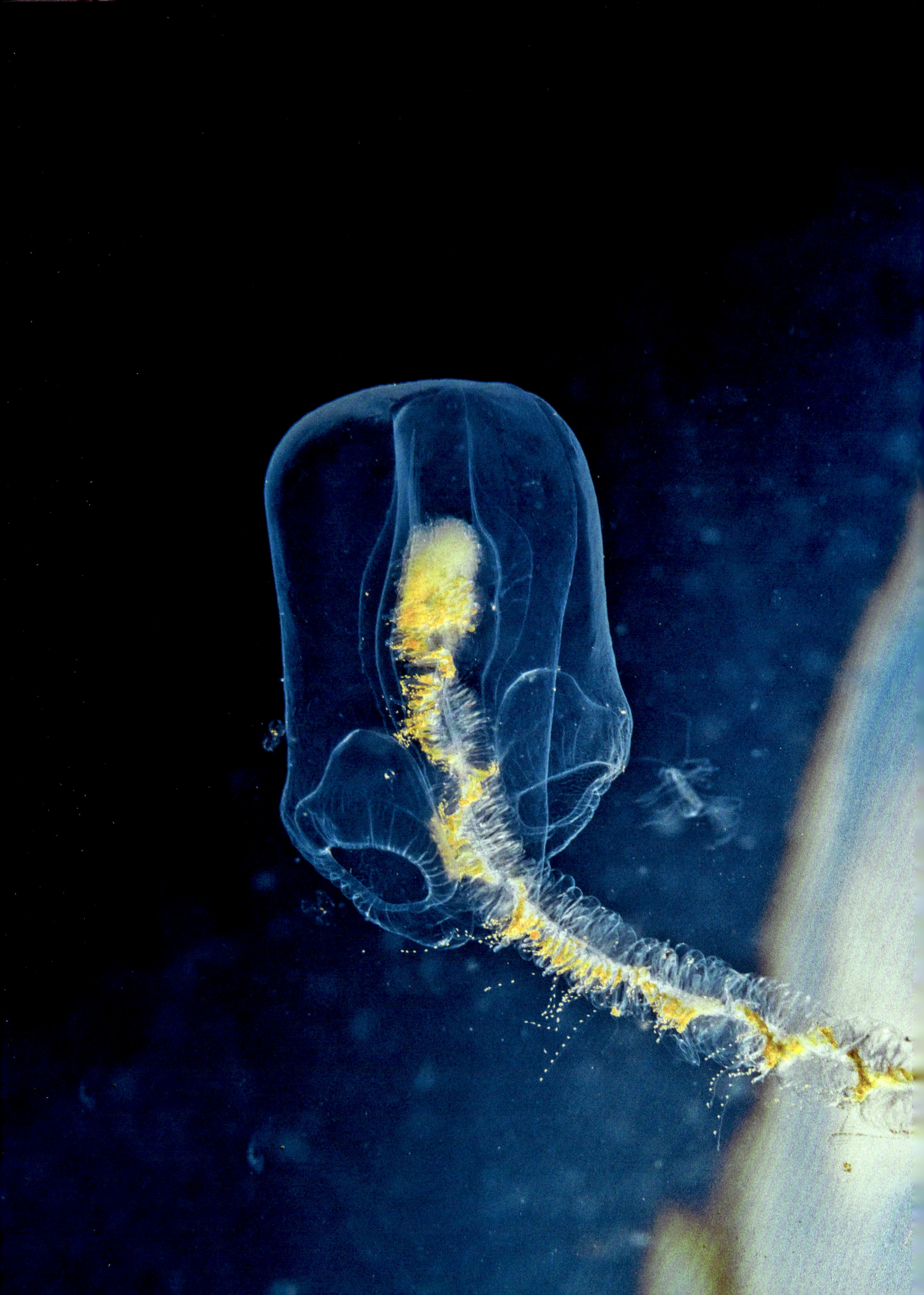

Giant Siphonophore

Praya dubia

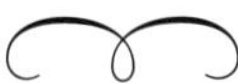

A strange-looking creature, *Praya dubia* has
a body composed of two lobes around a very long stem
of gelatinous, interlocking pieces, creating a broomstick-
width column. It is one of the world's largest organisms,
rivaling a blue whale in length, but is a mere thread in
comparison. Unlike the blue whale, however, *P. dubia* is
venomous. Its sting is a sharp zap, like an electric shock,
and can cause systemic symptoms, including breathing
problems and a rapid heartbeat. Also, weirdly, it kills
the surface of the skin, causing it to peel off like severe
sunburn or the shedding of a snake. Luckily, we are
unlikely to encounter *P. dubia*, since it lives in
the depths of the world's oceans.

SIZE: Colony length to 164 feet (50 m)

Thimble Jellyfish
Linuche unguiculata

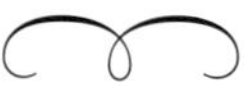

During spring and early summer, vast swarms of whimsically shaped, little brown thimble jellyfish drift into swimming areas throughout the Gulf of Mexico and Caribbean, creating misery. Seabather's eruption, as this bane of tropical swimmers is known, is an intensely itchy rash caused by exposure to *Linuche unguiculata*. Intriguingly, stings from the medusae are not the problem. Instead, the jellyfish and their microscopic larvae get caught under swimwear where they are crushed against the skin and discharge thousands of microscopic stinging cells, which cause the rash. A hot shower may sound like a soothing antidote, but freshwater just aggravates the reaction. The best protection from *L. unguiculata* is to wear as little as possible . . . or stay out of the water.

SIZE: Bell diameter to ¾ inch (20 mm)

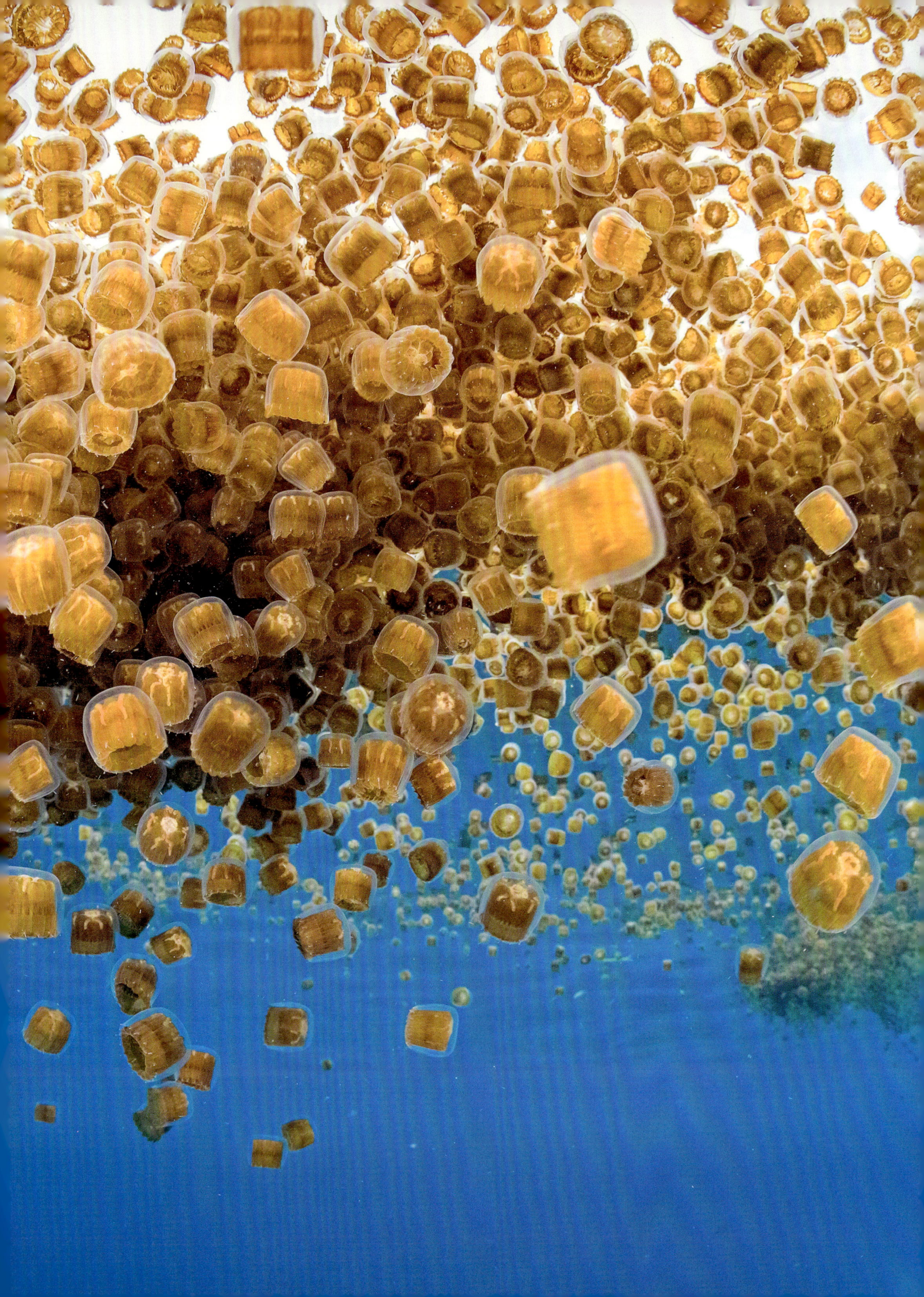

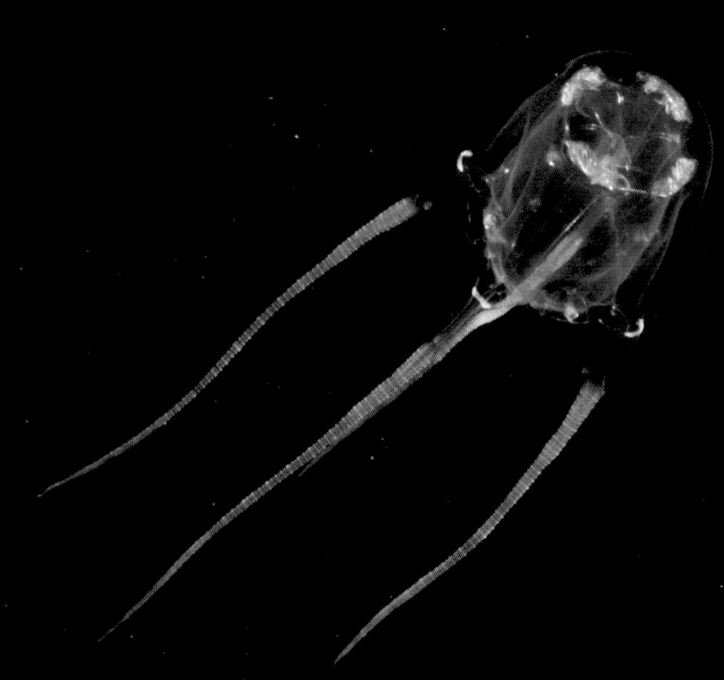

Jimble

Carybdea rastonii

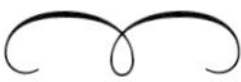

The jimble is a common type of box jellyfish found along southern Australian coastlines. It is one of the mildest of the box jellies, delivering a sharply painful sting to the skin, but, unlike some of its cousins, it does not appear to have potentially lethal properties. Its swarms, however, caused a great commotion leading up to the 2000 Sydney Olympics, threatening to derail the triathlon events. When not terrorizing Olympic organizers, the jimble uses its keen eyesight to swim in a vertically oblique pattern above the interface between sand and algal beds, hunting for food. Curiously, it is one of the few jellyfish that is more common in the winter than in the warmer conditions of summer.

SIZE: Bell height to 1¼ inches (3 cm)

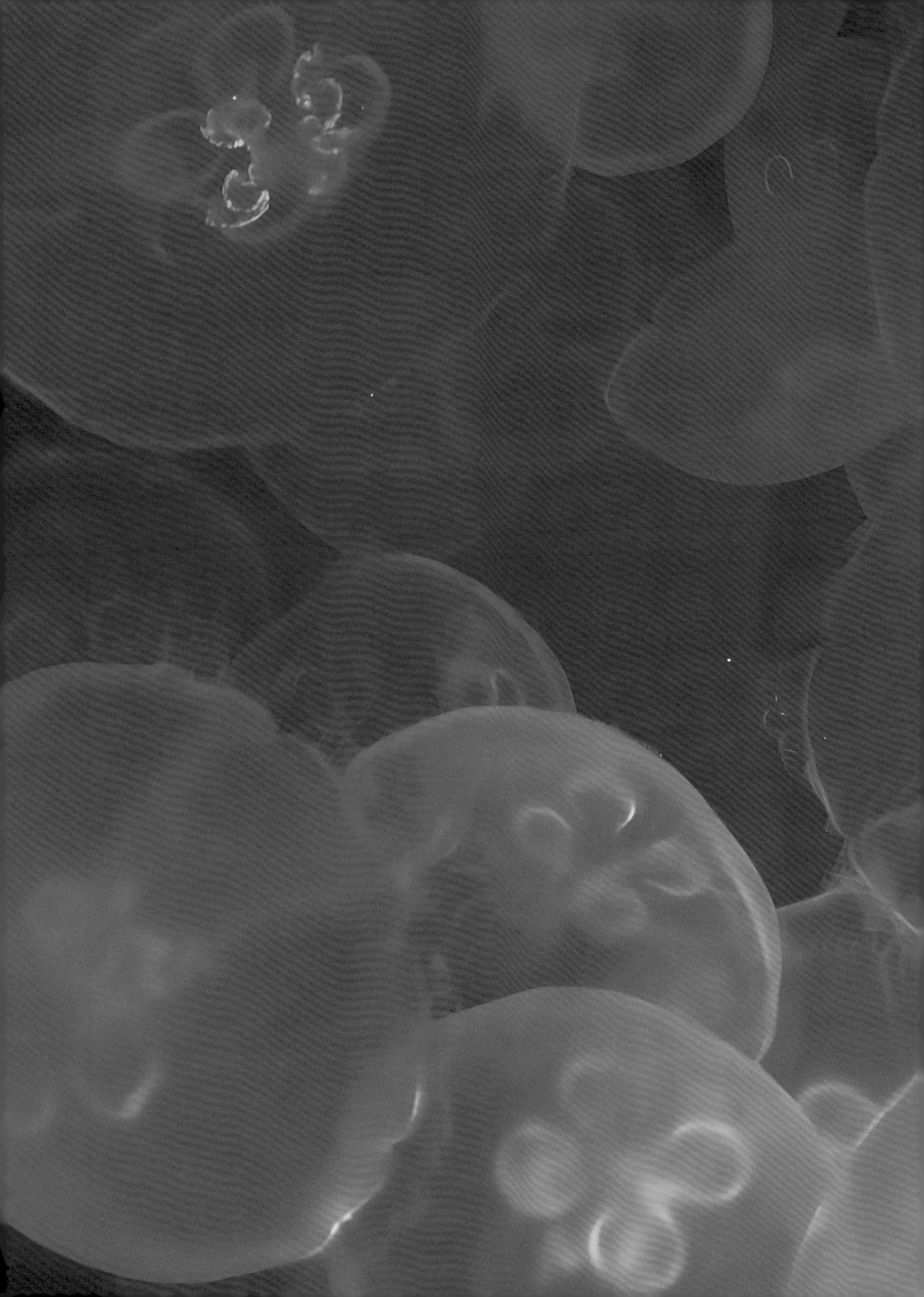

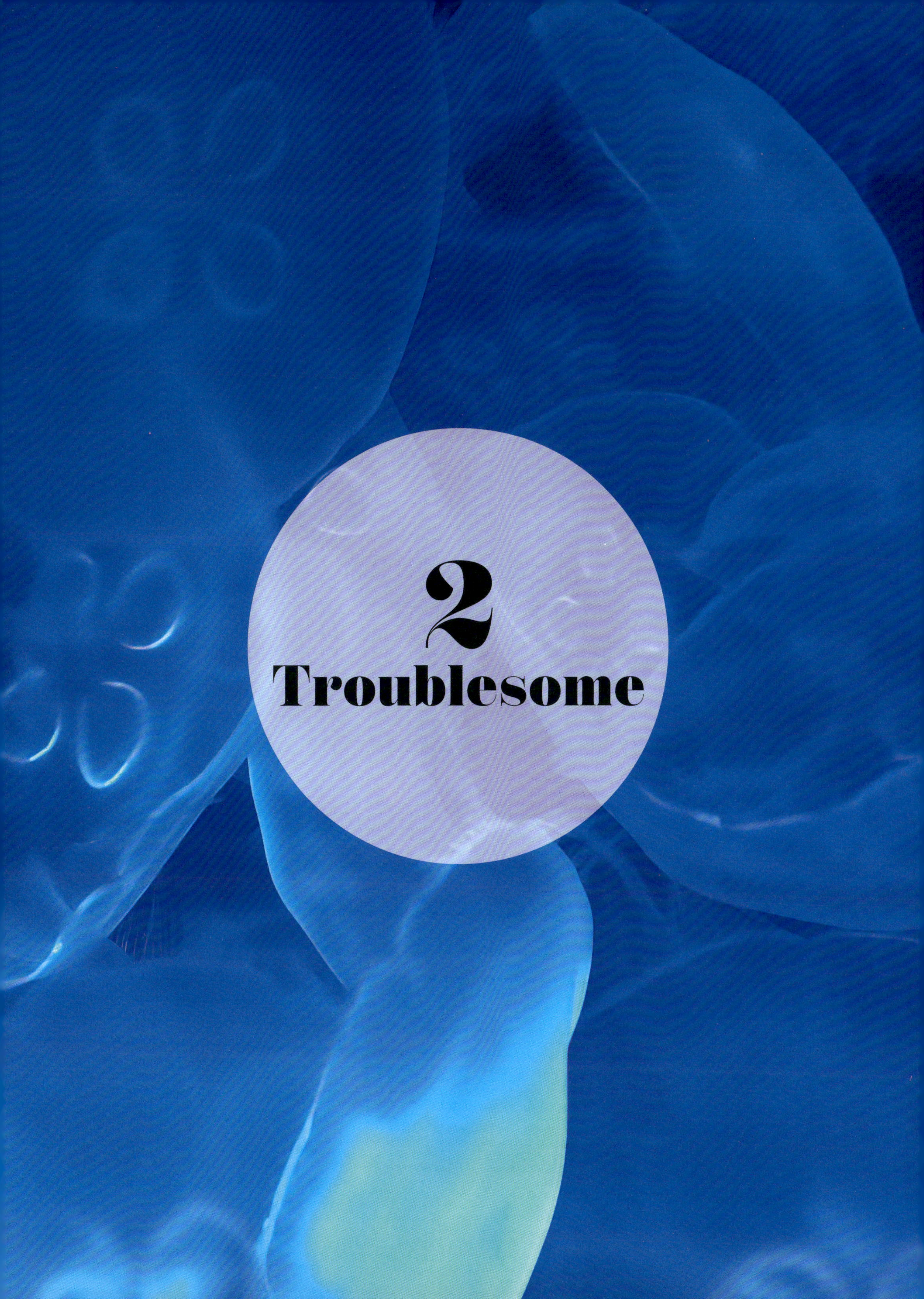
2
Troublesome

S tings are just one of the many hazards that jellyfish present. Another less intuitive, but far more difficult danger to prevent, is their problematic blooms, or swarms. Jellyfish bloom as a normal part of their life cycle when they alternate between the free-swimming sexual medusa stage and a fixed asexual polyp stage. The polyps spend most of their time cloning into large colonies. Under the right conditions, the polyps produce baby jellyfish, which grow very fast. Too often nowadays, both sides of the life cycle are opportunistically responding to changes in the ocean and exploiting them to their advantage.

Overfishing removes the other species that jellyfish compete with for food, as well as those that may prey on jellies directly. Either way, jellyfish win. Moreover, warmer water (caused by global warming) revs up the metabolism of most jellies, making them grow faster, reproduce more, and live longer. Warmer water also holds less dissolved oxygen, making it harder for fish and crustaceans to survive, but jellyfish are unaffected. And coastal construction projects such as ports and wharves, aquaculture installations, and oil and gas platforms offer additional space for jellyfish polyps to grow.

Jellyfish have a variety of tricks to torment us. They clog up the cooling-water intake pipes used by marine

industries, causing emergency shutdowns. They clog
fishing nets to the extent that these must be cut loose
to avoid capsizing the boat. They help create and
maintain "dead zones," where nothing else can survive.
They parasitize. They multiply. And most debilitating
of all, jellyfish eat the eggs and larvae of fish, as well as
the plankton that those larvae would eat. This "double
whammy" of predation and competition efficiently topples
the food chain from the base, positioning jellyfish as the
top predator. And once they dominate an ecosystem in this
way, they are difficult to control.

Some of the most troublesome species, surprisingly,
are among the most heart-achingly beautiful. To see them
in an aquarium, lazily pulsating with their tentacles gently
flowing in the current, it is hard to imagine the havoc they
can wreak. But wreak they do. The mild-mannered moon
jellies cost the farmed salmon industries and power plants
hundreds of millions of dollars per year. The nettles cost the
tourist industry billions. The lovely blubbers cost the fishing
and shipping industries even more.

Jellyfish are thriving like never before due to the
conditions we are creating in the oceans. Certainly,
they would thank us if they could.

Sea Walnut

Mnemiopsis leidyi

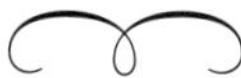

Prior to the 1980s, *Mnemiopsis leidyi* seemed
like such a gentle species. It doesn't sting. And its body
is as delicate as a cloud. But as it stealthily hitchhiked
across the Atlantic in ballast water, it found a happy home
in the Black Sea. Within a few years of this accidental
introduction, its population—estimated at more than a
billion tons, which is more than ten times all the world's
fish landings—had crippled the entire food chain by
preying on fish eggs, larvae, and plankton. By 1993,
it comprised 95 percent of the Black Sea biomass.
It then expanded into the Aegean, the Mediterranean,
and even the Baltic. Where it will stop—or
if it will stop—nobody knows!

SIZE: Body length to 4¾ inches (12 cm)

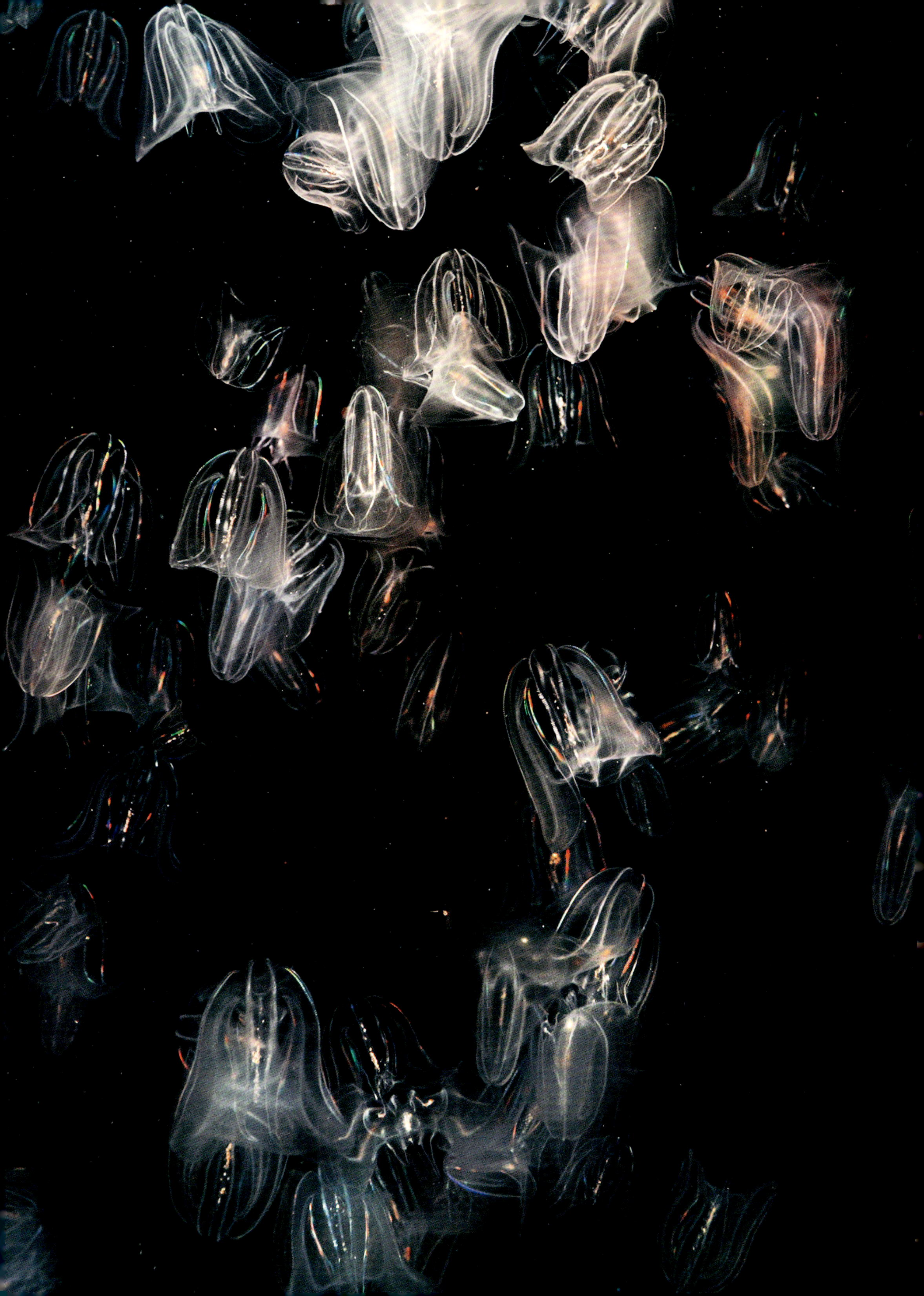

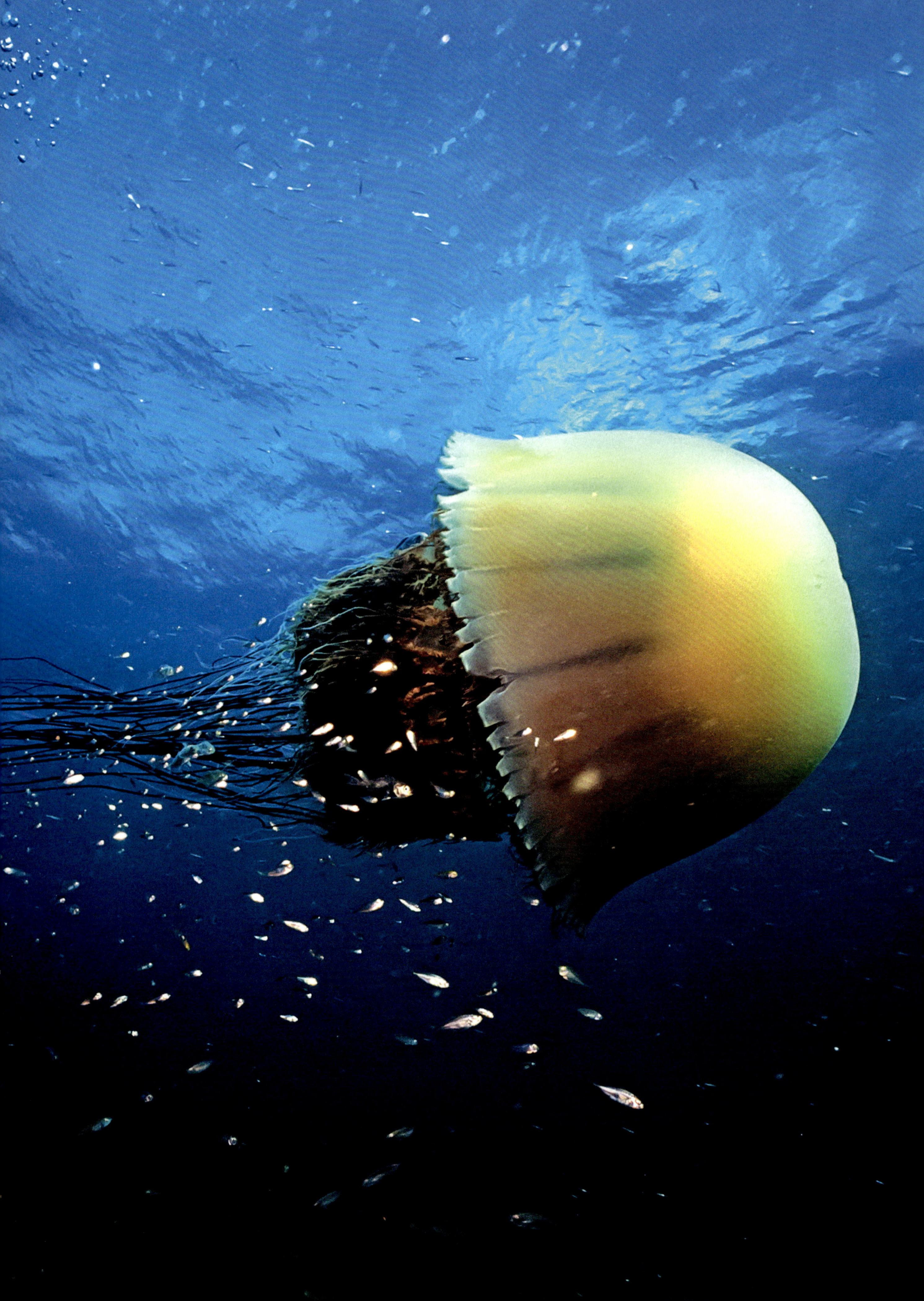

Nomura's Jellyfish

Nemopilema nomurai

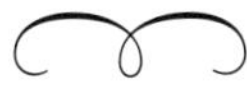

Imagine a jiggling behemoth, an enormous mass
of sting and slime. This is Nomura's jellyfish. China's
coastal waters are now a perfect nursery for these
jellies, since they are long depleted of fishy predators
and competitors. The jellyfish become caught up in
northward currents, feasting on vast amounts of
plankton and growing rapidly as they drift along. By
the time they reach the Sea of Japan's fishing grounds,
these jellyfish are the size of a refrigerator and have been
estimated at a staggering half a billion individuals *per
day*. Most fishermen don't even bother trying to fish in
these conditions, but those who do may lose their
nets or capsize their boats. Worse still, the sting
of these jellyfish can be deadly.

SIZE: Bell diameter to 6½ feet (2 m)

Jelly Blubber

Catostylus mosaicus

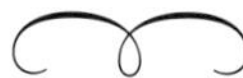

In October 2006, America launched its newest and most expensive and awe-inspiring nuclear supercarrier, the USS *Ronald Reagan*. It was built to withstand any threat from nature or a hostile military. But at its first port of call on its maiden voyage, the ship encountered its very own disabling "kryptonite"—*Catostylus mosaicus*. This is one of southeastern Australia's most common jellyfish. It is beautiful, but its blooms are a portentous warning for all marine industries since it may clog up cooling-water intake pipes, resulting in engine damage and costly shutdowns. And this is what happened to the *Ronald Reagan*. Curiously, the species is blue in Victoria and Queensland waters but brown in New South Wales due to symbiotic algae that are lacking in the blue forms.

SIZE: Bell diameter to 14 inches (35 cm)

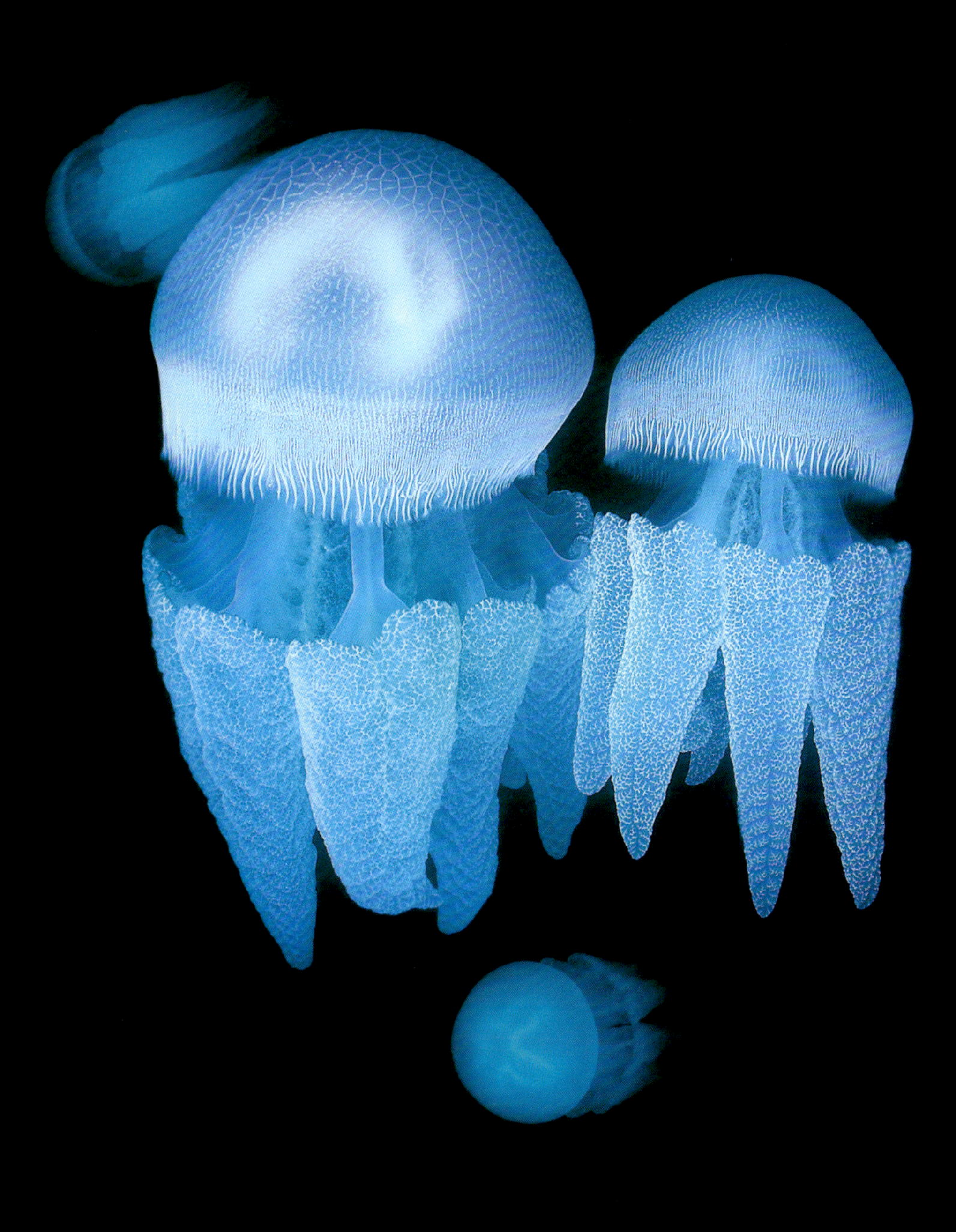

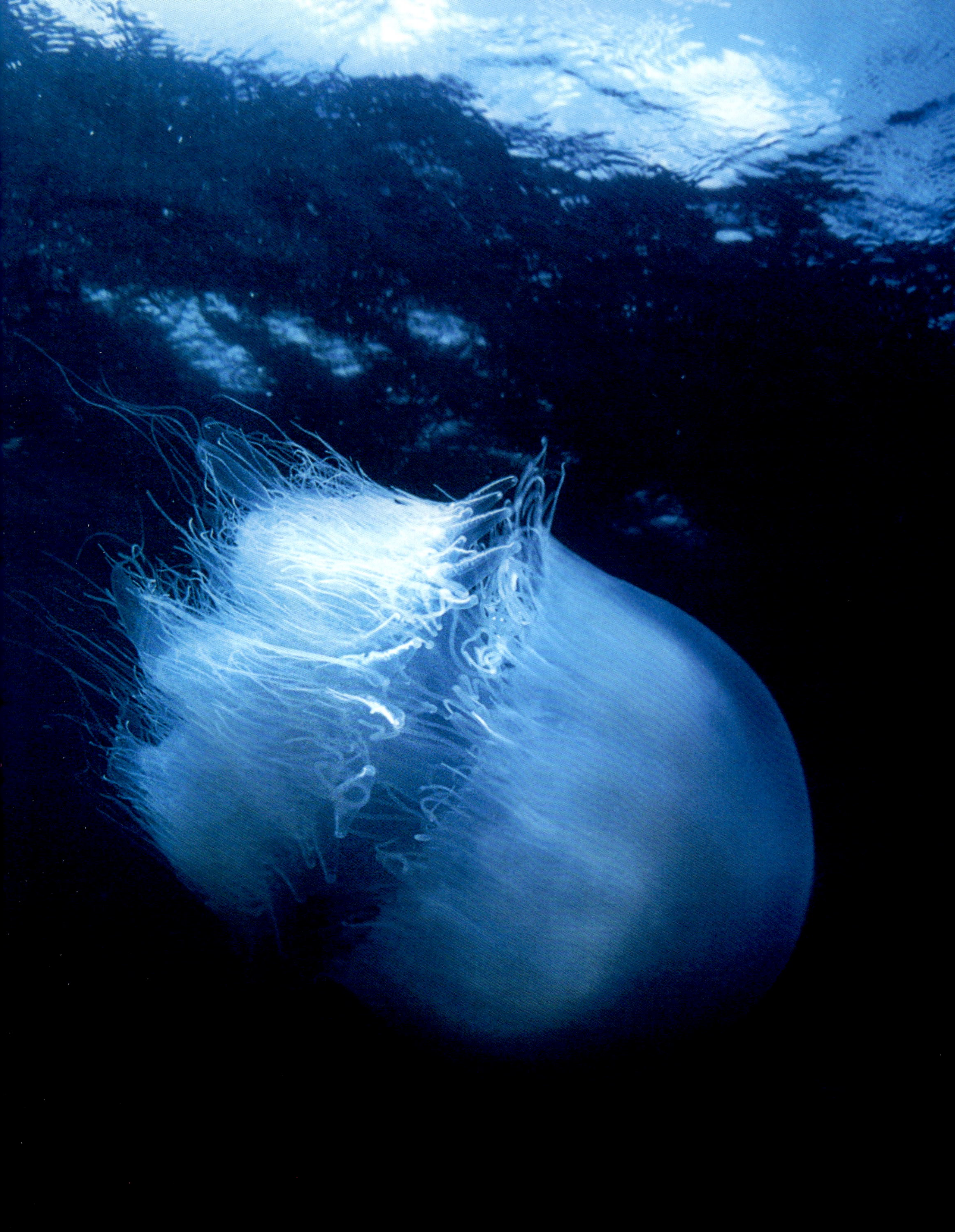

Nomad Jellyfish

Rhopilema nomadica

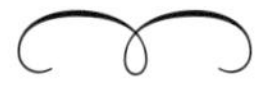

Jellyfish generally have a shocking propensity to clog the intake pipes of ships, power plants, desalination plants, and just about anything that sucks in seawater for cooling or other industrial purposes. When the facility is nuclear, an emergency shutdown goes far beyond being inconvenient and costly—it can be dangerous. The nomad jellyfish, which was only discovered in 1976, presents a dual threat, and its dreamy, ice-blue coloration offers a chilling reminder of this capacity for harm. Along the coasts of Israel, Lebanon, and Syria, *Rhopilema nomadica* reaches population densities of 500,000 per square mile. Its sting is severe, affecting unsuspecting bathers and fishermen alike. And too often, thousands of jellyfish clog the cooling systems of nuclear power plants, inching us closer to a disastrous meltdown.

SIZE: Bell diameter to 30 inches (76 cm)

Moon Jelly

Aurelia

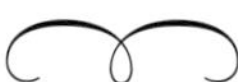

Moon jellies are among the most prolific and
therefore most conspicuous of all jellyfish. Their
pleasantly flattened body has a pale, ghostly whitish color,
typically with four obvious internal rings and a fringe
of hundreds of short, fine tentacles. The rings are the
reproductive organs, which line the stomach pouches.
Rarely and intriguingly, they may have up to eight.
And the moon jelly's sting ranges from undetectable to
a soothing warm sensation. But this seemingly mild-
mannered jellyfish is capable of unspeakable havoc.
In swarm densities, it clogs the intake pipes for the
cooling systems of power plants or ships, or its
slime and stinging cells get into the gills of farmed
salmon, killing millions within minutes.

SIZE: Bell diameter to 12 inches (30 cm)

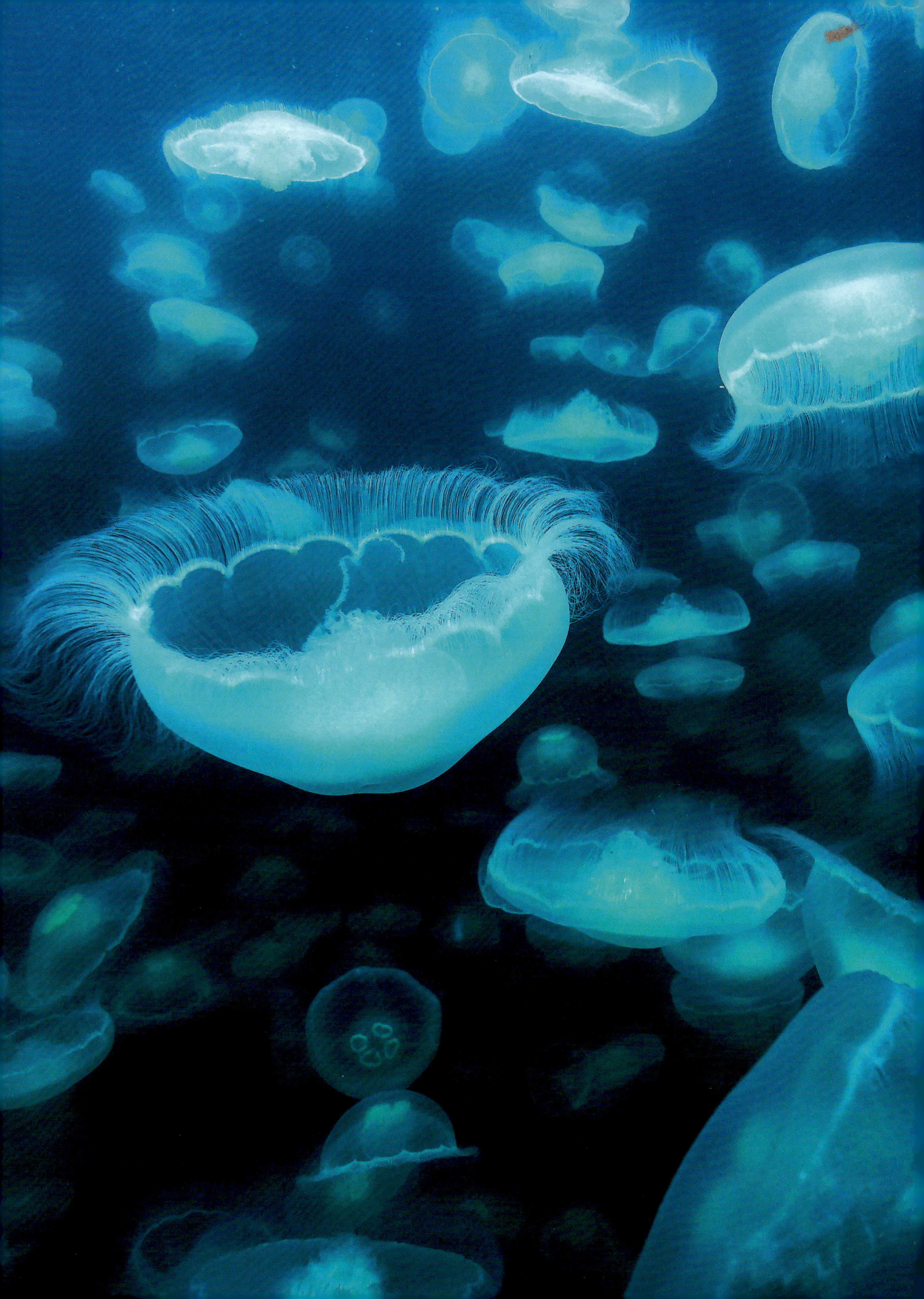

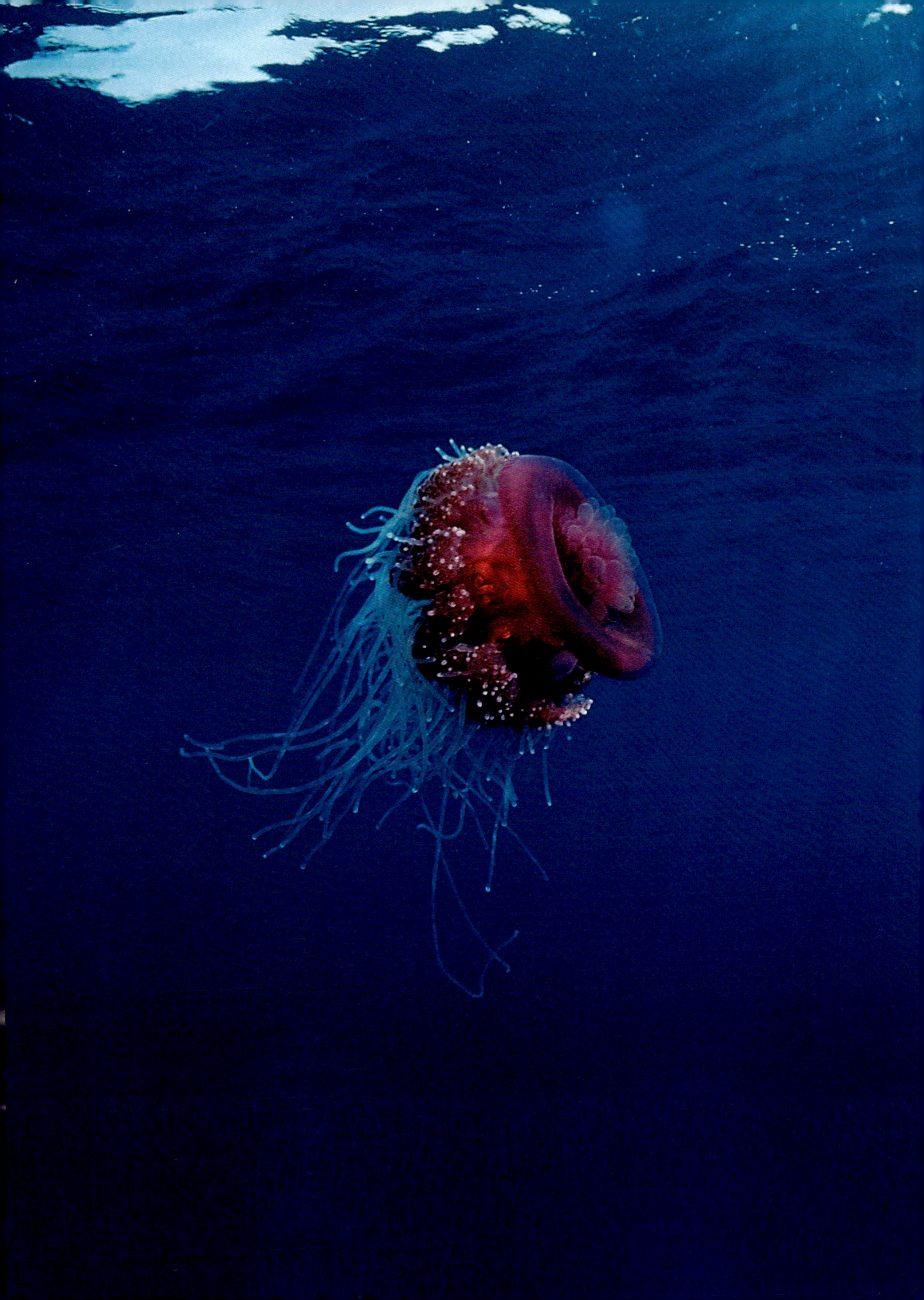

Crowned Jellyfish

Netrostoma coerulescens

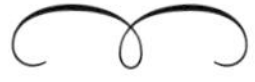

Among the most delightful of all jellyfish are
those in the breathtakingly beautiful genus *Netrostoma*.
This group is characterized by a bowl-like indentation
in the center of the bell, with a central hump bearing
one or more knobs or finger-like papillae. Species are
distinguished according to the number and arrangement
of the projections and by their body coloration, which
ranges from shades of blue to pinks and purples. But as
with so many jellies, one cannot decouple the beauty
from the beast. Along the coastlines of India, *Netrostoma
coerulescens* is one of half a dozen species of jellies
that take turns blooming throughout the year,
creating an ongoing health and socioeconomic
hazard for people and industries.

SIZE: Bell diameter to 8 inches (20 cm)

Japanese Sea Nettle

Chrysaora pacifica

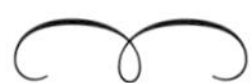

This beautiful species was discovered in the late 1800s,
but astonishingly, it spent the next hundred years hiding
in plain sight, largely ignored by the broader scientific
community. When public aquariums began exhibiting it
in the 1990s under a different name, *Chrysaora melanaster*,
the problem became clear. The northern sea nettle,
C. melanaster, is larger and has bold, chocolate-brown
bars radiating out from the center of its bell, while the
more demure *C. pacifica* has a more refined pattern.
This species is now more notorious for its troublesome
identity than for its sting or ecological impacts.

SIZE: Bell diameter to 8 inches (20 cm)

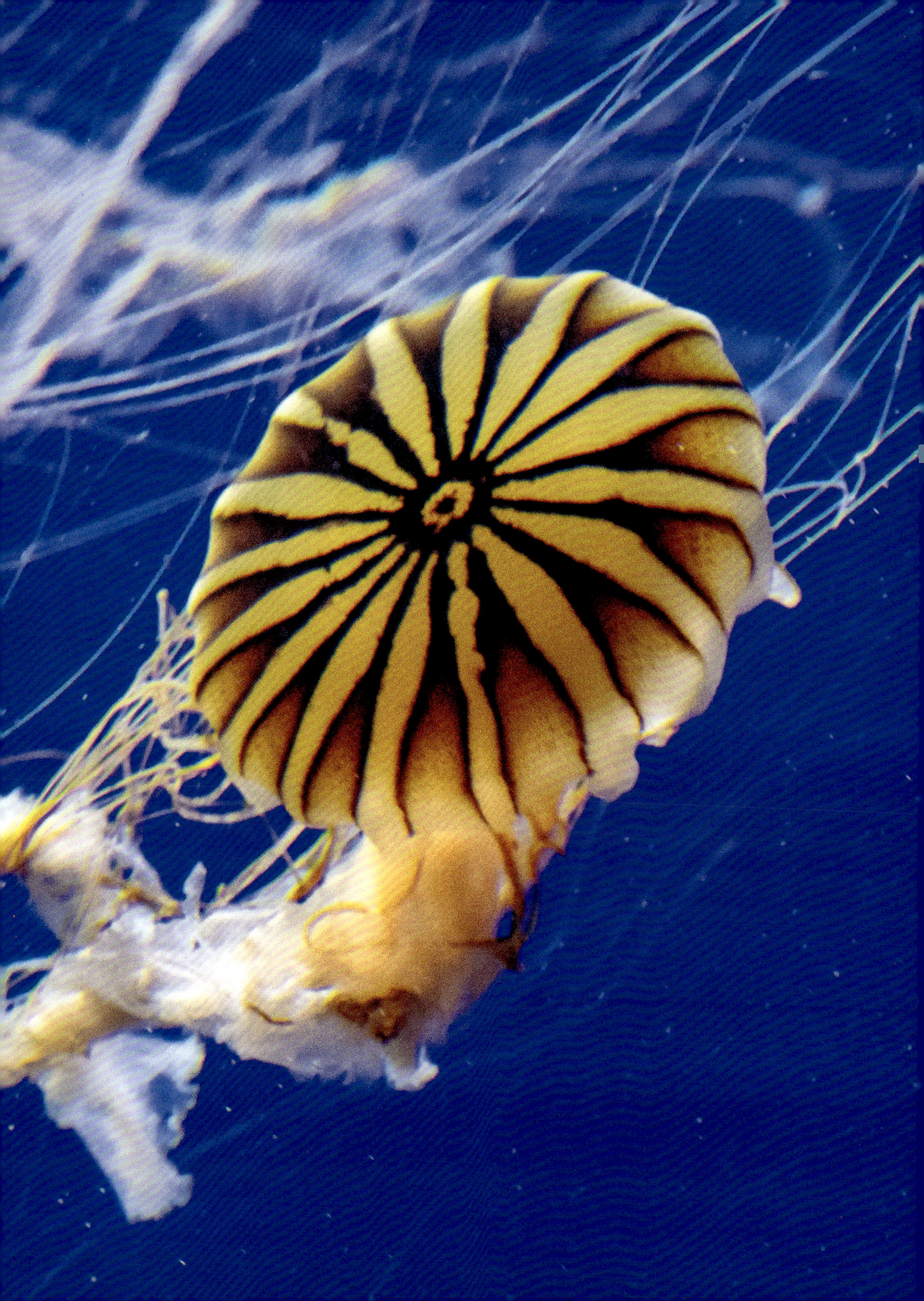

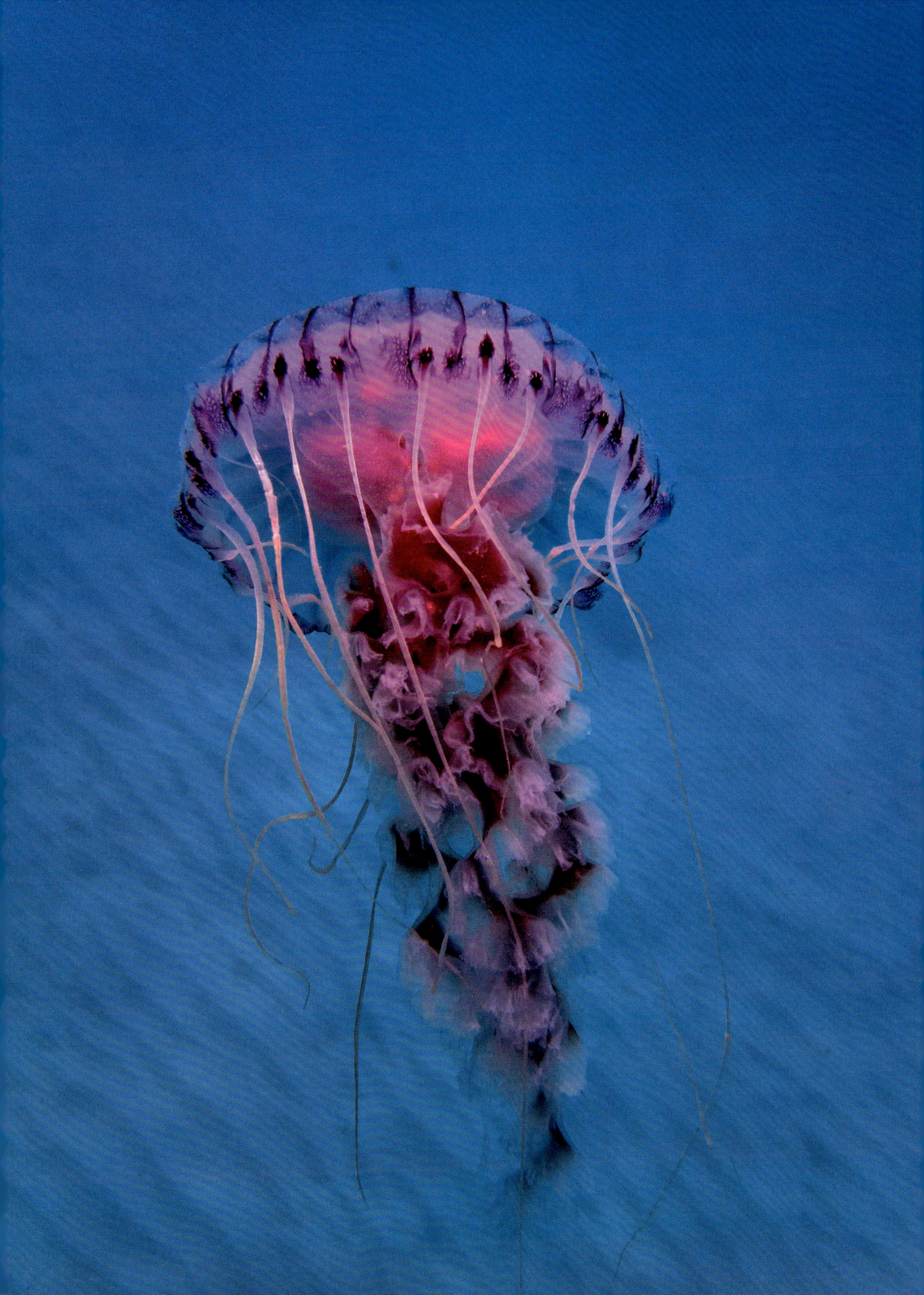

Purple Compass Jelly

Chrysaora africana

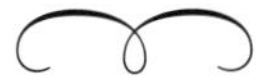

The purple compass jelly, like other members
of the *Chrysaora* genus, is showy and resplendent at first
glance—gracefully flowing and purple—but don't be
fooled. This species is a pest, and how that came to be is a
stern warning to all. Fisheries in the Benguela Current in
the South Atlantic Ocean were overexploited for decades,
leaving food and other resources for opportunists. By
the 1990s, jellyfish numbers had ballooned enormously,
creating a stingy-slimy killing field impacting over
30,000 square miles (78,000 square kilometers). The
seabed here is a "dead zone," where dead and dying
jellyfish and plankton rot, creating a low-oxygen zone
where nothing else can survive. Fish have vanished.
Fisheries have crashed. The whole ecosystem is now
dominated by jellyfish and showing no signs of recovery.

SIZE: Bell diameter to 12 inches (30 cm)

Fish Parasites
Subphylum Myxozoa

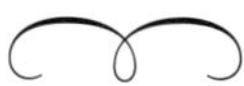

Certainly, the strangest of all jellyfish are the
myxozoans. To understand their weirdness, imagine an
offshoot group that has lost almost all its normal jellyfish
features, as well as the genes that code for its tentacles,
pulsations . . . everything. It has become a tremendously
simplified amoeba-like parasite. It still stings, though.
If being degenerate were its only party trick, perhaps
the myxozoans wouldn't be so important. But they also
infect fish. For example, one species targets the muscle
of farmed salmon. It doesn't hurt the living fish, but
once harvested, the parasite causes the fillets to liquify
and become unappetizing, costing the salmon industry
millions of dollars. Whether it can harm those who
consume infected fish is unclear.

SIZE: Length to 300 microns

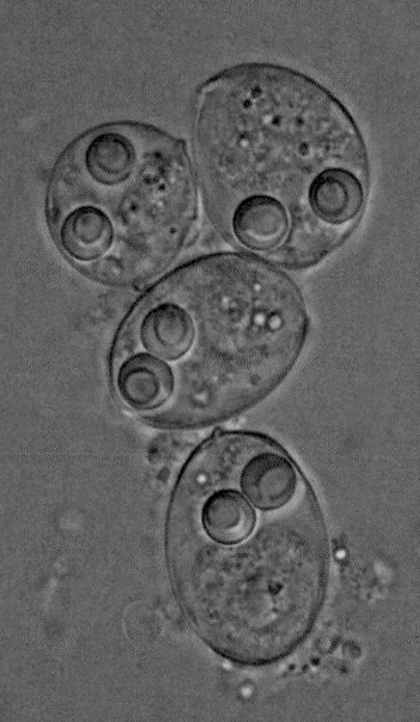

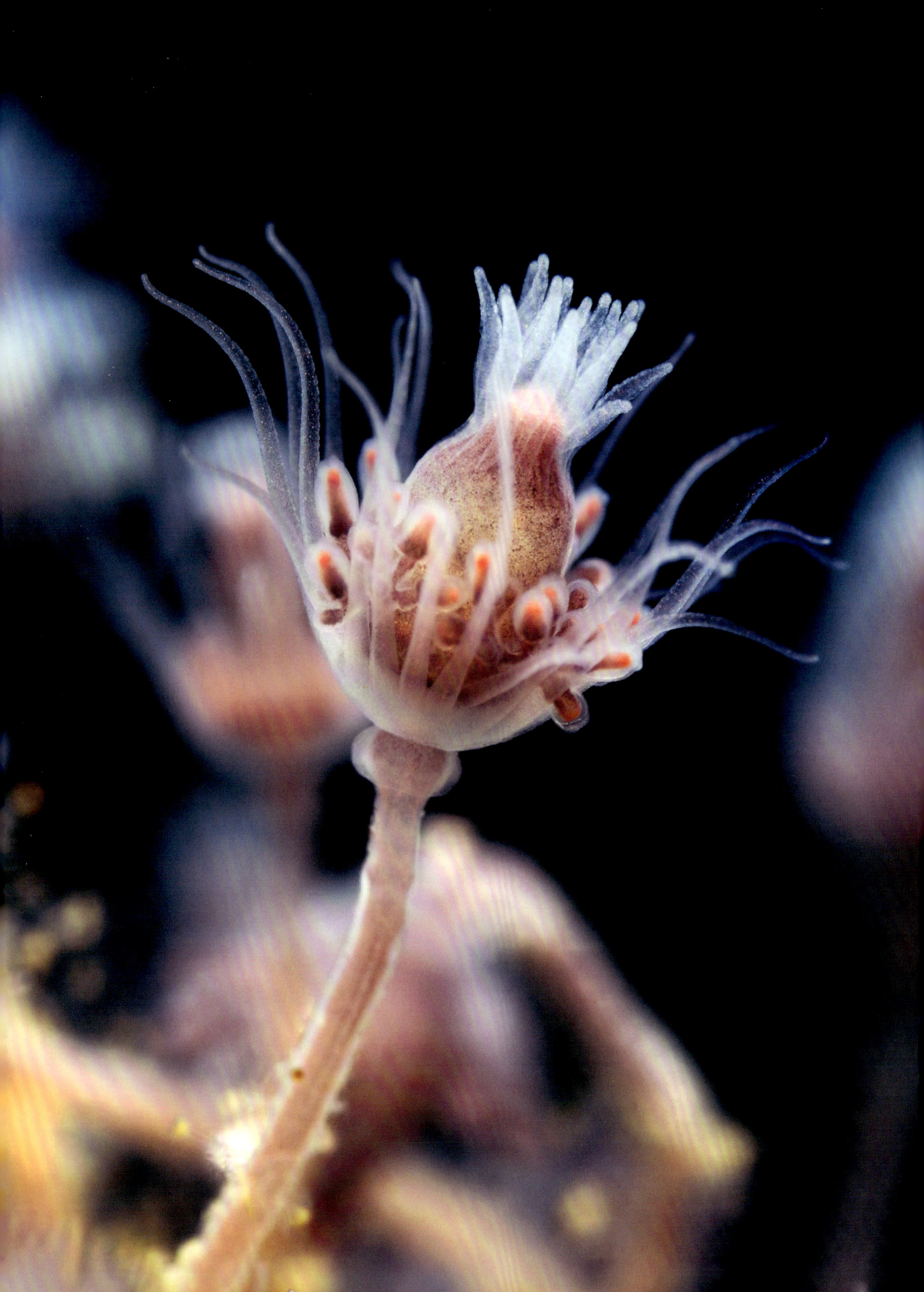

Flower-Head Polyp

Ectopleura

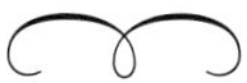

Many of the most problematic jellyfish species are quite large and conspicuous. *Ectopleura*, in contrast, is minute. Its small size and tremendous bloom densities enable it to penetrate and sting the gills of fish, causing disease. But the medusa stage is not alone in threatening farmed fish, because the hydroid stage (when the organism is attached to a solid substrate) is also troublesome. Hydroids grow incredibly fast. Scraping them away is only a short-term solution because this stimulates them to grow more vigorously. The scraping also causes them to fragment, which is another source of injury for delicate fish gills. But like a real-life version of the brooms in *The Sorcerer's Apprentice*, the fragments also act as the seeds for new colonies, simply multiplying the problem.

SIZE: Polyp height to 2½ inches (6 cm)

Sea Tomato

Crambione mastigophora

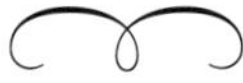

The soul-achingly rugged coastlines of Western Australia evoke solitude, contemplation, and serenity. But these seemingly pristine vistas also harbor many secrets. One is the amazing abundance of sea tomatoes. Occasionally, and increasingly in recent years, the coastlines are inundated with these blood-red jellyfish, in such quantities that they are said to scare away the whale sharks that come there to feed. And when these blooms wash ashore and blanket the sand so thickly that it looks like a red carpet, birds and turtles fail to nest. The reason for these blooms is unknown, but it is thought to be the result of decades of intense trawling, which leaves the seabed vulnerable to opportunists like jellyfish.

SIZE: Bell diameter to 10 inches (25 cm)

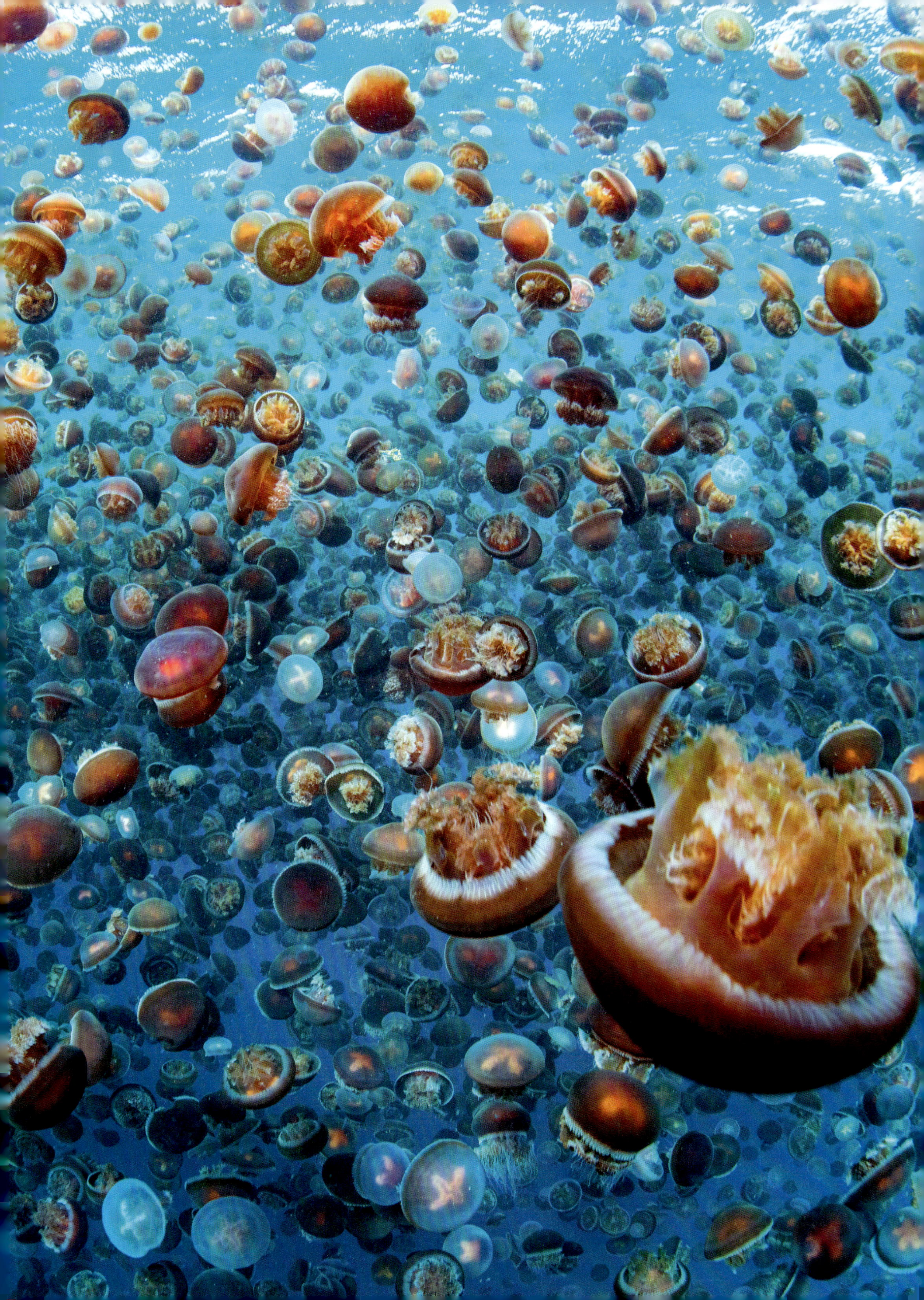

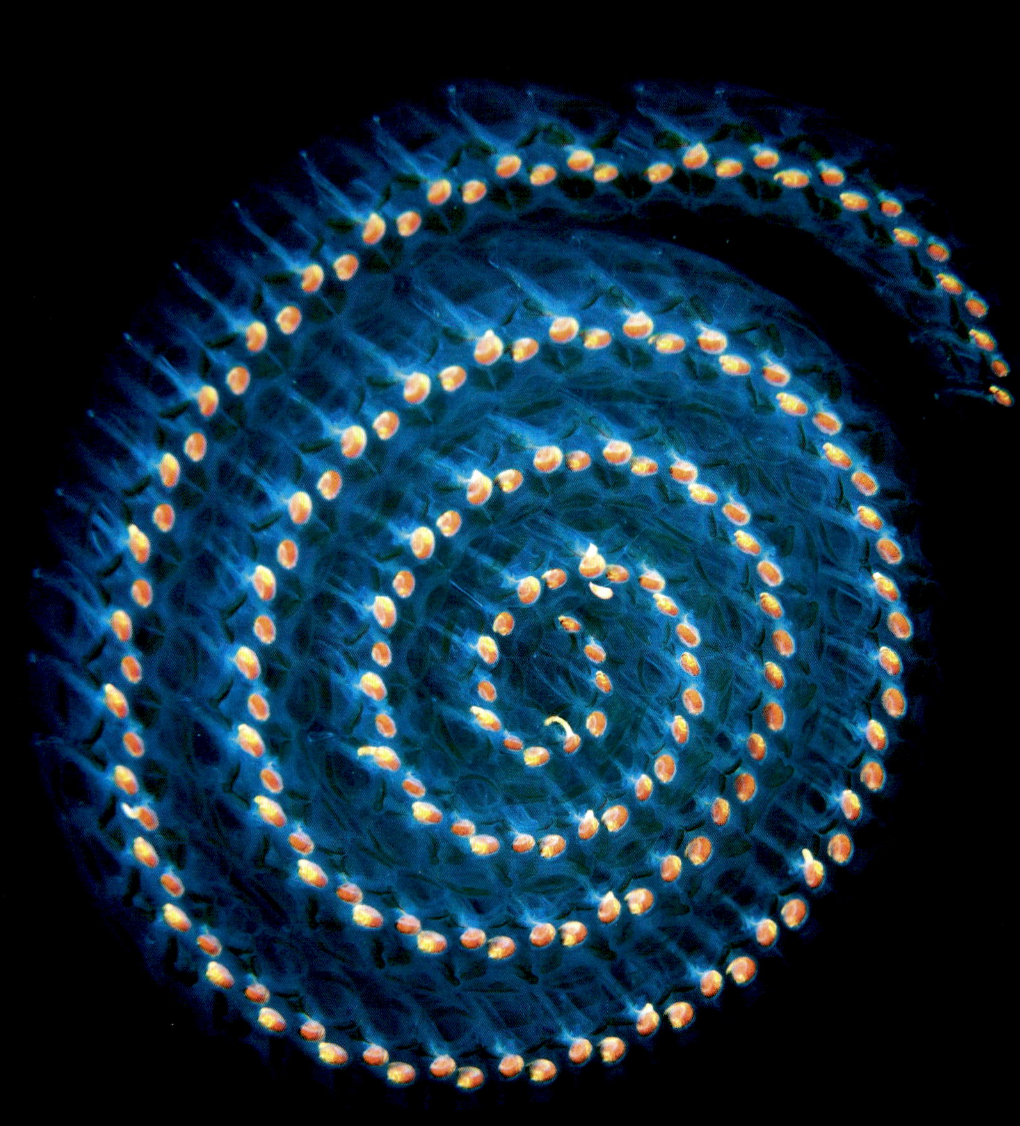

Salps

Pegea

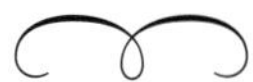

Salps are one of the least understood of all the oceans' creatures. They are related to sea squirts, also known as tunicates, but spend their life swimming and drifting. *Pegea* is one of the most striking of all salps, with its colonies naturally coiling into mesmerizing patterns. And though they look like jellyfish, they are, in fact, more closely related to humans than to other jellies. Salps are not venomous, but they may be dangerous nonetheless. Gorging on vast quantities of phytoplankton, it appears that salps may concentrate toxic algae, becoming poisonous bullets to their predators. Scattered reports exist of mass deaths of dolphins, dugongs, seabirds, or fish, where the stomach is found during autopsy to be stuffed full of salps. This is an emerging area of research.

SIZE: Body length to 5½ inches (14 cm)

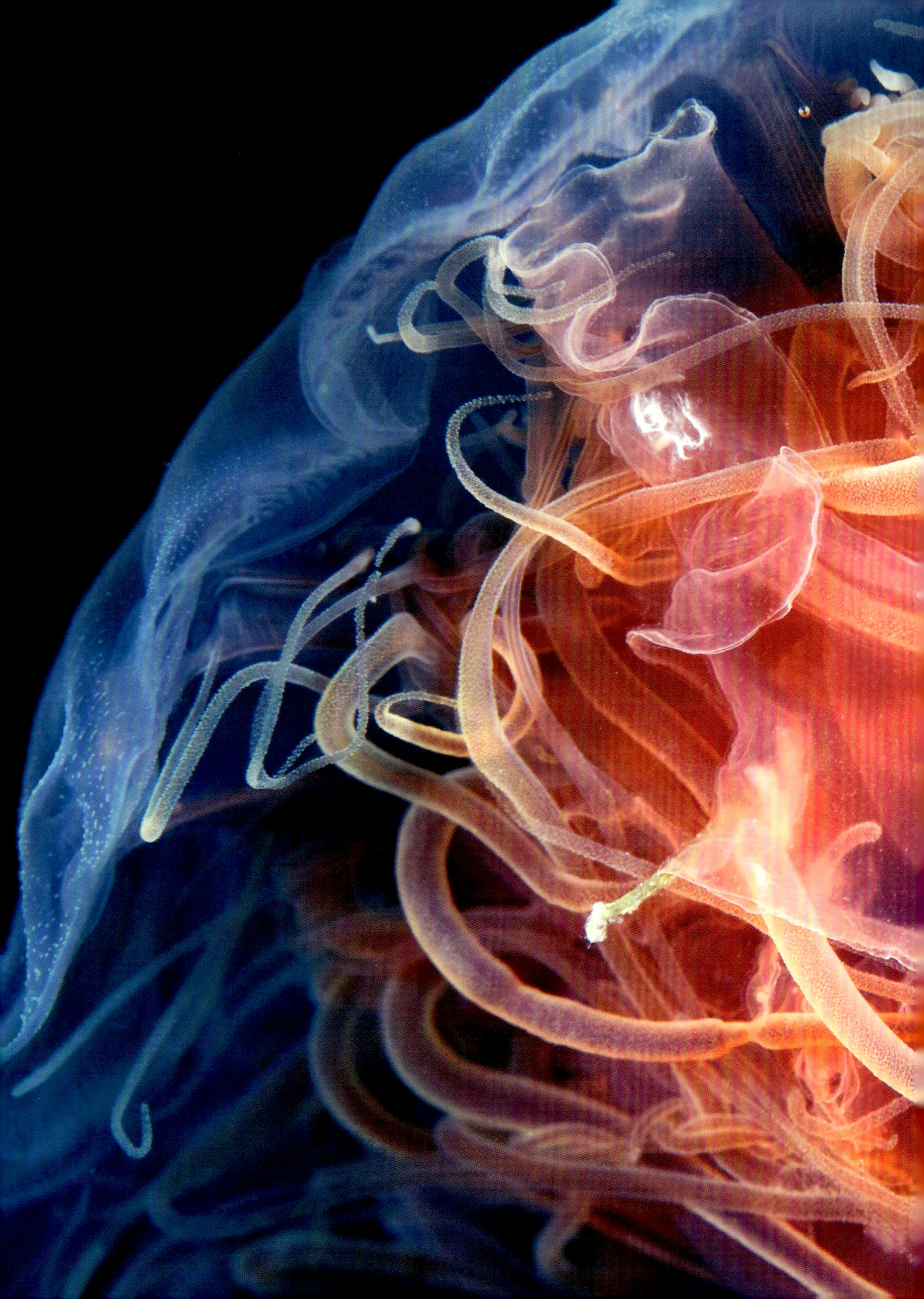

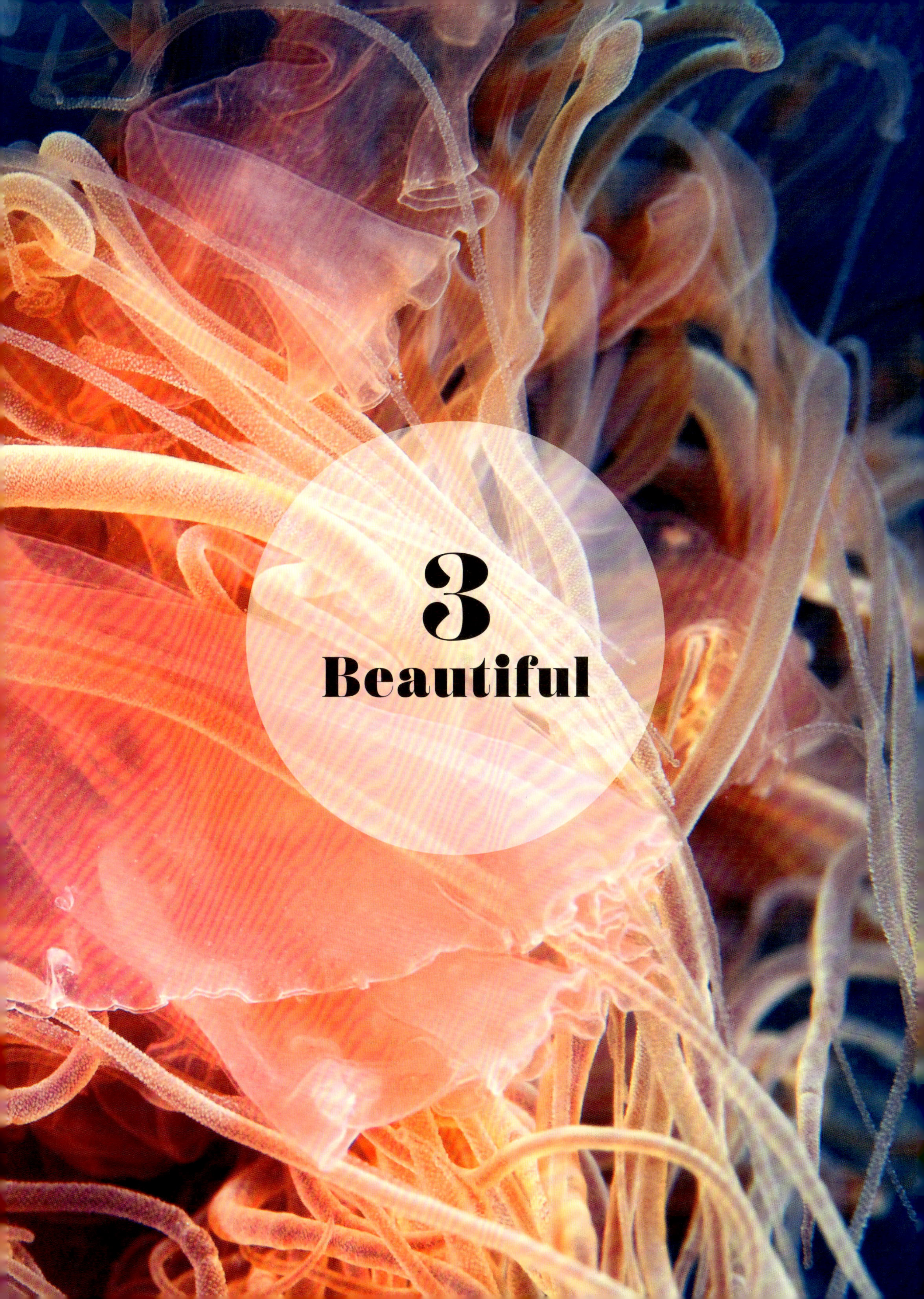
3
Beautiful

M esmerizing. Captivating. Fascinating. The beautiful-but-lethal nature of jellyfish strums at our heartstrings when we see them in their element. Their flowing tentacles appear to dance with a primitive rhythm as the animal pulsates, driven by ancient instincts.

Some species, like the sea nettles, come in dazzling colors and patterns: The purple-stripe sea nettle with its silvery white body and bold purple star; the Japanese sea nettle (*Chrysaora pacifica*, see page 52) with its ghostly whitish background and chocolate-brown streaks radiating to the edge; and the black sea nettle (*Chrysaora achlyos*, see page 152), which is such a uniformly deep red that it almost looks black in the water, with a pale star emanating from its center. If their showy colors don't beguile you, their long, ruffly oral arms certainly will, being many times as long as the jelly's body is wide, as will their thread-like tentacles, passively trailing behind.

Or behold one of the most dreamy and whimsical of all jellies, the blue button, whose small, flat disk floats upon the surface of the ocean, with dozens of almost neon blue tentacles radiating out, each studded along both sides with tiny knobs. Driven to shore in their thousands, blue button strandings invite us to wonder about the wanderings of these beautiful little beings.

Another type of jellyfish, which most people wouldn't recognize as a jellyfish at all, are the Stauromedusae. Stuck at the bottom of the sea instead of drifting on the currents, they are easy to miss but splendid to behold. Their tulip-shaped or fluted bodies bear eight tufts of tiny tentacles, each tipped with a stinging knob. Stauromedusae look almost unbearably exquisite and elegant, suspended lazily from a blade of seagrass or the underside of an algal frond. Well camouflaged, to the keen observer they may vie for the most treasured of all finds.

The flower hat jelly, however, leaves nothing to chance. Its body and tentacles are streaked in bubblegum-pink and black, two of the rarest jellyfish colors. It sits unmoving, resting among algae or on sediment, then with a great flourish, it alights and flaps wildly to move to another perch. But this most magical of jellies reveals its full glory under ultraviolet light, glowing an eerie blue with tentacles tipped in yellow.

Whether enchanting us by glowing in the dark with fluorescence or bioluminescence, or charming us with their delightful shapes or striking colors, jellies are, in essence, the flowers of the sea, as lovely as lilies, as resplendent as roses, as beautiful as bluebells.

Purple-Stripe Sea Nettle

Chrysaora colorata

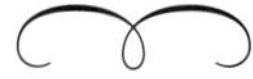

Scuba divers and swimmers along southern
California's coastline are often treated to a delightful
summertime surprise. The purple-stripe sea nettle is
common, huge, and unmistakable with its dazzlingly
bold purple-and-silver color pattern. It begins life as a
tiny, daisy-shaped larva in the warm waters off Mexico
and grows rapidly as it feeds on the rich plankton
that drift northward on the California Current. It is
capable of catching fish much larger than its mouth and
digesting them externally within the frills and ruffles
of its pleated oral arms, the fleshy structures that trail
behind its massive body. As its common name suggests,
this sea nettle can sting, though not severely.

SIZE: Bell diameter to 28 inches (70 cm)

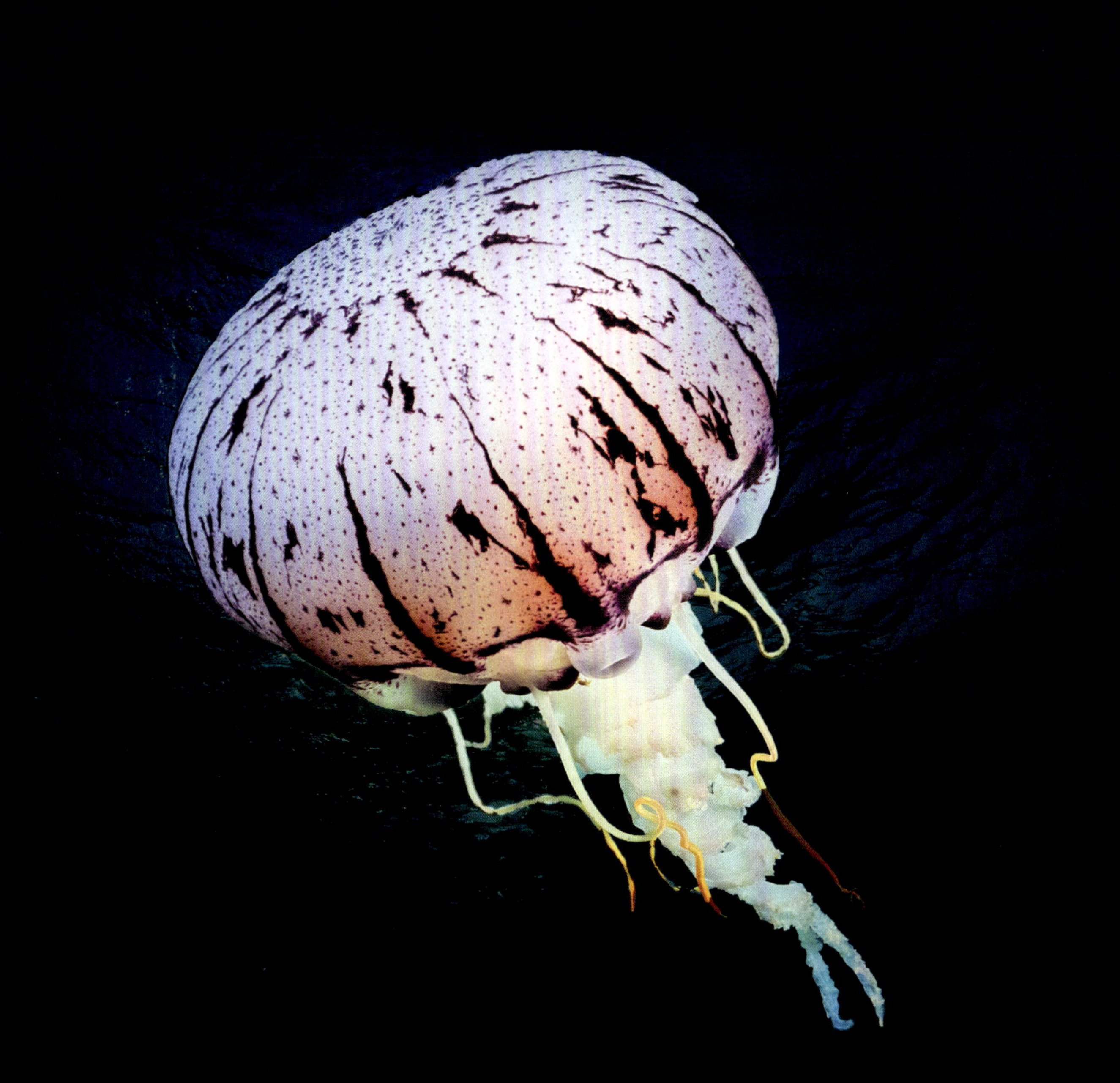

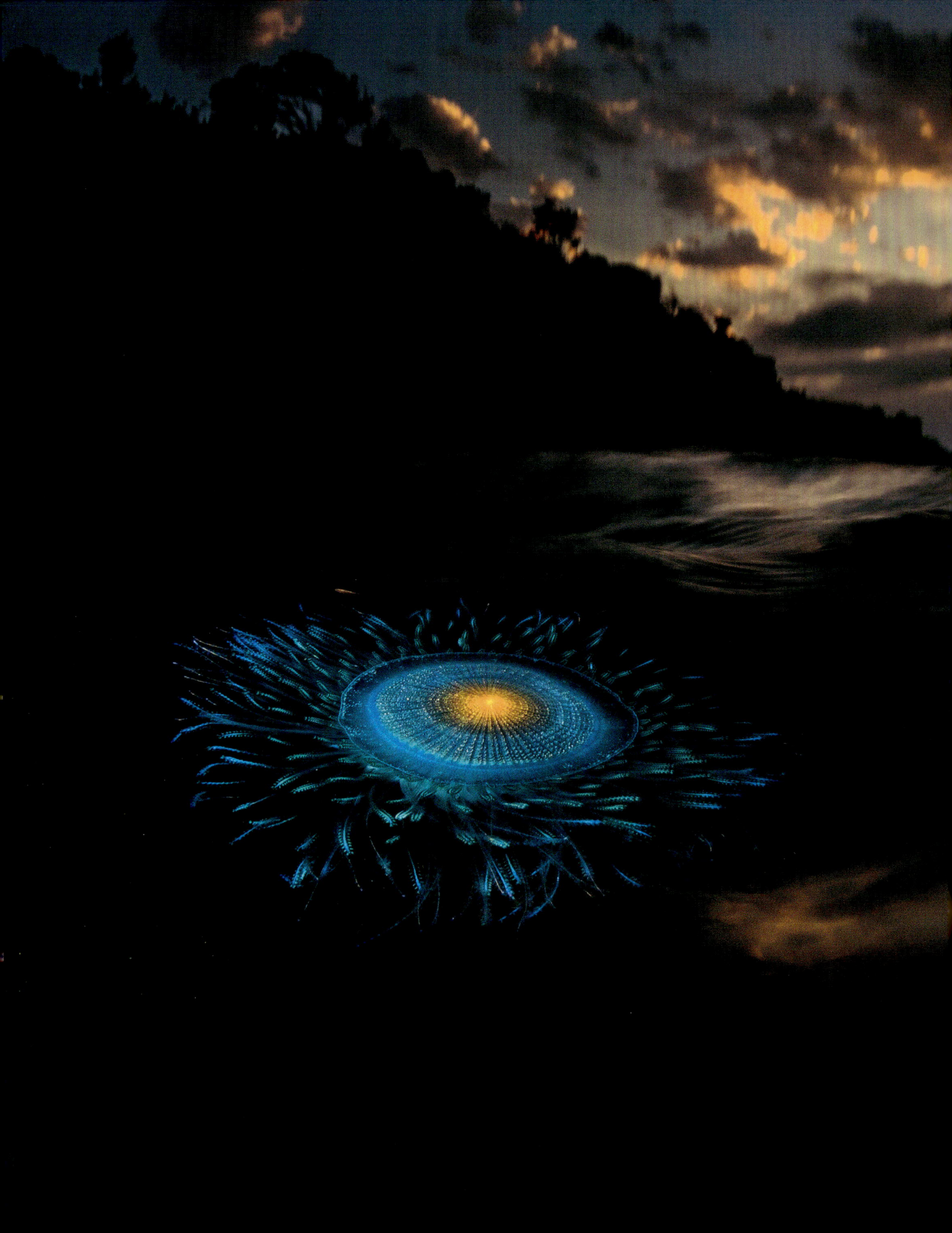

Blue Button

Porpita porpita

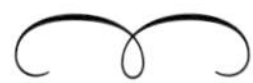

The blue button, like its close cousin, the by-the-wind sailor (*Velella velella*, see page 110), is a floating polyp colony. Both have a lightweight, air-filled "shell" made of chitin, which keeps them pinned to the surface as they travel the seas. And both have a forest of polyps attached to the underside, which release tiny, short-lived medusae. Whereas the by-the-wind sailor has a perpendicular sail, the blue button lacks any such projection, having only a small, round, chambered disc. Many dozens of whimsically knobbed tentacles radiate out from this, skimming the underside of the air as they gather food and deter would-be predators. Their intense blue color is thought to help camouflage them from predators and possibly act as sunscreen from ultraviolet light.

SIZE: Float diameter to ⅝ inch (15 mm)

Golden Blubber

Bazinga rieki

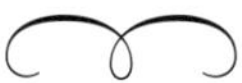

This remarkable little jellyfish was discovered hiding in plain sight in the waters near Sydney, Australia, earning it the genus name *Bazinga* in reference to the meaning of "Ha ha, fooled you!" as used in the hit TV show *The Big Bang Theory*. Its species name, *rieki*, honors Denis Riek, the photographer who found it and brought it to the attention of scientists, highlighting the important role of citizen science. While most people might marvel at its diminutive size, delightful golden coloration, or rapid pulsations as it swims, a closer look at its structures reveals a fascinating secret—it is as different from other jellyfishes as marsupials are from other mammals.

SIZE: Bell diameter to ¾ inch (20 mm)

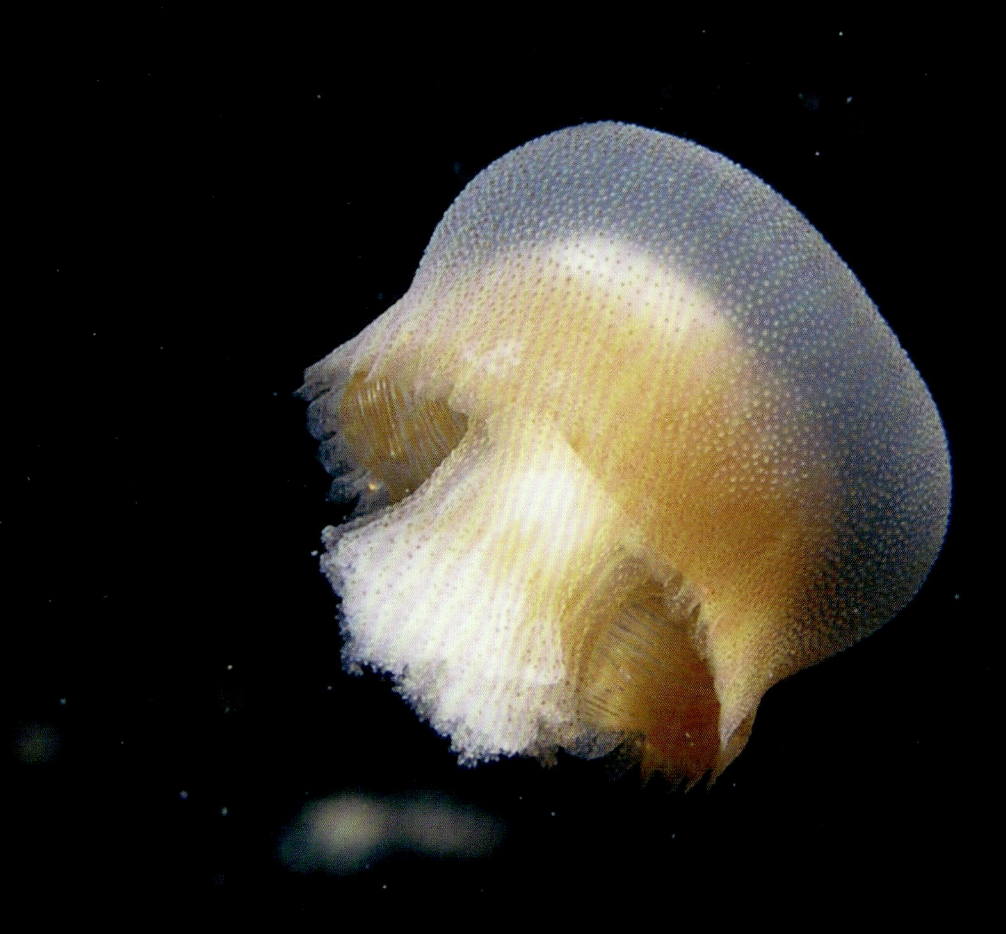

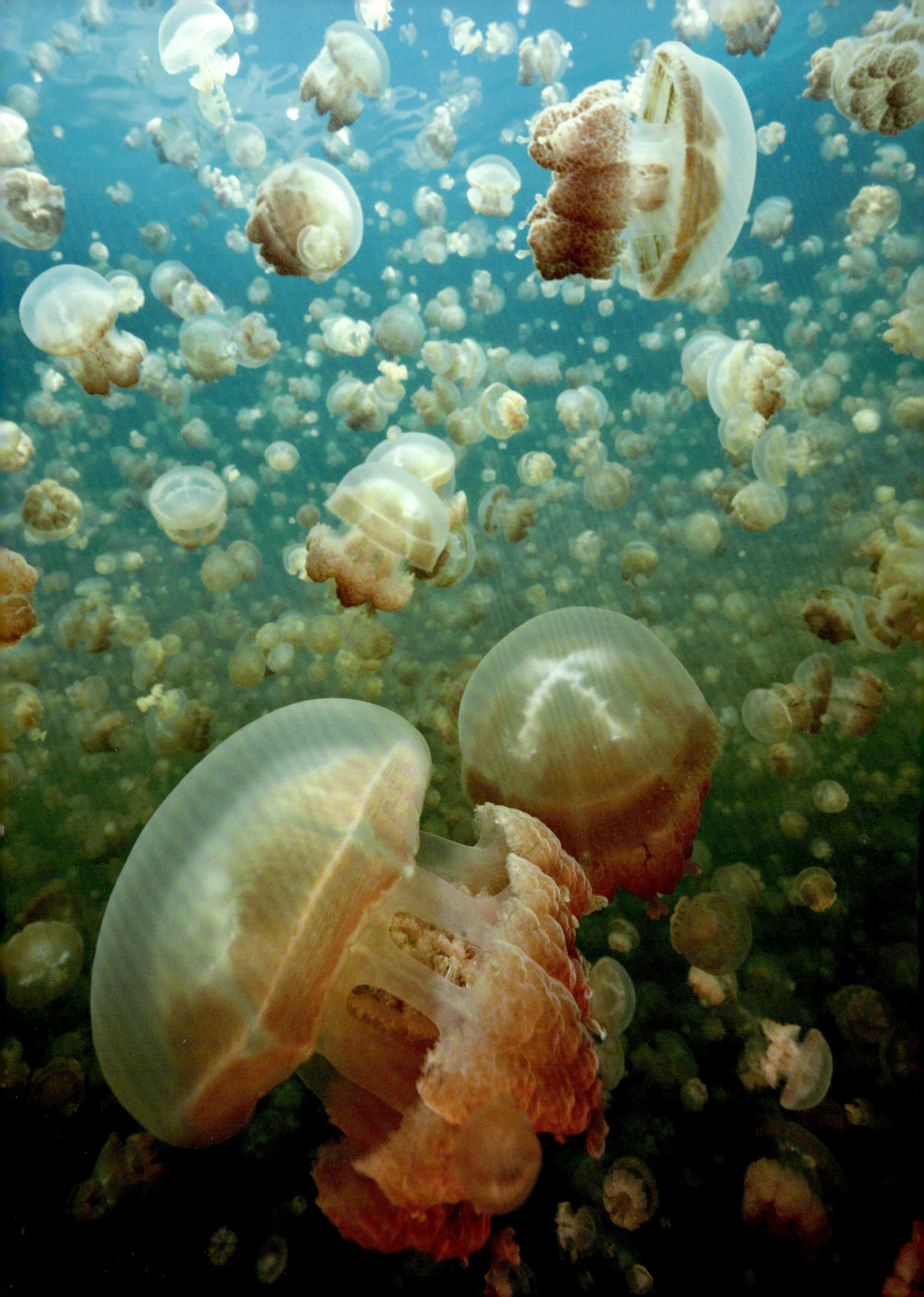

Lagoon Jelly
Mastigias papua

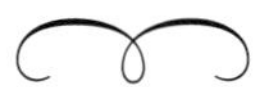

The lagoon jelly is both amusing and amazing. Its golden body seems to dance as it swims about by rapid pulsations. This beautiful species is also safe to swim with! *Mastigias papua* is found throughout the western Pacific Ocean, including the inland marine lakes of the Palau archipelago. Here, at least five different subspecies each inhabit their own lakes. Separated from predators, these isolated populations of *M. papua* have lost the need to defend themselves. Likewise, the species lives in lives in symbiosis with microscopic algae, as corals do, so it does not kill prey. As a result, over evolutionary time it has lost its stinging cells. The lagoon jelly is now just a harmless agriculturist, farming the algae that feed it.

SIZE: Bell diameter to 2¾ inches (7 cm)

Violet Bubble Jelly

Cephea cephea

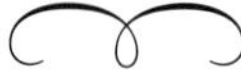

This jellyfish is glorious to behold, but it is as
pestilent as it is pretty. Its body is a glassy, bluish-
violet above and brown and lacy below, with dozens
of transparent filaments streaming down. The upper
surface of the body is sculpted like an island in a moat,
with around twenty finger-like projections sticking out
in all directions from the hump. It really doesn't look
real . . . but it is. *Cephea cephea* is common throughout
the tropical and subtropical Indo-Pacific, where it
is harvested as a delicacy for Chinese and Japanese
consumers. Occasionally, it blooms in vast numbers,
reaching densities of up to twenty medusae
per 35 cubic feet (1 cubic meter), where it may
disrupt the local ecosystem.

SIZE: Bell diameter to 16 inches (40 cm)

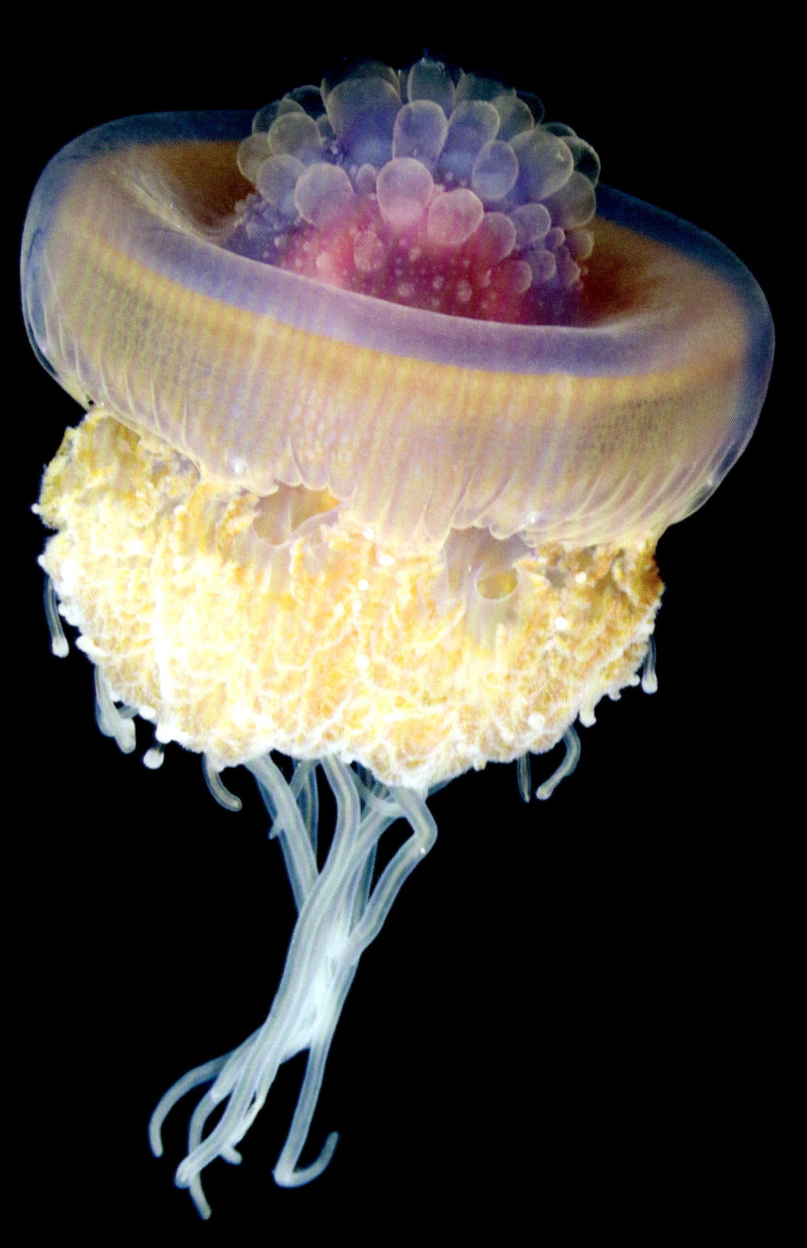

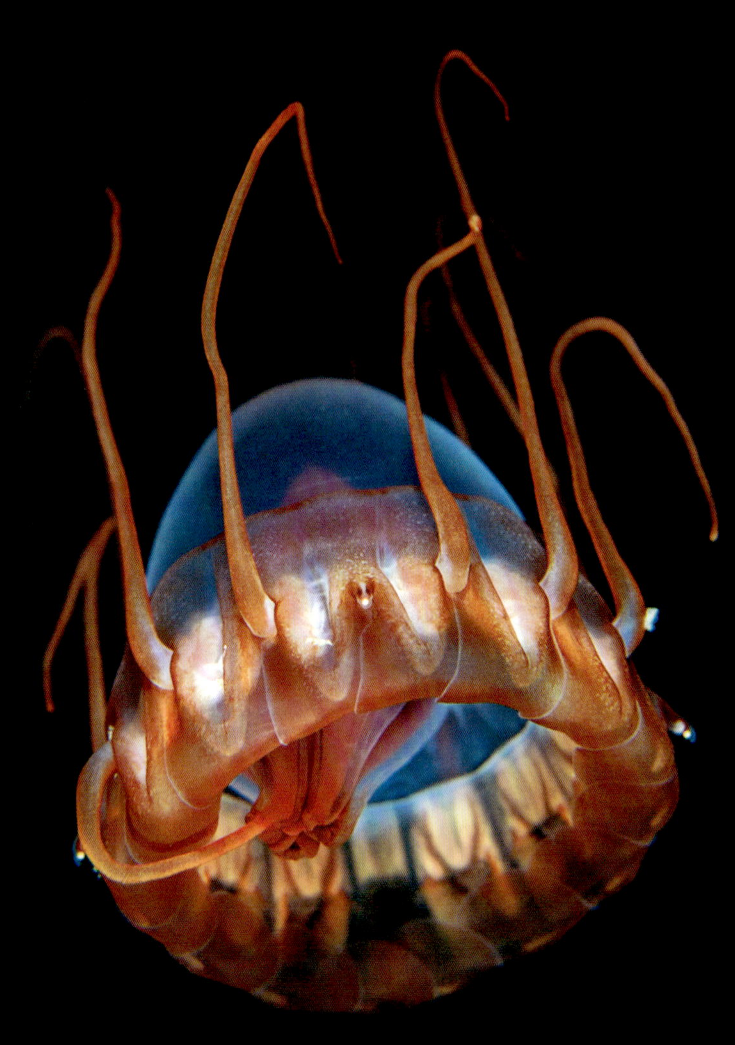

Helmet Jellyfish

Periphylla periphylla

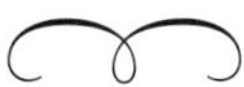

Also known as the Santa's hat jellyfish, *Periphylla periphylla* is common throughout the deep seas of the world, living in the part of the open ocean often called the mesopelagic, or twilight zone, which is so deep, in fact, that even at high noon, light only penetrates faintly. Here, when disturbed, *P. periphylla* provides a glittering light show, with faint blue twinkles around its body. Its dark red stomach, however, is believed to mask the bioluminescent flashes of ingested prey, giving their last cry for help before succumbing. Overfishing in the deep, dark habitats of the Norwegian fjords has enabled *P. periphylla* to invade and take over the role of top predator, preventing fish populations from becoming reestablished.

SIZE: Body height to 14 inches (35 cm)

Bell Jellyfish

Polyorchis penicillatus

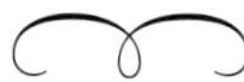

One of the most charismatic of all medusae is the
bell jellyfish, which is found in protected bays and
harbors along the west coast of North America. It whiles
away the day resting on the seabed, with its lips at the
end of a long, slender manubrium, or throat, probing the
sediments for tiny prey. The bright red spots around the
margin of the bell act as light-sensitive eyes, allowing it to
sense shadows. When disturbed, it rises from the seabed
in a great flurry of pulsations and tentacles, before
drifting down again, slowly, with the tentacles extended
in exquisite elegance. Once abundant, *Polyorchis
penicillatus* seems to be vanishing, though
the cause remains a mystery.

SIZE: Body height to 2¾ inches (7 cm)

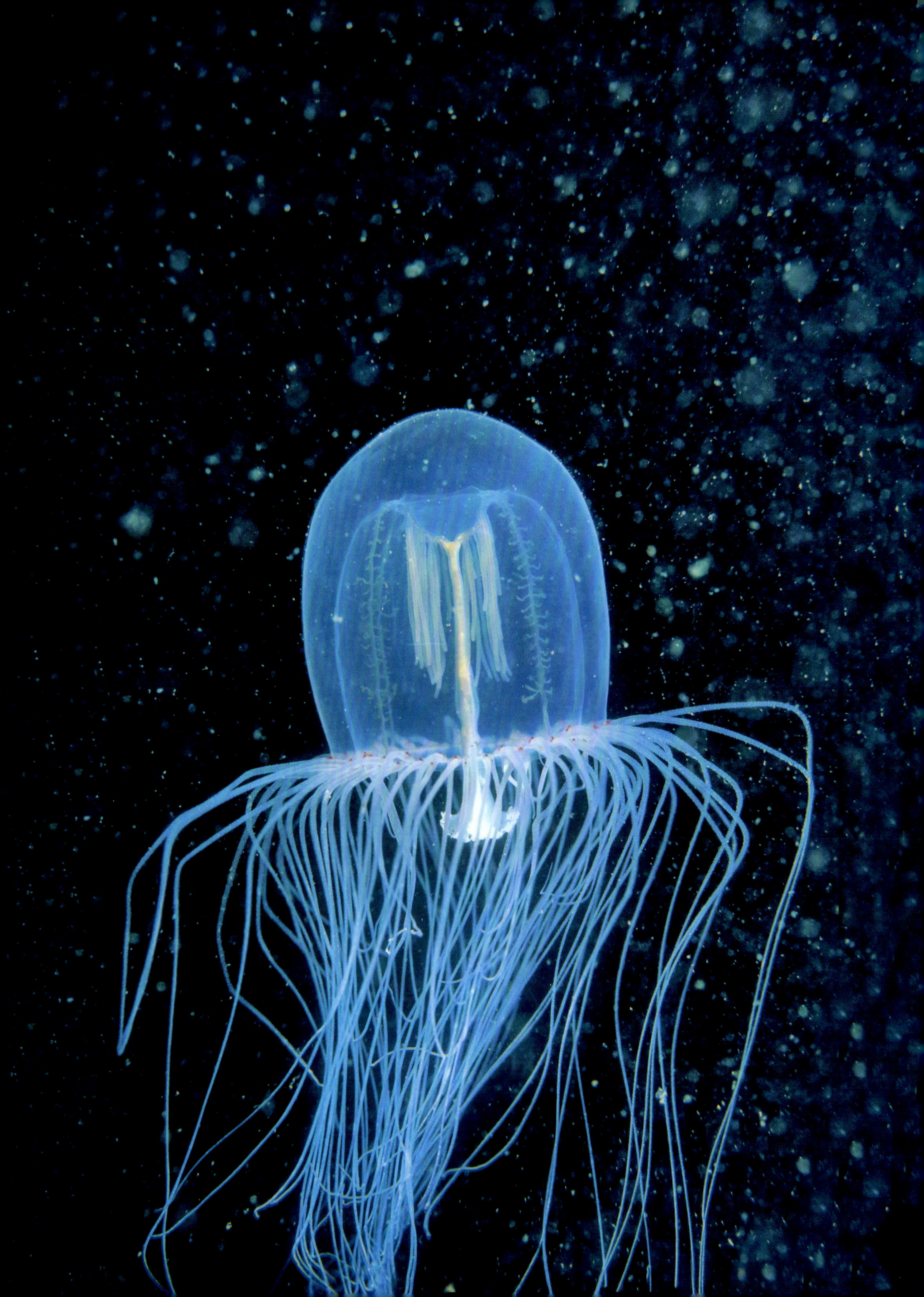

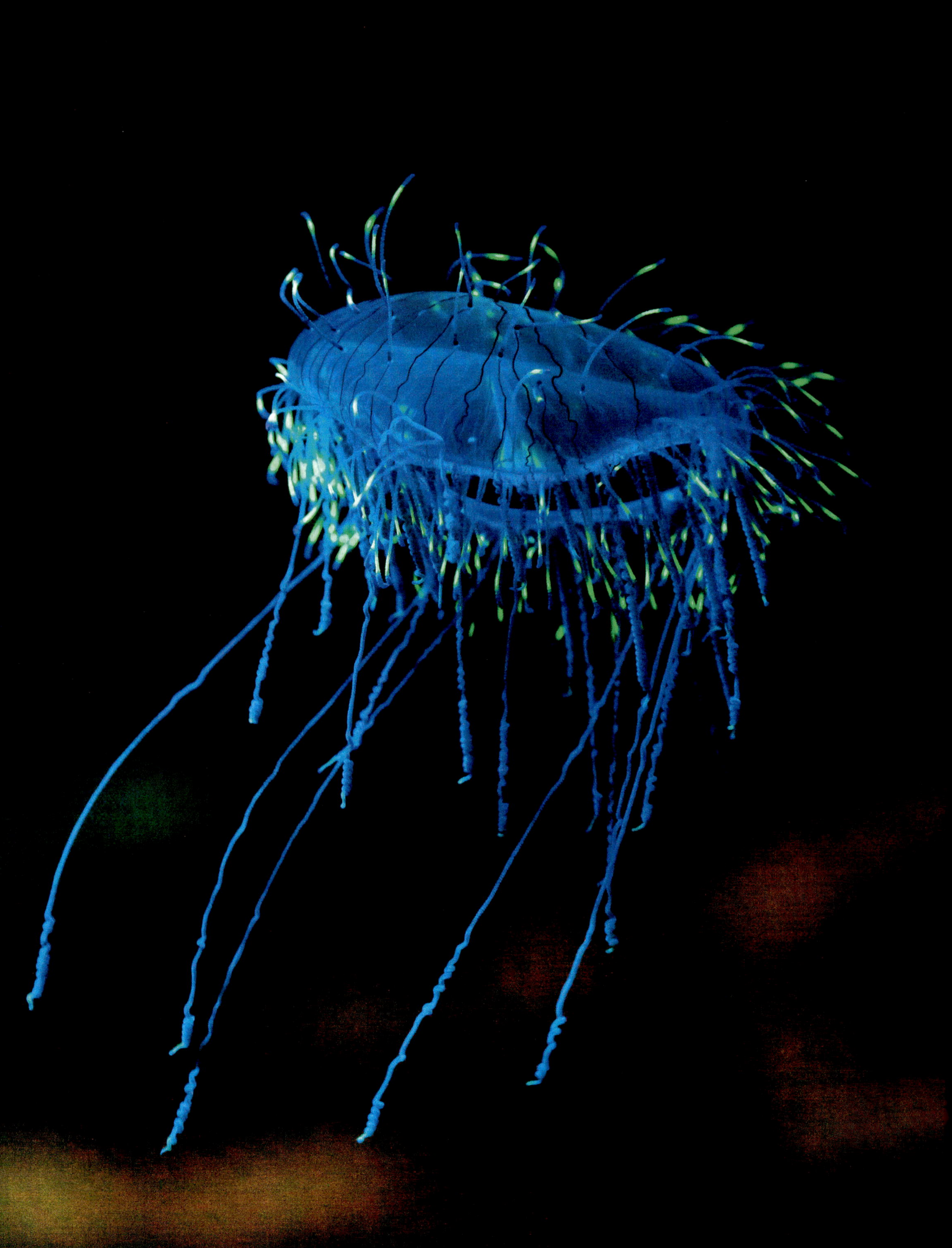

Flower Hat Jelly

Olindias formosus

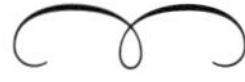

By day, the flower hat jelly dazzles with the
bright pink and bold black streaks that decorate its
body, offering camouflage in its native reedy and
weedy habitat. But by night, or under ultraviolet light, it
becomes radiantly beautiful, with the body glowing softly
blue, accentuated by an aura of luminous, golden-tipped
tentacles. *Olindias formosus* spends its time perched on
marine plants such as kelps and seagrasses, occasionally
relocating by means of full-body flapping. Native to
Japan, it is now a common display species in public
aquariums, where it fulfills two important criteria, being
both easy to raise and glorious to behold. But beware,
O. formosus delivers a painful sting that has proven fatal.

SIZE: Bell diameter to 6 inches (15 cm)

Fluted Jellyfish
Class Stauromedusae

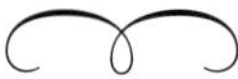

These delightful little jellyfish are unable to swim, instead spending their life affixed to rocks or seaweed. They attach by means of a sticky foot, which connects to the body by a long stalk. The body is goblet-shaped and rimmed by eight arms, each bearing a tuft of fine tentacles. Stauromedusae come in a variety of striking colors and patterns, which helps camouflage them in their intertidal and shallow subtidal habitats. Fewer than a hundred species are known worldwide. Remarkably, being stuck to the seabed doesn't mean they can't move around when necessary, since Stauromedusae simply bend over to one side, use their tentacles to stick to the surface, then release their foot and somersault away.

SIZE: Body length to 1½ inches (4 cm)

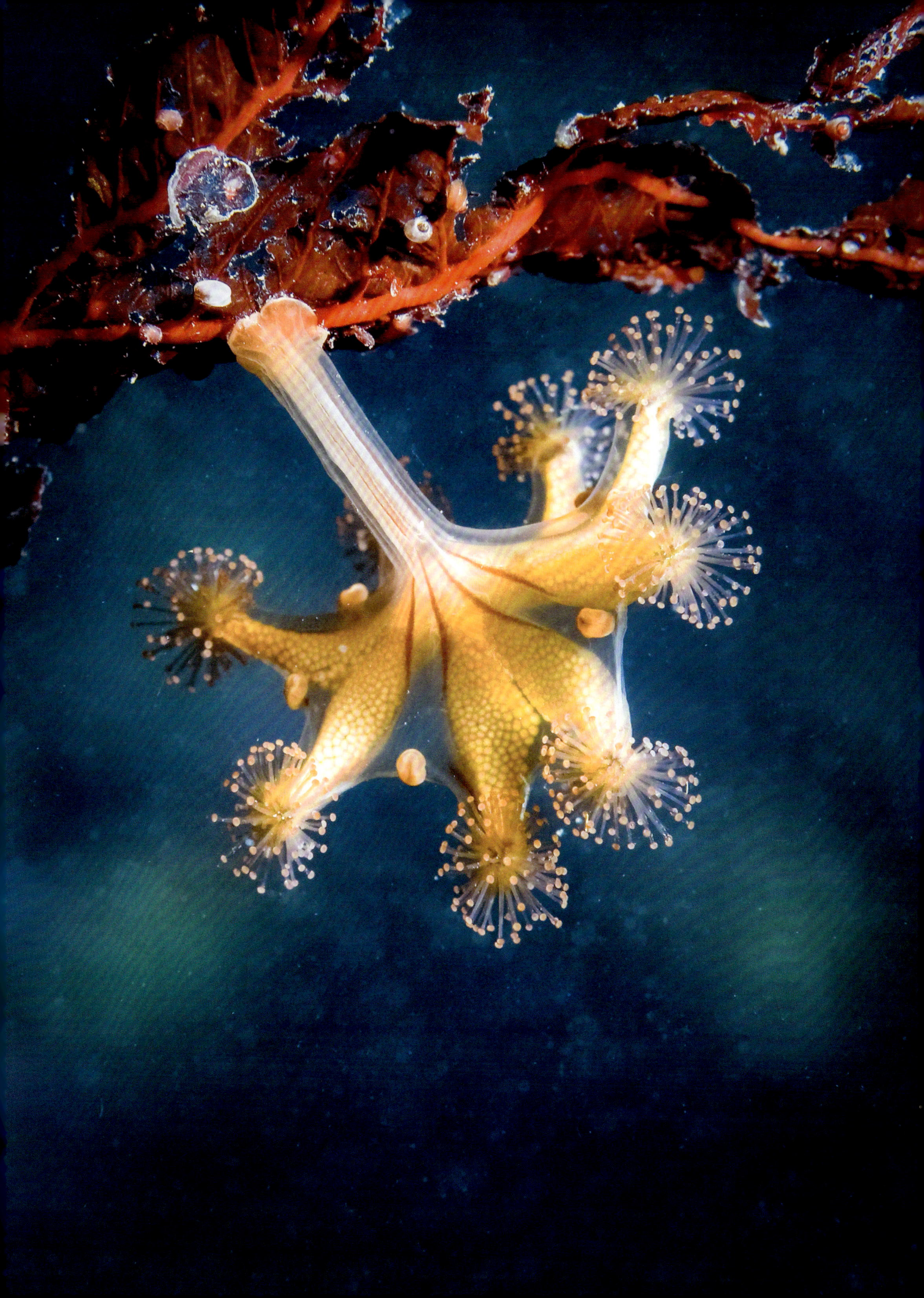

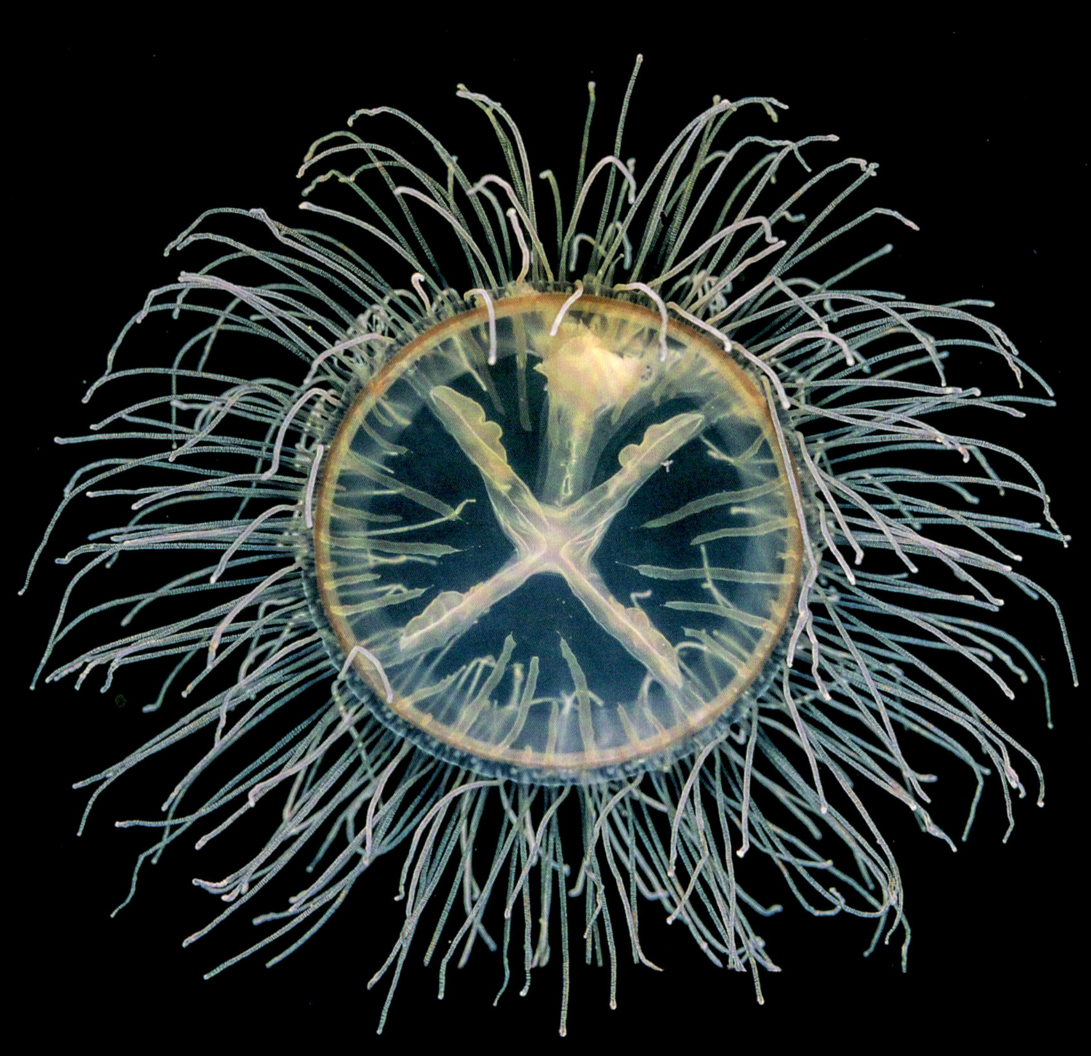

Black Sea Jellyfish

Maeotias marginata

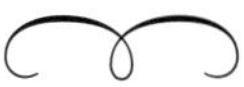

Native to the Black and Azov Seas of Eastern
Europe, *Maeotias marginata* is one of only a handful
of jellies that makes its home in brackish estuaries,
that is, low-salinity river mouths. This feature makes
it the perfect candidate to be carried from port to
port by ships. And this is exactly what has happened
in California. By poetic coincidence, *M. marginata* has
invaded the upper delta of San Francisco Bay and is now
found in abundance in the shadow of the Jelly Belly
jellybean factory. Here, they delight and mesmerize
visitors as they pulse upward to the water's surface,
then flip over and slowly sink, upside down, with their
hundreds of tentacles fanned out to catch tiny plankton.

SIZE: Bell diameter to 2¼ inches (5.5 cm)

Giant Bell Jelly

Scrippsia pacifica

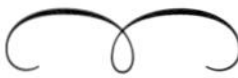

As a rule, hydromedusae (medusae in the cnidarian class Hydrozoa) are typically small and colorless, and easy to overlook. *Scrippsia pacifica* thumbs its tentacles at those rules— being large and flamboyant, it is impossible to miss. Unlike many jellyfish species, it was once abundant, but today is rare. With few historical studies of its ecology, its vanishing is a mystery. Maybe it cannot tolerate warming water, or perhaps it is harmed by chemical changes or sedimentation in the bays where it makes its home. Or perhaps its polyp stage is commensal with another species, which has since been fished out, polluted out, or just died out. Regardless, the world will be a little less delightful when the last *Scrippsia* lays to rest.

SIZE: Bell height to 4 inches (10 cm)

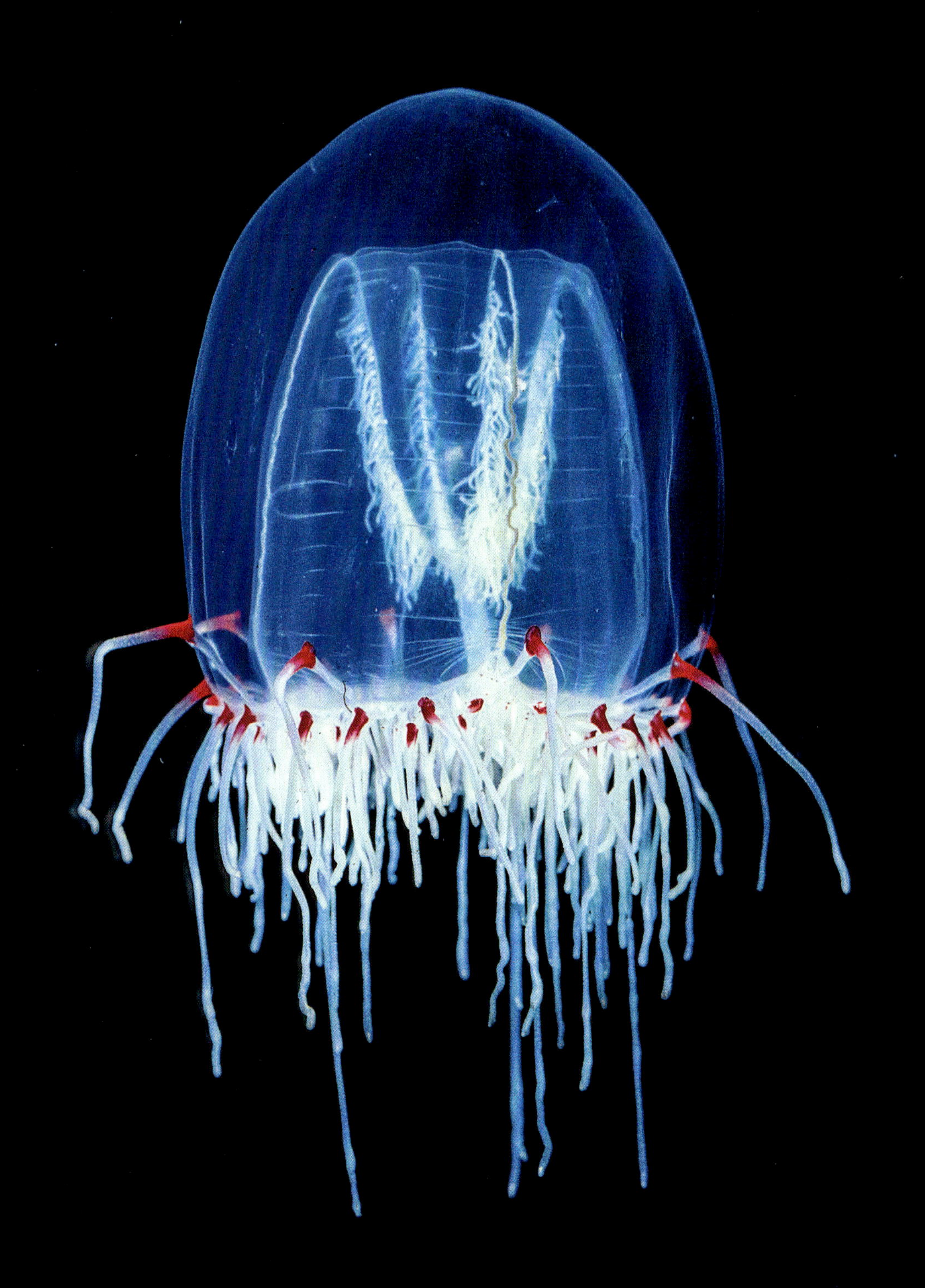

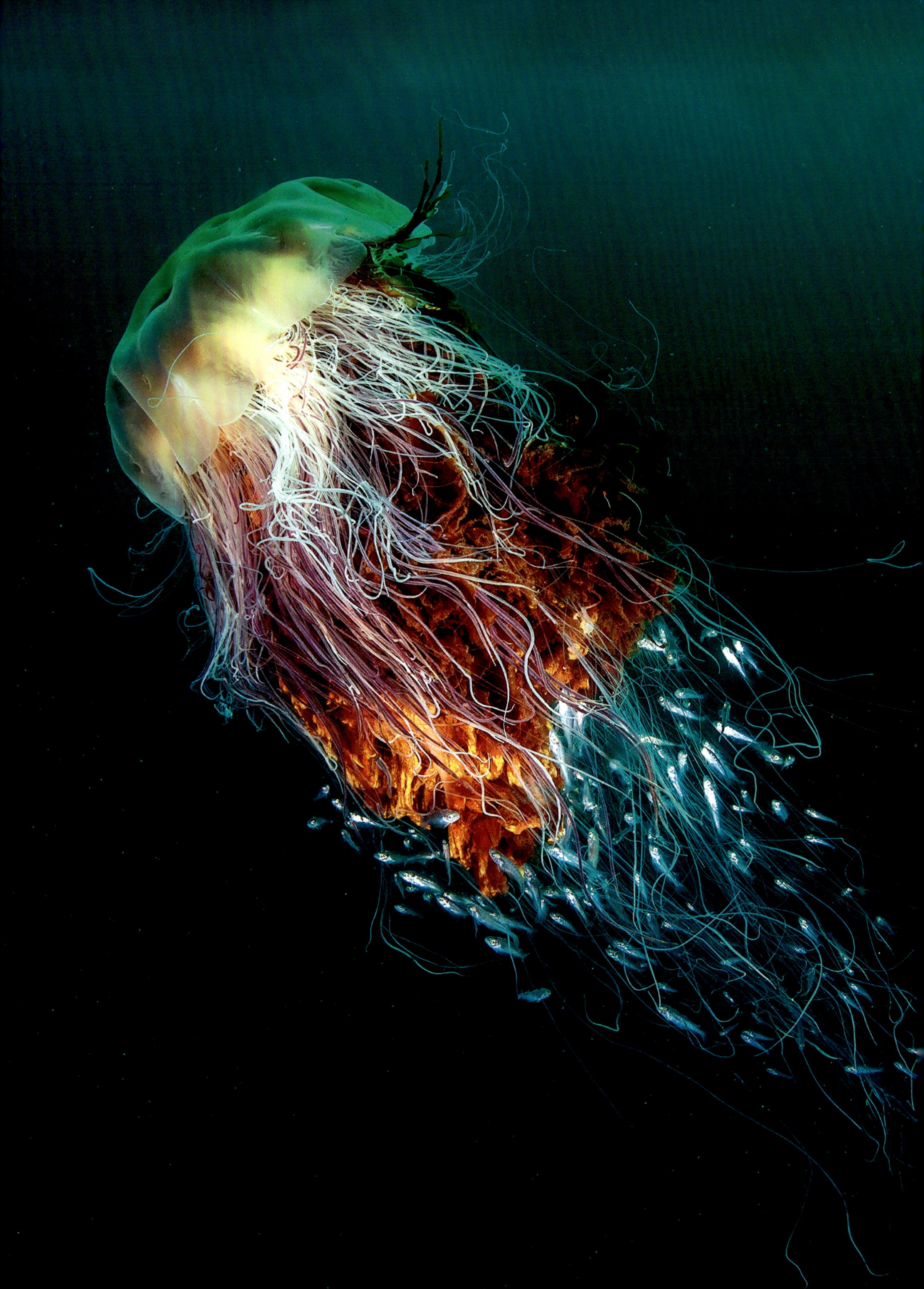

Lion's Mane Jellyfish

Cyanea capillata

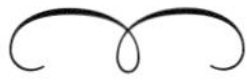

Lion's mane jellies are widespread from the
North Pole to the South Pole. Many different forms
around the world have been mistakenly identified
as *Cyanea capillata*. The true *C. capillata* is brown and
found in the waters around Western Europe. It is easy
to distinguish from two other species that occur in the
region: the bluefire jelly (*C. lamarckii*, see page 22) is
typically bright blue, while the more northern *C. arctica*
is brownish and reaches more than 6½ feet (2 m) across
the body, with tentacles that have been recorded at an
incredible 118 feet (36 m), one-and-a-half times the
length of a blue whale! Lion's manes can deliver a
painful sting, although most are not life-threatening.

SIZE: Bell diameter typically to 20 inches (50 cm)

Ropy Jelly

Thysanostoma

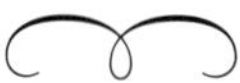

Thysanostoma are helmet- or dome-shaped blubber jellyfish found in tropical seas throughout the Indo-Pacific. Their eight very long, ropy oral arms make them instantly recognizable. The body is generally purple, ranging from electric purple to purple-streaked to purple-rimmed. Like so many other species occurring in poorly studied waters of faraway places, very little is known about any of the three documented *Thysanostoma* species, other than that they are quite rare and spectacular to behold. All sorts of information about these remarkable species, from their biology and ecology to their stings and distribution, are ripe for the taking for curious scientists or citizen scientists to discover and share, to enrich the world's scientific knowledge.

SIZE: Total length to 2 feet (60 cm)

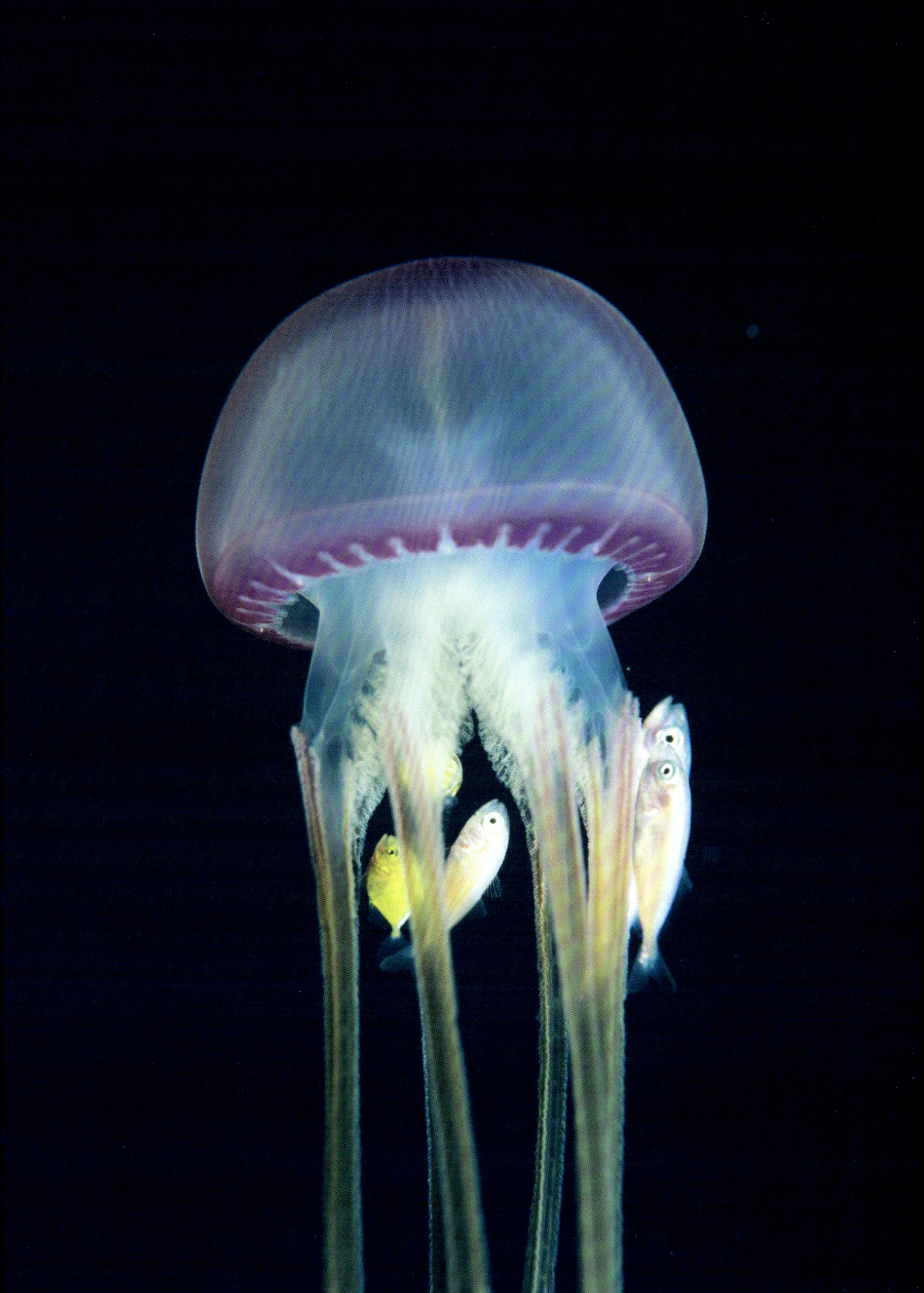

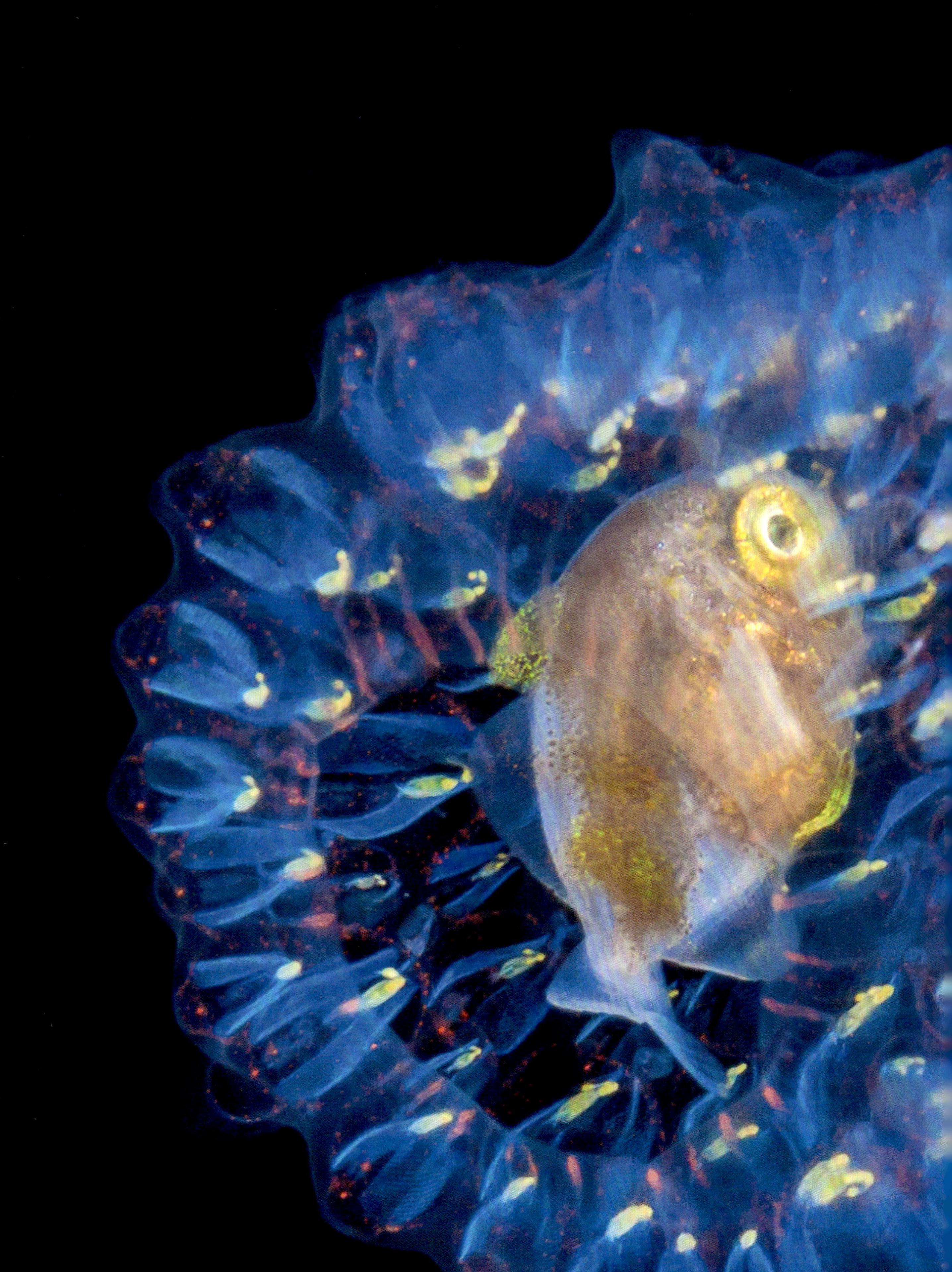

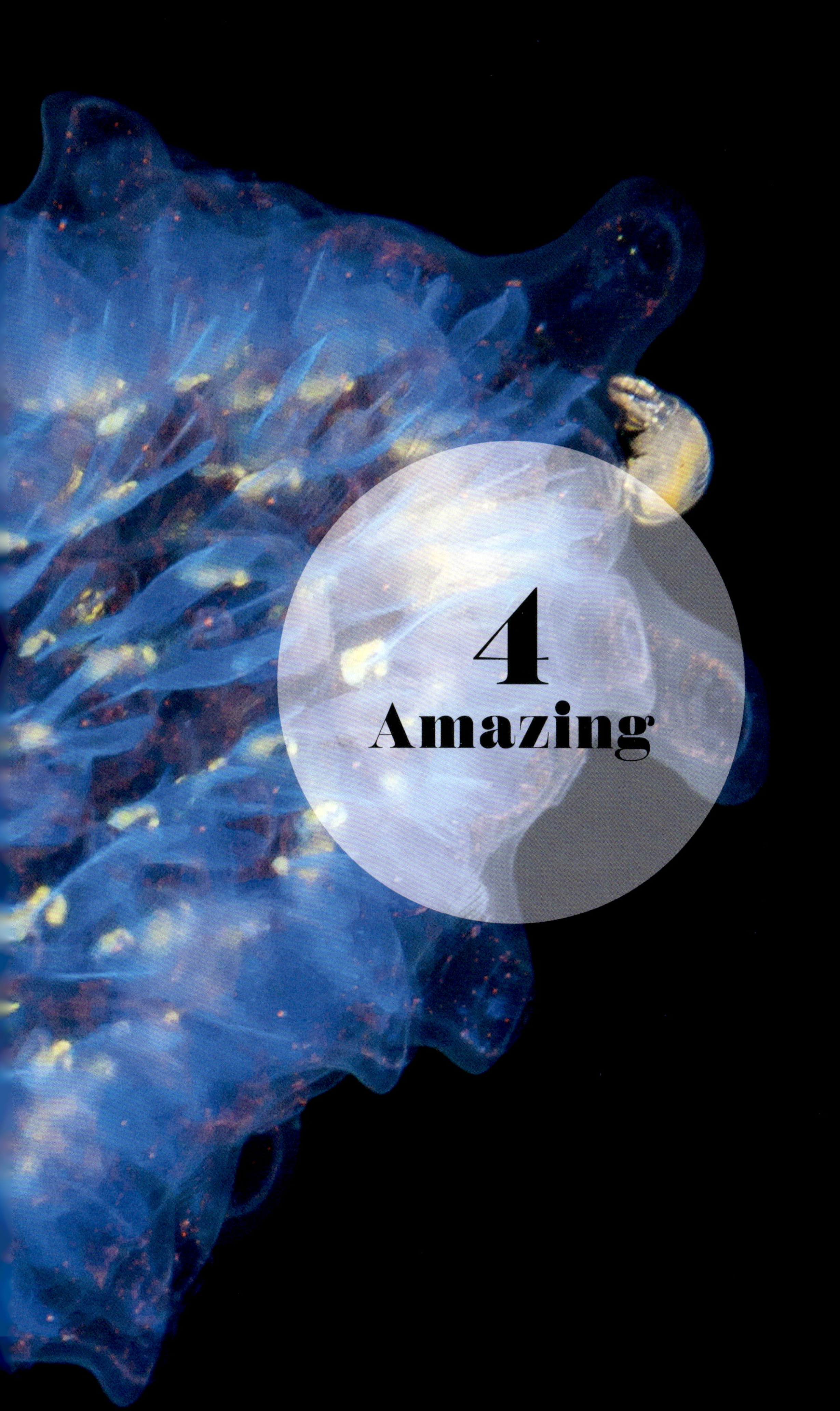
4
Amazing

After looking at jellyfish as the embodiment of both beauty and beast in the first few chapters, we now shift gear to examine these unusual creatures through the lens of awe and wonder.

The creatures that we loosely call "jellyfish" are, in fact, a diverse group of animals that aren't necessarily all that closely related. But amazingly, they all have evolved transparent, gelatinous bodies, a primarily passive drifting lifestyle, and the ability to opportunistically exploit changes to their habitat for their own benefit. Some of these different groups include the stinging species with a free-swimming medusa stage; comb jellies in a dazzling array of shapes but without the ability to sting; colonial siphonophores that are related to medusae but are so highly evolved they no longer resemble them at all; and salps, which are more closely related to humans than to other types of jellyfish.

Jellyfish today have invaded every aquatic habitat, from the deepest seas to the air-water interface, from freshwater streams and reservoirs to fish farms where they parasitize our favorite fish. Most are free-living in the water and have evolved a variety of ways to get around. Many are at the mercy of the currents; regardless of their size, these are classified as plankton, from the Greek word *planktos,* meaning "drifter." Some are quite strong swimmers; those able to swim against a current are called nekton. A few have structures that protrude from the water and are pushed around by the wind.

There is something hauntingly alien about these survivors from a time long passed, ancient beings still operating as they did hundreds of millions of years ago. While almost every other living thing with which they share this planet has evolved anew in their shadow, they haven't changed through the eons because they haven't needed to. Their way of life works. They have survived every mass extinction. Time after time, they persisted. These highly adaptable, opportunistic, hearty survivors have been here since the dawn of animal life and will persist long after we are forgotten.

In this chapter, we will visit species with sophisticated behaviors, such as courtship and navigation without a brain; a species whose proteins have profoundly changed the course of medical research; another species that may extend the date of animal origin *by double*; and the first known organism that is truly biologically immortal. Jellyfish are, in the fullest sense of the word, amazing.

Immortal Jellyfish

Turritopsis

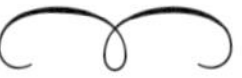

Throughout human history and across cultures, many
people have wondered what it would be like to live
forever. Jellyfish in the genus *Turritopsis* are small and
thimble-shaped, with a beautiful red stomach and a
fringe of exquisite, thread-fine tentacles. Several species,
including *T. dohrnii* from Italy's Adriatic Sea, are more
than just pretty. They are truly biologically immortal.
When the jellyfish dies, its cells reform into a larval
state and it comes back to life, able to bud off more baby
jellyfish. The genetics underlying this miraculous process
are not yet fully understood. In most species genes are
programmed to age and die, but in these immortal
species they continue, seemingly on an endless loop.

SIZE: Bell height to ⅜ inch (1 cm)

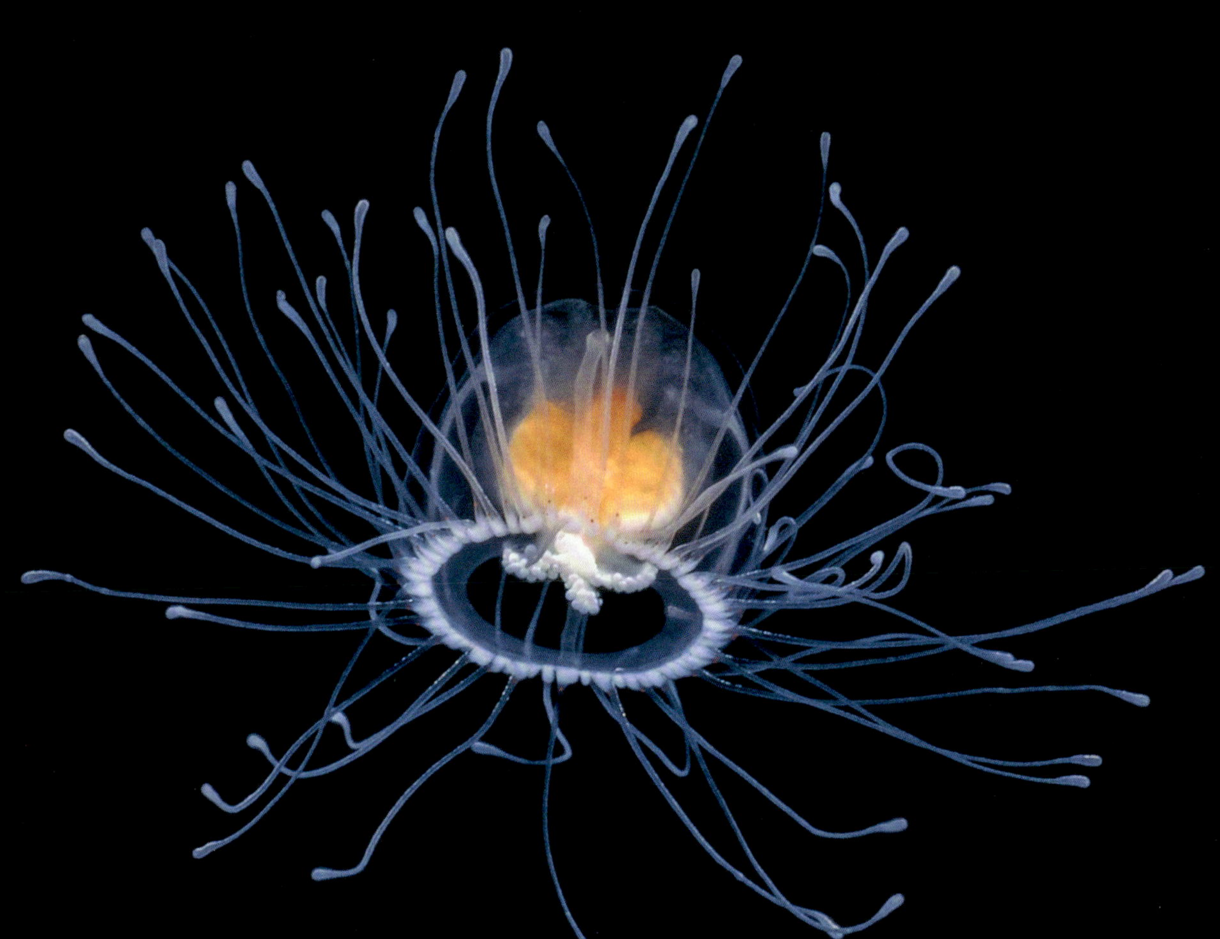

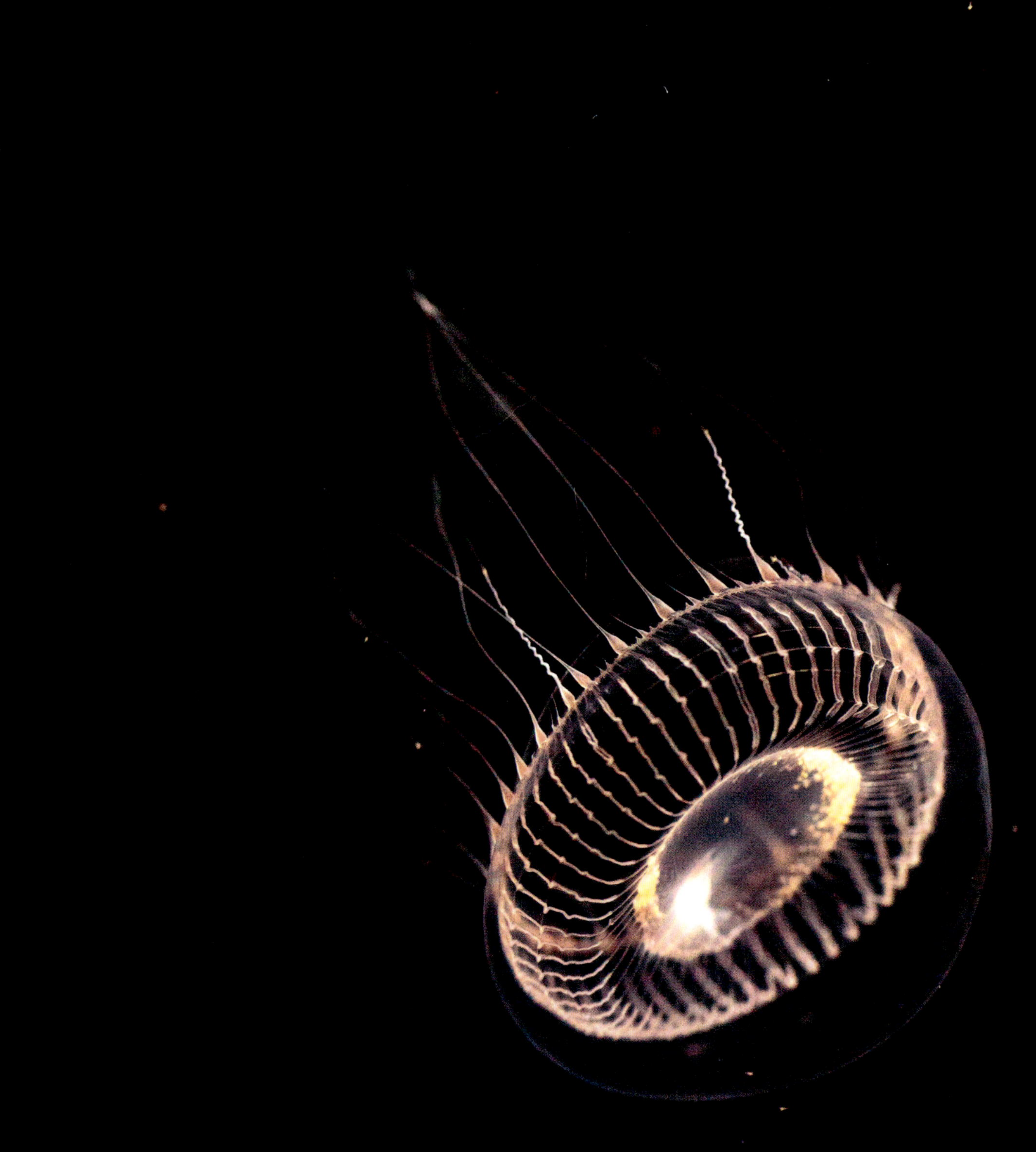

Crystal Jelly

Aequorea victoria

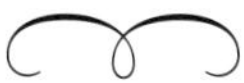

The crystal jelly, native to west coast Canada's
British Columbia, drifts motionless on marine currents
with its long, fine tentacles streaming out behind. Its
humble and elegant appearance belies a splendid secret.
Many jellies are bioluminescent—they produce their own
light—and some are fluorescent, reflecting light when
stimulated by an external source. But the crystal jelly is
both. At night, it reacts to disturbance with a bright blue
flash (bioluminescence), while tiny dots of brilliant green
around the margin can be stimulated by ultraviolet
light (fluorescence). The green fluorescent protein (GFP)
involved in the fluorescence has been harvested and
synthesized from these dots, and it is now a critically
important part of neurological and developmental
research, earning its discoverers a Nobel Prize in 2008.

SIZE: Bell diameter to 4¾ inches (12 cm)

Courtship Jelly

Copula sivickisi

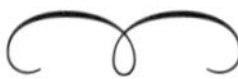

Most of the time, this demure species uses its
adhesive pads on the top of its bell to stick to seagrasses
and seaweeds. But during breeding season, it does
something truly remarkable. Fertile females develop
pigment spots, and when males see these, a courtship
dance begins, culminating with the male depositing a
packet of sperm inside the female to fertilize her eggs.
The reason that this is so amazing is that *Copula sivickisi*
has no brain. Like other box jellies, it has well-developed
complex eyes, and its courtship dance is the pinnacle
of complex behavior, but scientists are yet to
explain how these work without a brain.

SIZE: Bell height to ⅜ inch (10 mm)

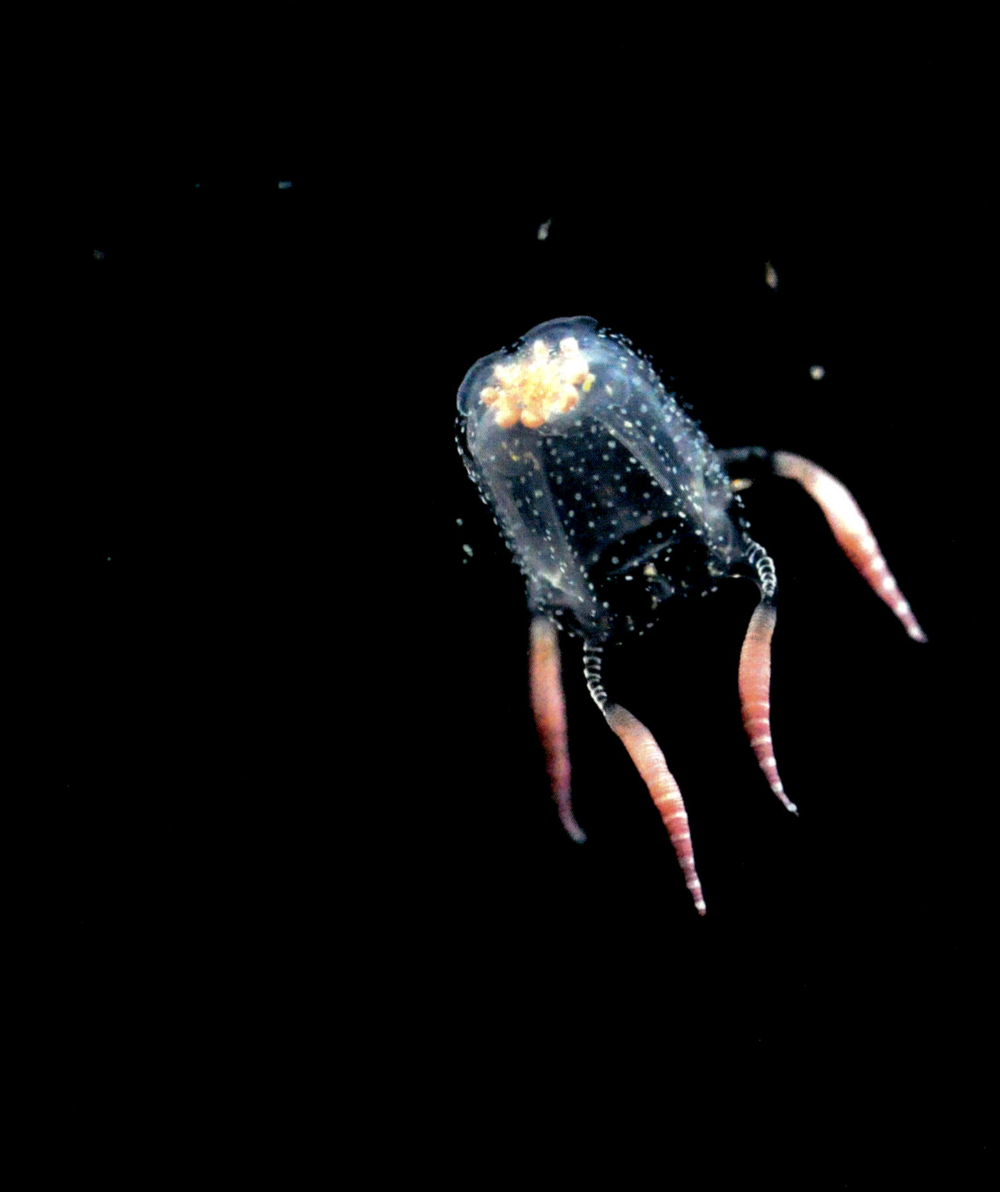

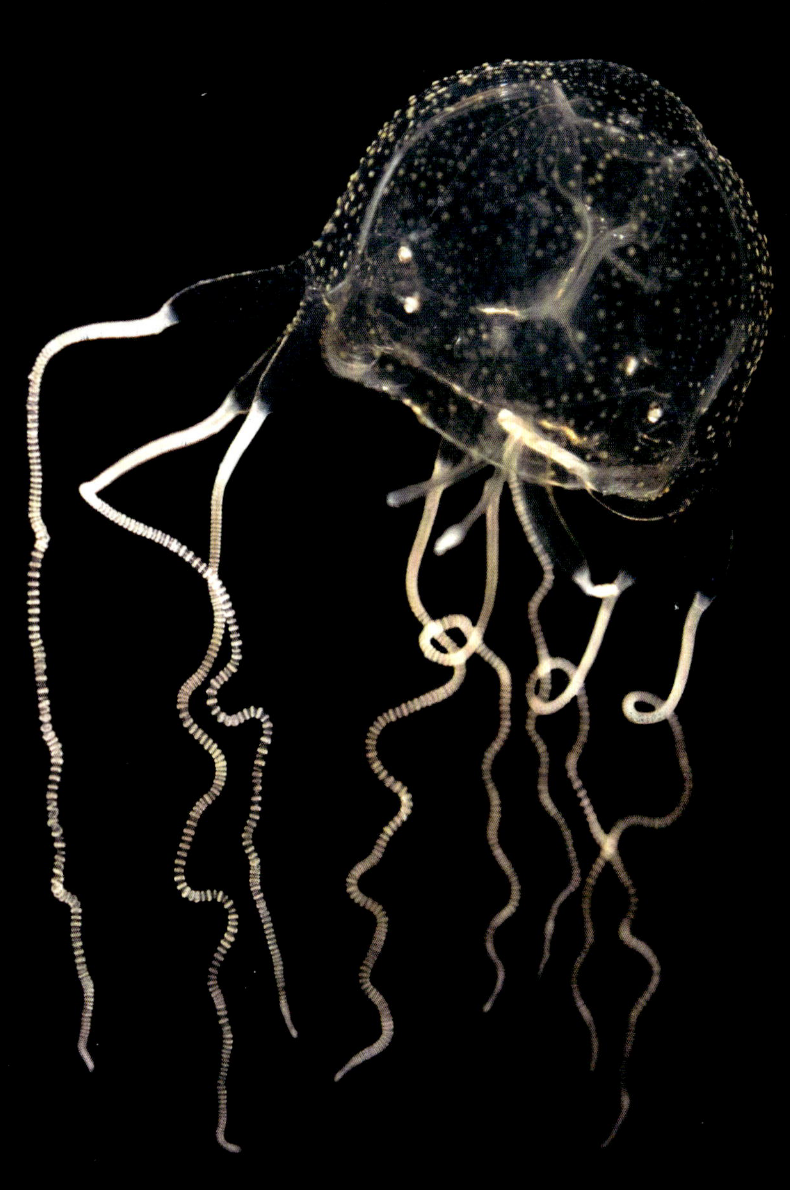

Mangrove Box Jellyfish
Tripedalia cystophora

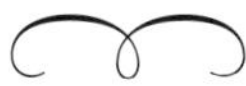

What the mangrove box jellyfish lacks in size, this diminutive species makes up for in its fascinating biology and ecology. Its native habitat is tropical mangroves, where it uses shafts of light to hunt copepods, or tiny crustaceans, and other plankton. *Tripedalia cystophora* is an agile swimmer, thanks to its well-developed eyes. On each of the four flat sides of its cube-shaped body, it possesses a knob of six eyes. The central two are complex with a lens, retina, and cornea, both facing inward, one toward the mouth and the other upward toward the mangroves. The other four are merely light sensory. Despite having no brain, it easily navigates this complex environment, swimming in a pattern between the mangrove roots in its hunt for daily sustenance.

SIZE: Bell height to ½ inch (13 mm)

Freshwater Jellyfish

Craspedacusta sowerbyi

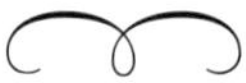

Among the most surprising of all jellyfish are those that are normally found in freshwater. These lacy little beings are found in lakes, streams, and especially artificial reservoirs all over the world, on every continent except Antarctica. They may form seasonal blooms so dense that drifting among them can seem like swimming in a blizzard. The sting of *Craspedacusta sowerbyi* is not known to be painful, but caution should still be exercised when swimming around them *just in case*. Scientists believe that *C. sowerbyi* is carried between water bodies by its polyp stages clinging to sediments between the toes of birds. Intriguingly, freshwater jellies readily eat mosquito larvae, which may one day prove to be useful as a mosquito control measure.

SIZE: Bell diameter to ¾ inch (20 mm)

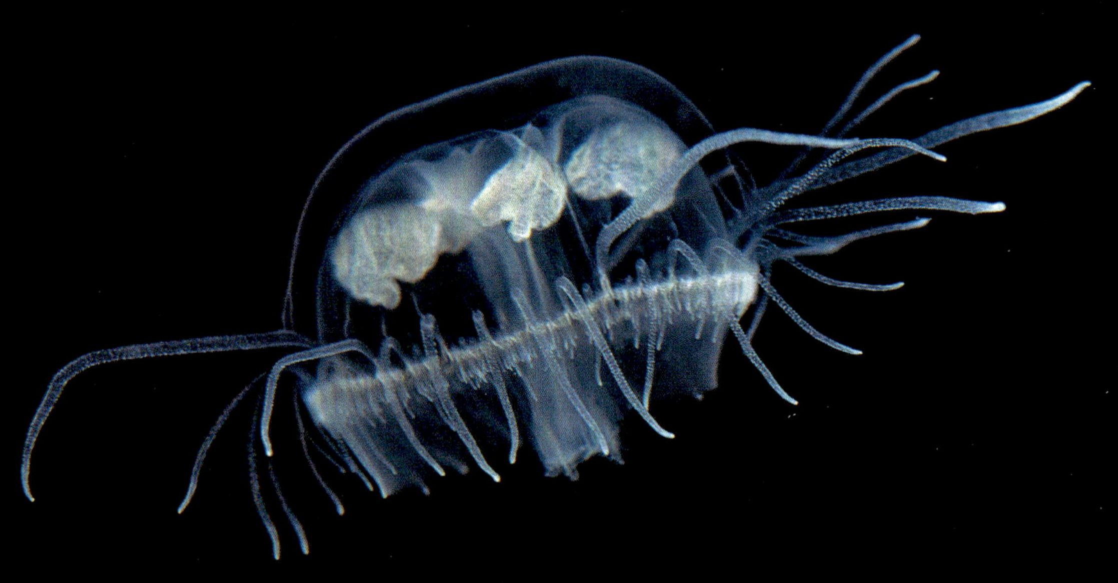

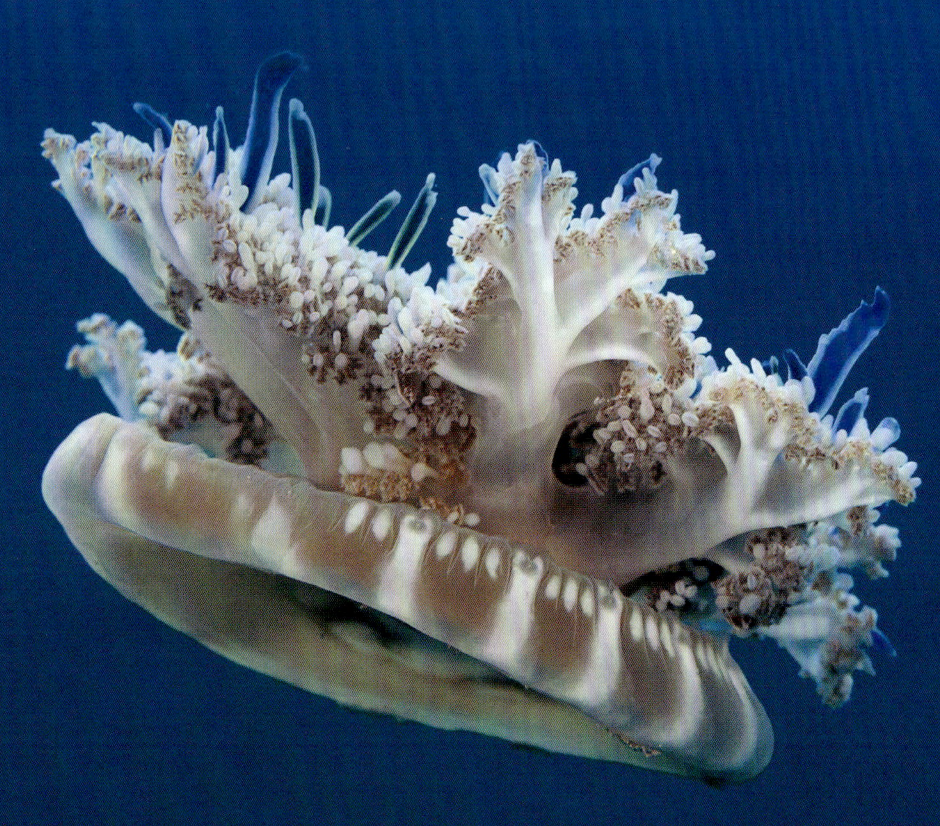

Upside-Down Jellyfish

Cassiopea

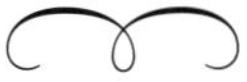

The upside-down jellyfish comprise a
group of more than a dozen species, which are some
of the most intriguing of all jellies. Native to tropical
lagoons, members of the *Cassiopea* genus are but humble
farmers, perched on rocks and stones, with the bell
angled downward to give the algal symbionts in their
tissues maximum exposure to sunlight. They pulse from
time to time to propel themselves away from stale water
and flood their algae with fresher, oxygenated water.
They are able to swim, but most of the time they don't.
Cassiopea may look gentle, but looks can be deceiving.
They release tiny packets of stinging cells into the
water above, where unsuspecting divers and
swimmers may be quite fiercely stung.

SIZE: Bell diameter to 14 inches (35 cm)

By-the-Wind Sailor

Velella velella

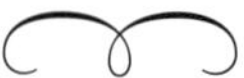

Organisms living at the air-water interface must contend with both terrestrial and aquatic factors such as temperature, salinity, and drying out. But those who also have a sail that sticks up into the air lead an especially dangerous existence. Utterly at the mercy of winds and breezes, either the winds die down or they drive the jellies to their death. Nature has a ploy, however, for ensuring that only a fraction of the *Velella velella* population is stranded and lost at one time. On the high seas, *V. velella* is either right- or left-handed depending on how the crest is angled obliquely along the main body axis. For example, if the jelly is left-handed, then the crest runs from upper left to lower right along the body. When a breeze arises, it pushes only those with the crest oriented at the corresponding angle.

SIZE: Float length to 4 inches (10 cm)

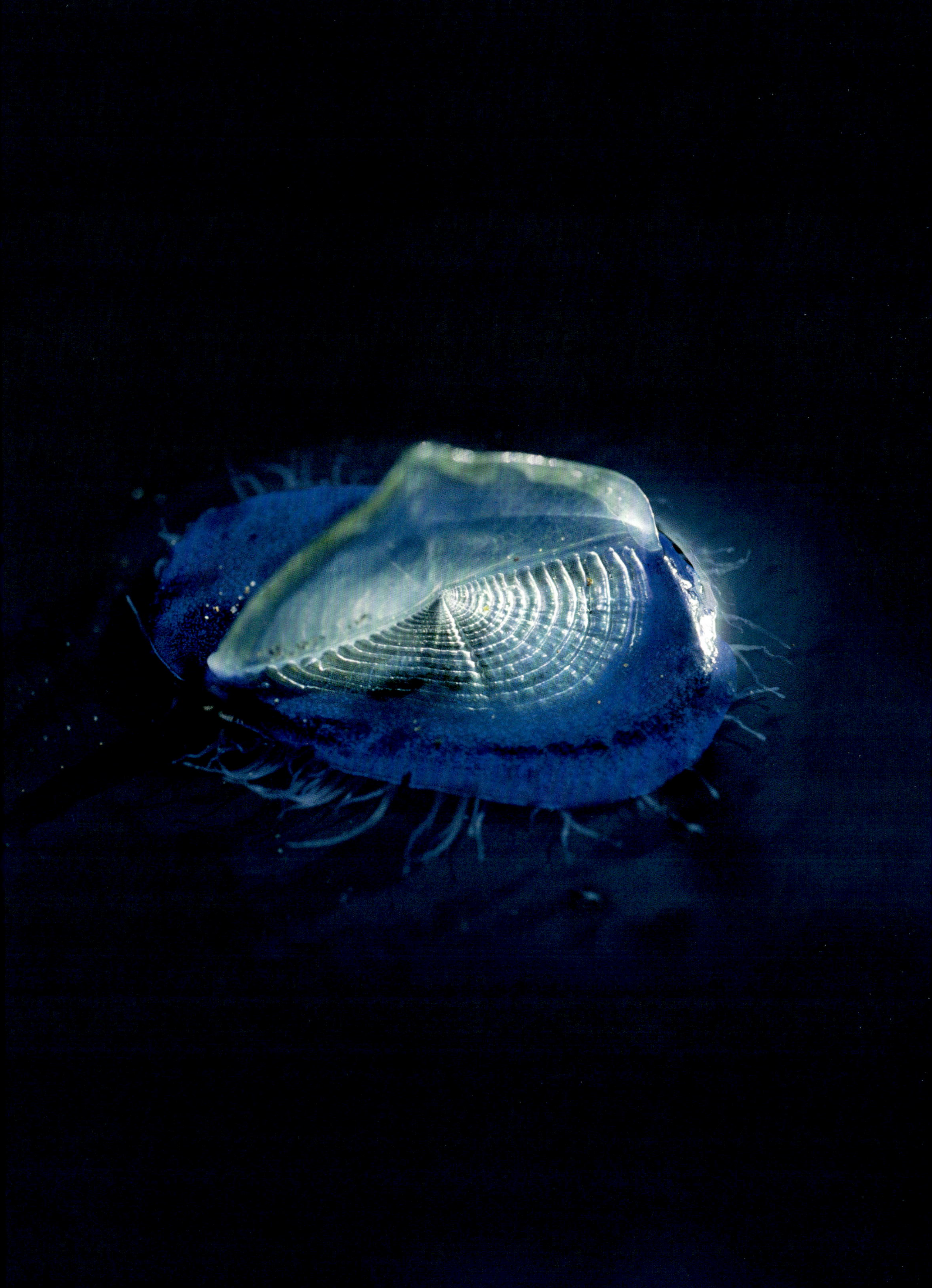

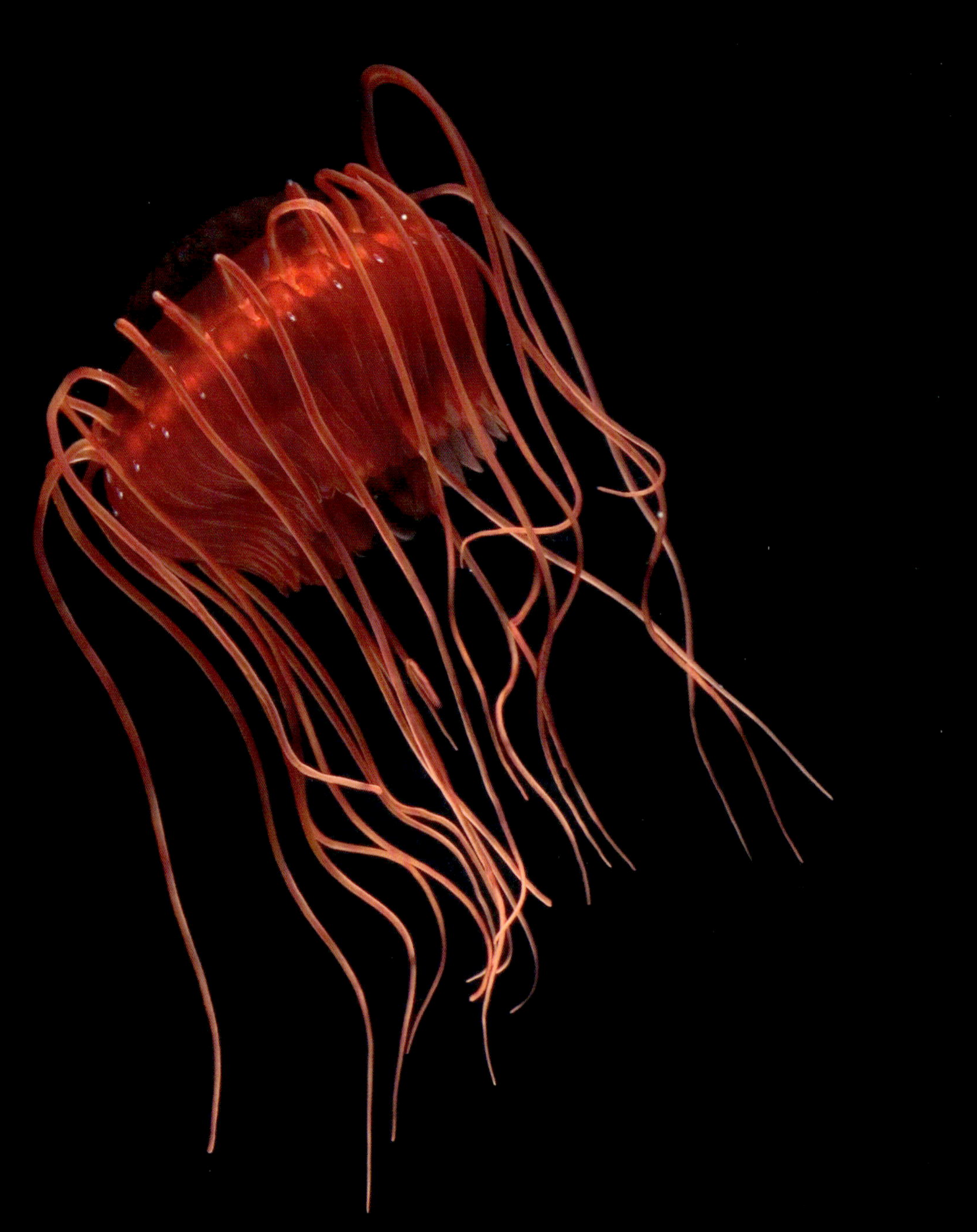

Flying Saucer Jellyfish

Atolla wyvillei

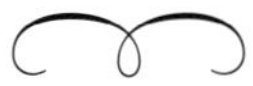

The flying saucer jellyfish inhabits the deep oceans across the world, so deep that light barely penetrates. At these depths, the color red appears black, allowing *Atolla wyvillei* to hide in plain sight. One of this flying-saucer-shaped jelly's tentacles is often observed to be much longer than the others, providing endless fodder for speculation. Is it a lure for catching prey, or a trawl for accumulating prey? Is it used to capture and hold a mate, or a way for males to inseminate females? Is it sensory? Like its cousin *Periphylla periphylla*, it is thought that the opaque red stomach of *A. wyvillei* shields the frantic bioluminescent flashes of its prey from other species who might attack the predator; once harpooned and ingested, the prey stands no chance.

SIZE: Bell diameter to 6 inches (15 cm)

Haeckel's Jelly

Pseudorhiza haeckeli

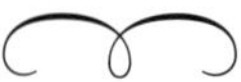

Haeckel's jelly might be mistaken for just an ordinary
purple blubber, but it bears a mysterious organ that has
stumped scientists for more than two hundred years.
Nestled off to one side within the lacy "mouthlets"—the
hundreds of tiny mouths that cover its oral arms—most
specimens grow a single long, fleshy, three-winged
appendage. Jellies are, as a rule, radially symmetrical,
but this structure makes *Pseudorhiza haeckeli* very
strongly asymmetrical. No one has ever offered a
satisfactory hypothesis as to what the jellyfish might use
this appendage for or why it is off-center. Besides this
mysterious palp, *P. haeckeli* is unmistakable due
to its lilac body color and red mesh accentuating
its bumpy surface.

SIZE: Bell diameter to 16 inches (40 cm)

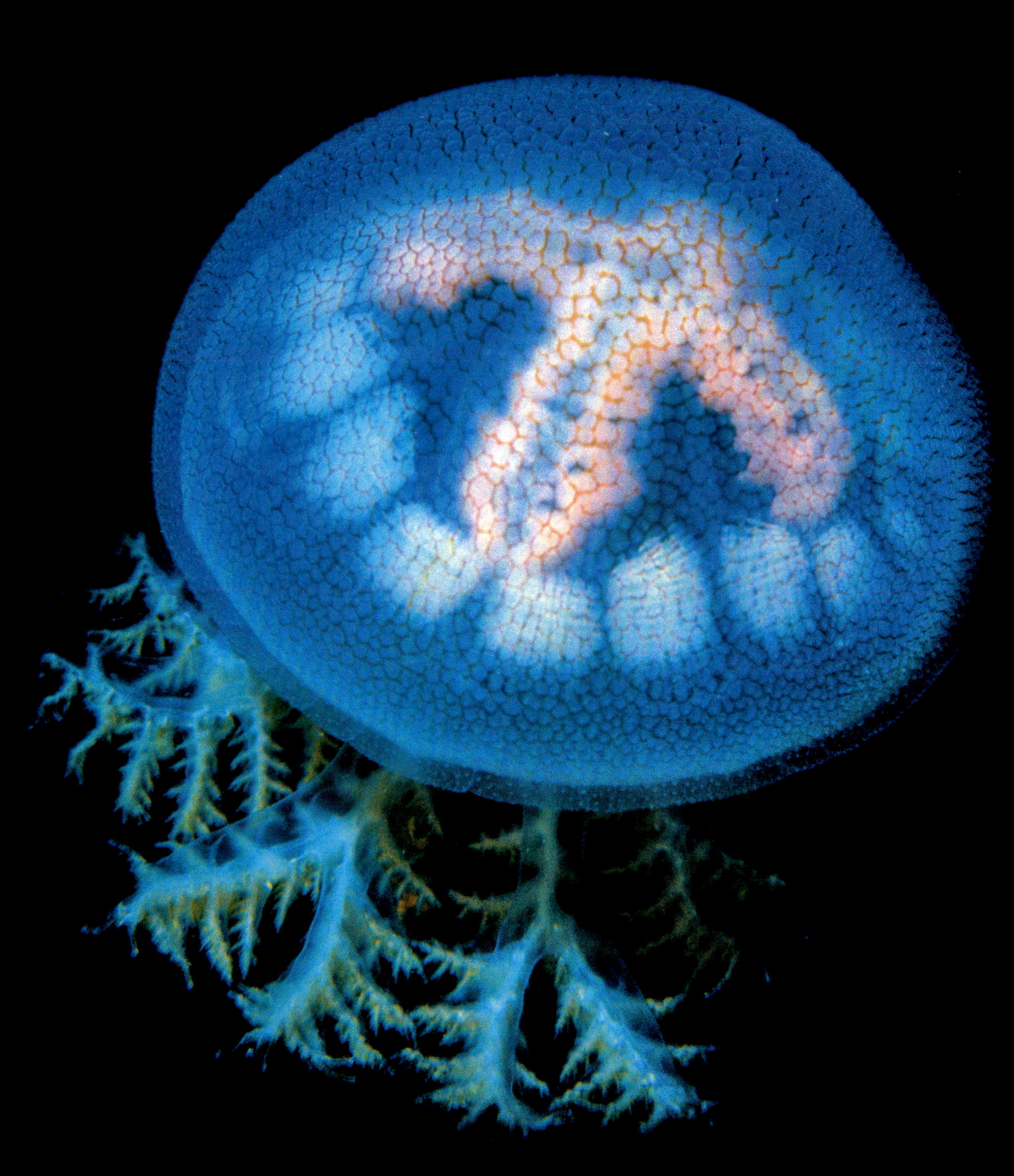

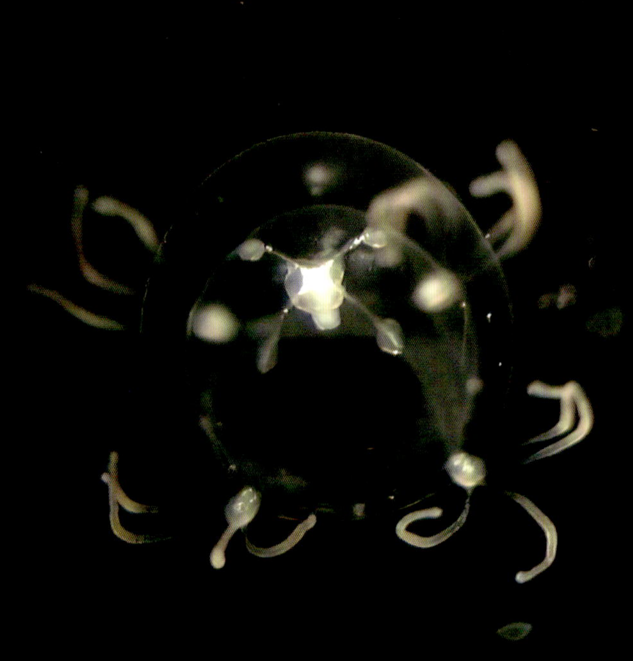

Saltwater Lake Jelly

Australomedusa thrombolites

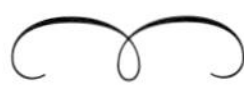

The oldest living organisms on Earth
are the stromatolites, columnar colonies of
cyanobacteria, or bluegreen algae, which date back
3.5 billion years and only survive today in rare
populations. An often-overlooked relative is the
thrombolites, which form low, broad mounds in hyper-
saline inland lakes scattered throughout southern
Australia. *Australomedusa thrombolites*, so named because
of its most peculiar neighbors, makes its home in and
among these sentinels from the ancient world. Lake
Clifton in Western Australia is steeped in Aboriginal
mythology because of the thrombolites, and yet most
people making the journey to see these living rocks
would never imagine that the water is also thronging
with minute medusae the size of a poppy seed.

SIZE: Bell height to $\frac{1}{16}$ inch (1.5 mm)

Paradoxical Jelly

Eucheilota paradoxica

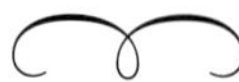

Most jellies that attract attention are large
and showy or frighteningly dangerous. *Eucheilota
paradoxica* is neither. It is, however, menacing in its own
right. This diminutive species clones baby jellies off its
own reproductive organs on the underside of its body,
circumventing the need for sexual reproduction. A
mature medusa may have half a dozen babies growing
at any one time before they are released into the
surrounding water, allowing the species to multiply
rapidly. Native to the eastern United States, it now
forms seasonally dense blooms in Australia. Its
sting isn't painful to humans, but it may threaten
the healthy functioning of coastal habitats due to its
voracious consumption of eggs and larvae.

SIZE: Bell diameter to ⅛ inch (3 mm)

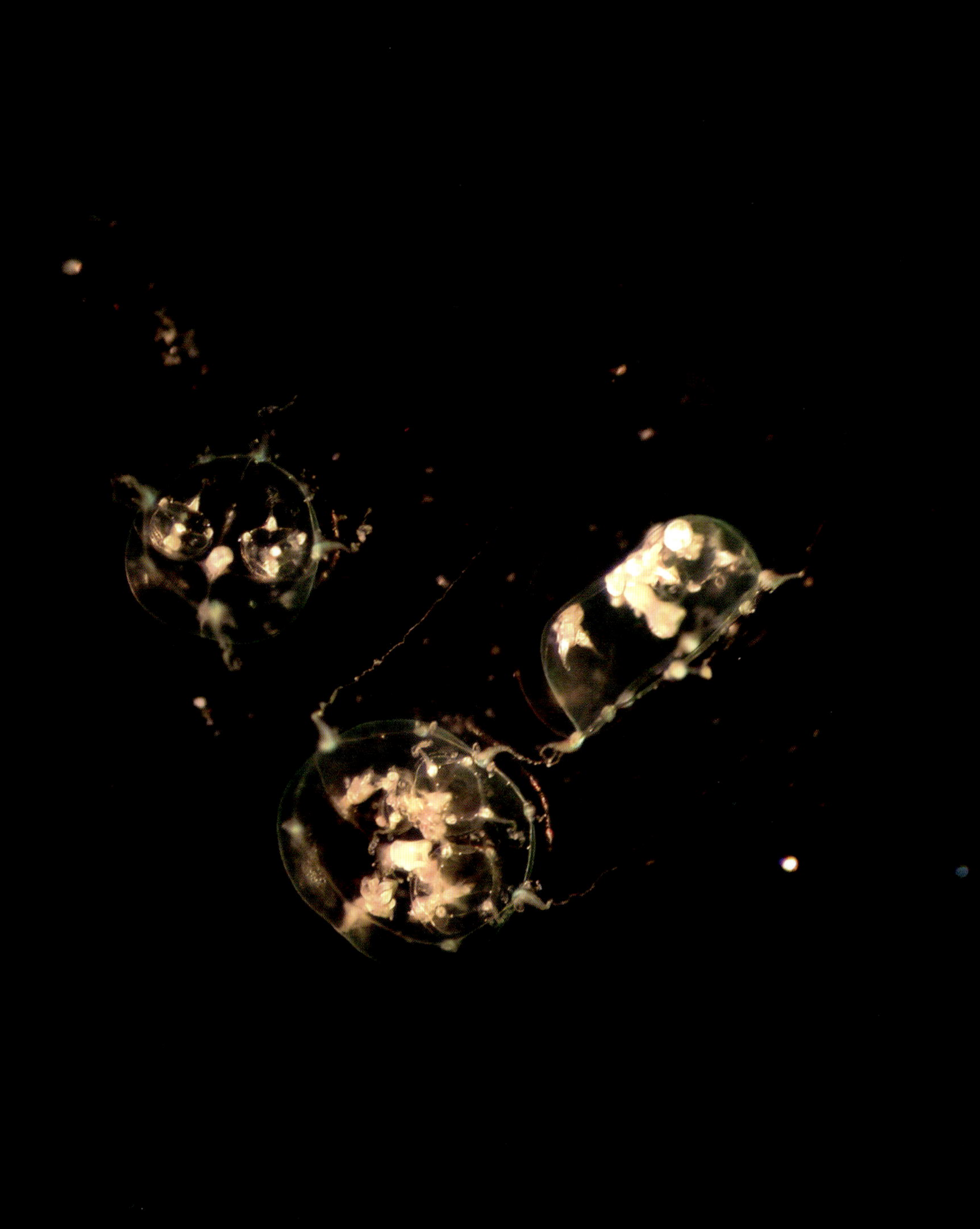

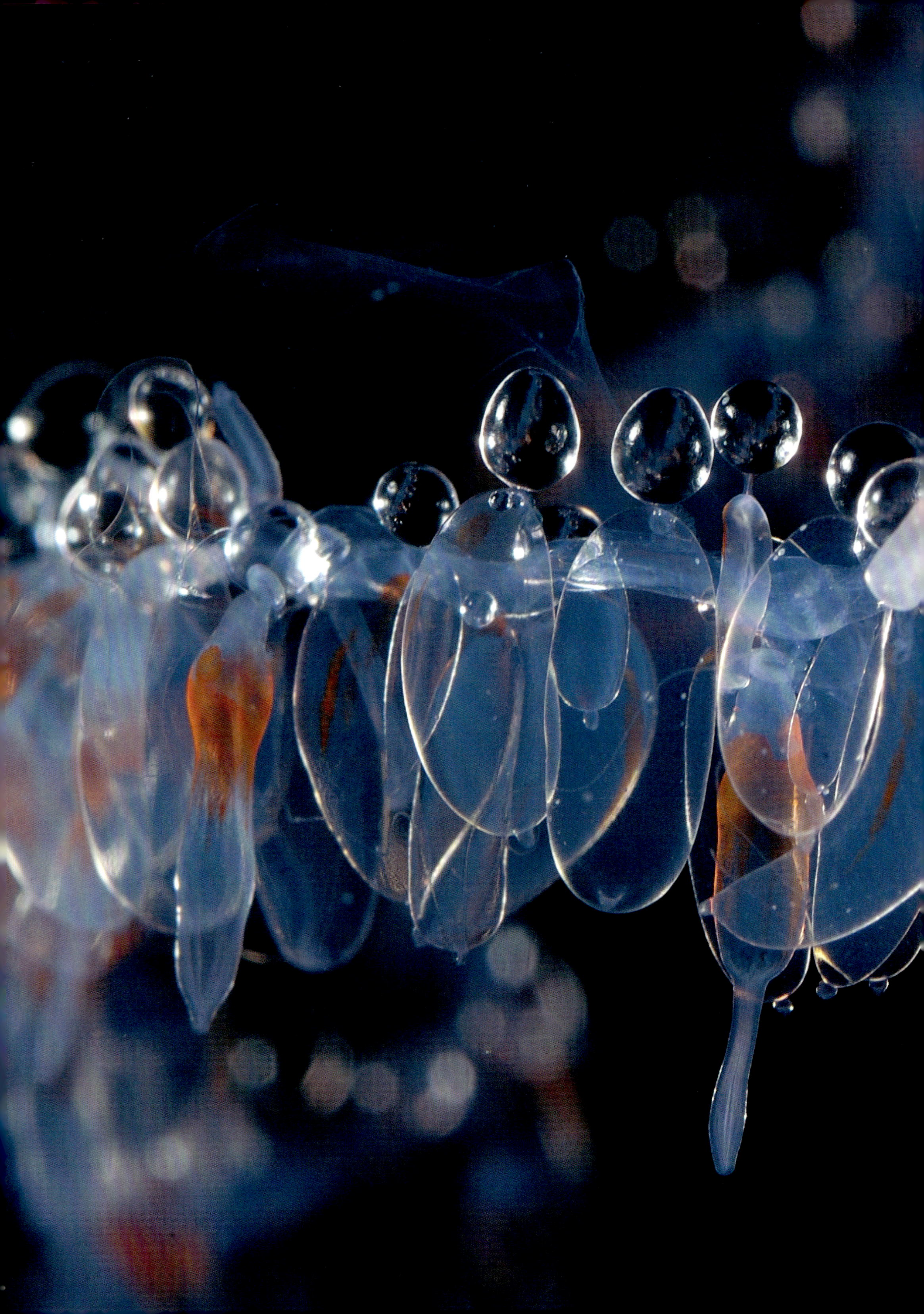

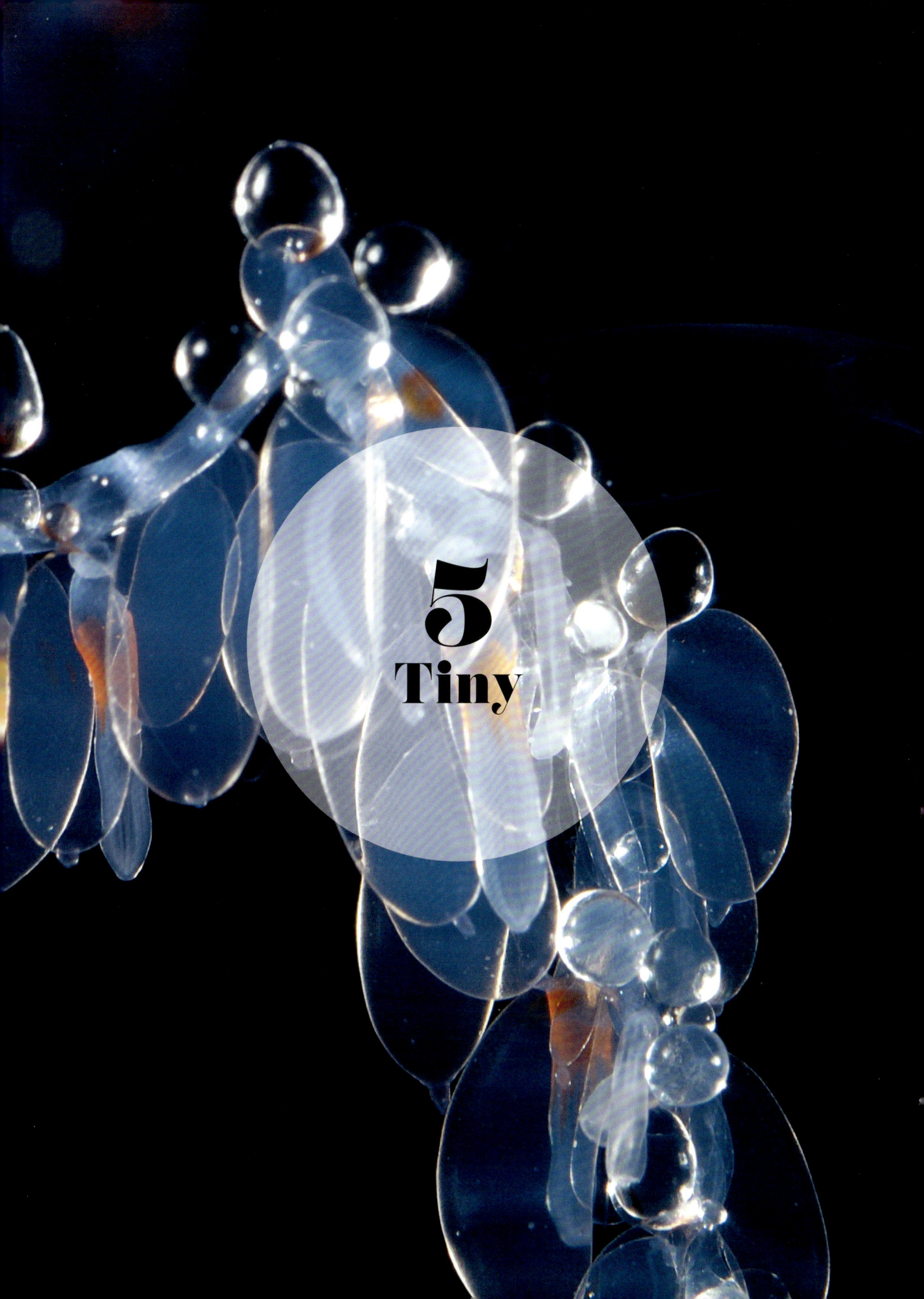
5
Tiny

Jellyfish range in size from the absolutely huge to the microscopically small. In this chapter, we take a dive into the miniature world and focus on the really small ones. Roughly 90 percent of all jellyfish species found globally are small, ranging from the size of a dot to just 1 inch (2.5 cm), and around 90 percent of these are tiny, less than ⅜ inch (1 cm). These tiny species are normally overlooked because you can't see them when you look over the side of a boat or off a jetty. And most people don't hover underwater staring at what drifts by. But with a plankton net—or even just a stocking—to catch them and a low-power microscope or even a hand lens to observe them, you will see that micromedusae are delightfully dainty, often whimsically sculpted, and frequently fantastically colored.

They range from lacy to blobular to pointy to flat, from barrel-shaped to star-shaped to ribbon-shaped. Understandably, there are small species in all the different groups of jellies and they may be found around the world. Almost as a rule, however, the smallest species tend to be more common in shallow nearshore and inshore waters, and often at tropical latitudes. It appears that a small body size may be an effective strategy for camouflage when you have nowhere else to hide. Also, perhaps not surprisingly, most very small species generally have very brief lifespans. They don't really die off, of course, as their polyps continue to thrive and clone, until it is time to bud off more babies.

Many of the most fascinating micromedusae are classified in the cnidarian class Hydrozoa. In this chapter, we will examine only a few of the more remarkable tiny species, including the ones with highly sculpted bodies and strange tentacles, from *Amphinema* to *Zanclea*, along with those that are genuinely strange, such as the aberrantly "quintessential" hydrozoan *Obelia* since it is very small, as well as the fabulous *Phialella zappai* because, being named after the musician Frank Zappa, it is just too interesting to leave out. This chapter also includes a few small jellies from other groups, such as the colonial *Nanomia* and the splendid little *Nausithoe*, as well as a couple that are the young of larger species, such as the baby Irukandji and the ephyra, both interesting in their own right.

So, let's take a journey down the microscope together, to see those lovely little jellies that are otherwise so tiny they are normally out of sight, out of mind. Most are so small you could fit dozens atop your pinky fingernail and so harmless that you wouldn't hesitate.

Ornate Jelly

Proboscidactyla ornata

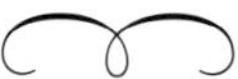

The medusa of *Proboscidactyla ornata* is, as its
name suggests, ornate. Most hydromedusae have
relatively straight radial canals, or internal vessels that
shuttle nutrients and waste between the stomach and
the tentacles, muscles, and sensory organs on the outer
periphery of the body. But in *P. ornata*, these canals
branch a few times, with each branch connecting to a
tentacle along the margin of the body. The clonal polyp
stage of *P. ornata* is a funny little organism, as the two
tentacles sticking up from the slender body give it
the appearance of an orchestra conductor. *Proboscidactyla
ornata* may be seasonally common enough to become
an irritant to marine life, but it does not appear
to be harmful to people.

SIZE: Bell height to ³⁄₁₆ inch (5 mm)

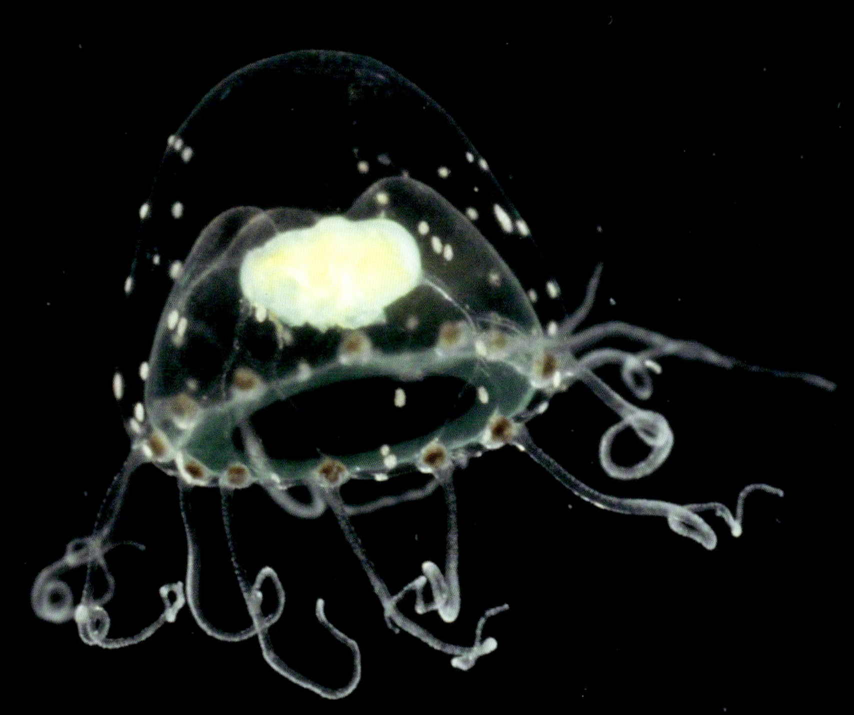

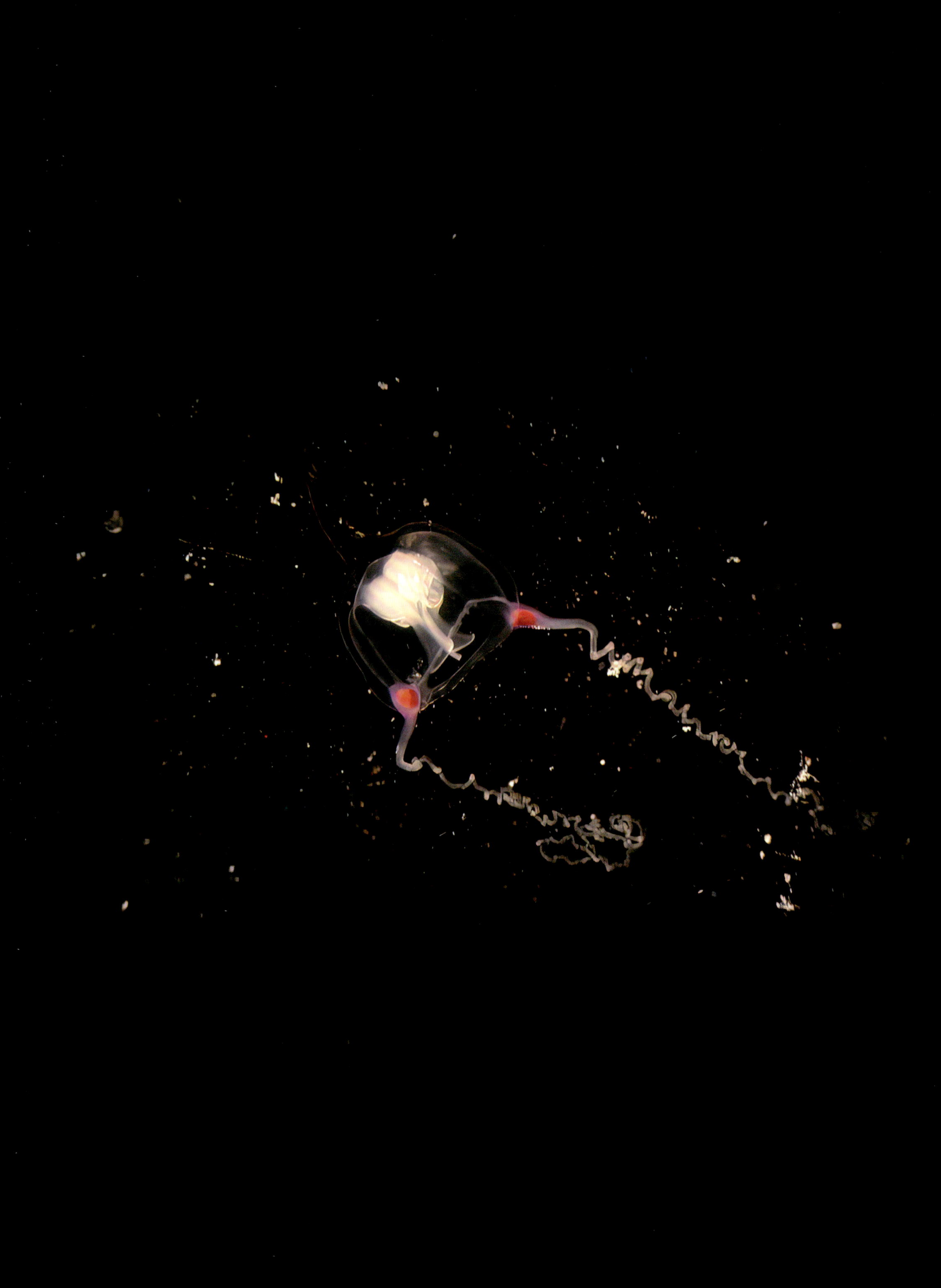

Two-Legged Jelly
Amphinema

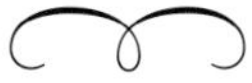

Species of *Amphinema* are immediately identifiable from other micromedusae, in that they only have two long, slender tentacles and most also have a solid, gelatinous projection pointing upward from the body, reminiscent of the hat of a garden gnome. They are often brightly colored inside the body or near the base of the tentacles. Like other species of micromedusae, under the right conditions *Amphinema* may bloom so prolifically as to be potentially troublesome for aquaculture: their tiny bodies can easily penetrate nets and get into sensitive fish gills, where the stings may stimulate debilitating or even lethal outbreaks of amoebic gill disease. *Amphinema* medusae pose no danger to humans and, in fact, are unlikely even to be noticed.

SIZE: Bell height to ¼ inch (6 mm)

Fairy Lights
Zanclea

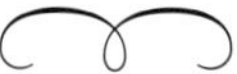

In comparison to *Amphinema* (see page 126),
species of *Zanclea* look more like highly ornate brooches
or perhaps microscopic Christmas ornaments. Their
overall body shape is similar to that of *Amphinema* in
being typically pointy, while their tentacles are studded
with dozens to hundreds of tiny side branches, each
bearing a ball of stinging cells. Like other hydromedusae,
they have a clonal polyp stage; theirs is found in
intimate association with other marine creatures such
as bryozoans, bivalves, corals, and algae. Members of
the *Zanclea* genus aren't toxic to humans, nor are they
particularly problematic to most marine industries like
tourism or power plants or shipping. These splendid little
creatures are just part of the typically unseen,
amazing world of the micromedusae.

SIZE: Bell height to ³⁄₁₆ inch (5 mm)

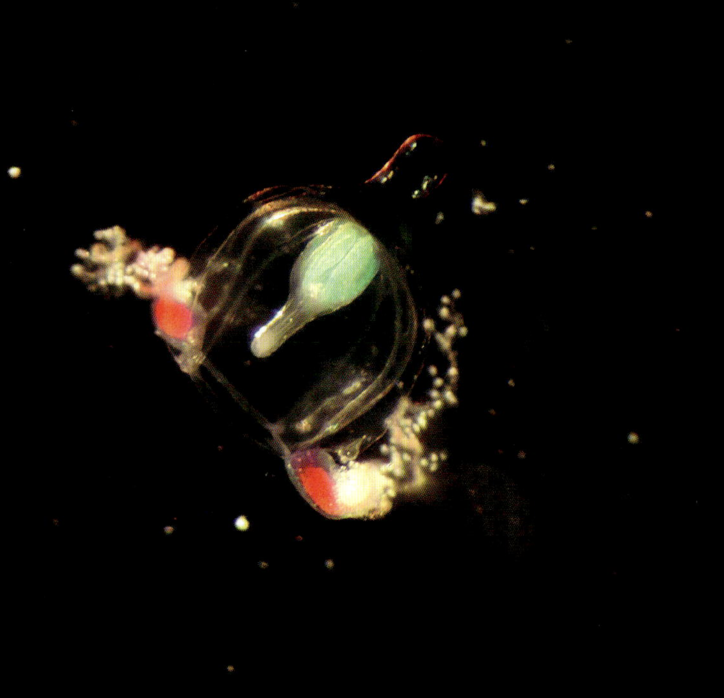

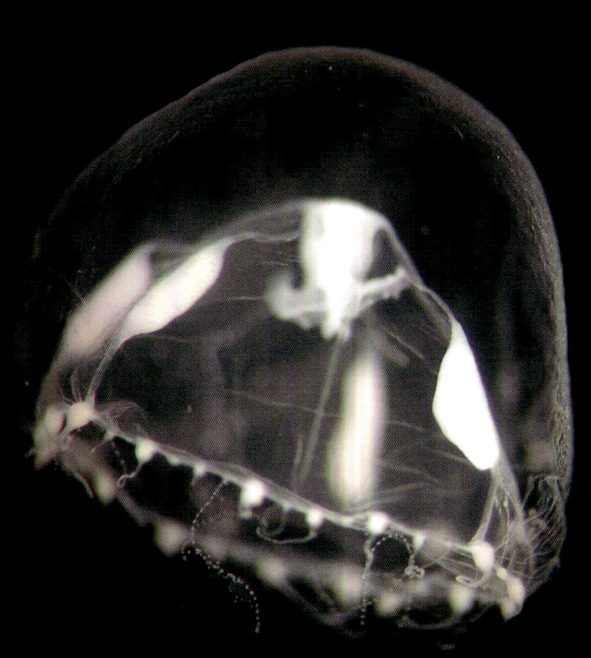

Zappa Medusa

Phialella zappai

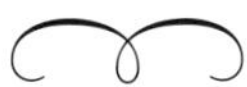

This tiny, seemingly humble micromedusa has one of the best origin stories in zoology. Its discoverer, Dr. Nando Boero, was a big fan of the musician Frank Zappa, so he named the species to honor his idol. Zappa soon found out about this and arranged front-row tickets for Nando at his next concert. With Nando in the audience, Zappa debuted a song he had written about Nando and the jellyfish. You can look it up—it's called "Lonesome Cowboy Nando." It's a splendid inspiration for becoming a taxonomist, a type of scientist who studies the naming and classifying of species. Apart from discovering new species, you might just have a song written about you!

SIZE: Bell height to 3⁄16 inch (5 mm)

Doliolids

Doliolum denticulatum

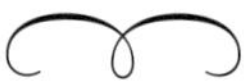

Doliolids are small, fantastically abundant and fascinating. They are transparent, barrel-shaped creatures rarely observed by swimmers and beachcombers. But those with a plankton net, even if only fashioned out of stockings, are in luck. In a bowl of seawater they will dart around in long bursts. But a closer look reveals their strange life cycle, which alternates between clonal and sexual stages. The clonal, or asexual, stage produces hundreds of buds, which align on a ribbon that resembles a strip of machine-gun bullets and protrudes like a long tail from one end. Depending on a bud's position on this ribbon, it may become either a feeding machine for the entire colony or a free-swimming breeder for the next generation.

SIZE: Body length to ⅜ inch (10 mm)

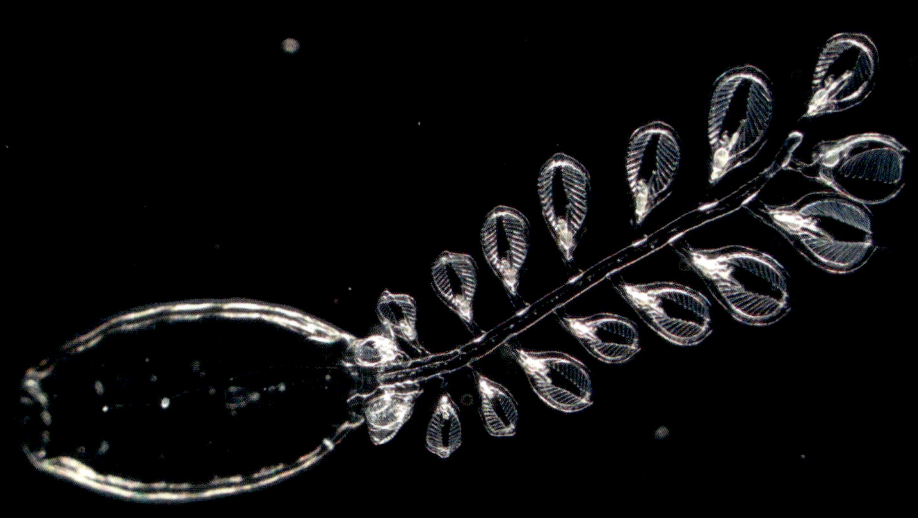

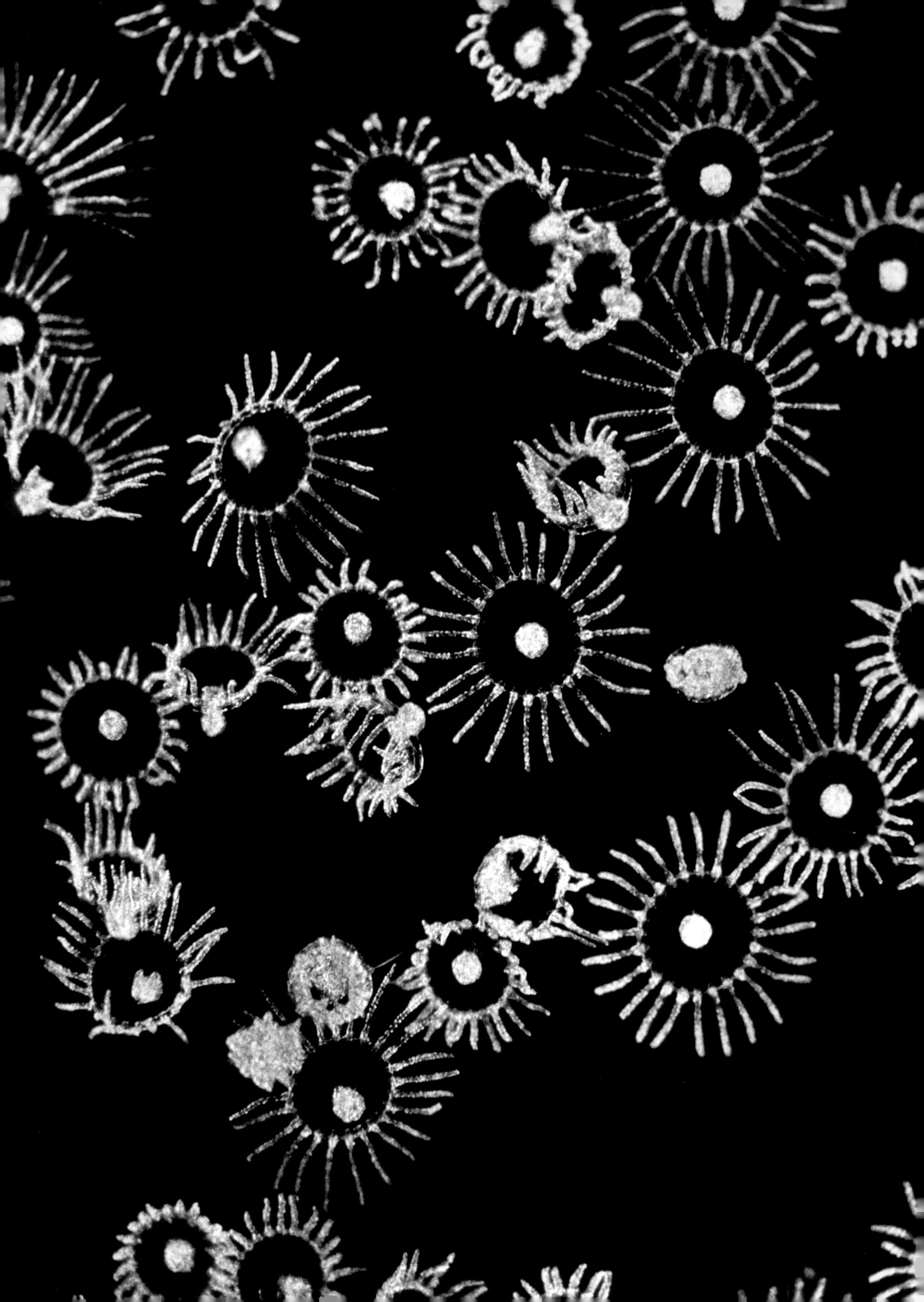

Sea Fur

Obelia

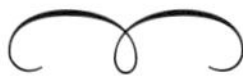

High school and university students alike
are often familiar with this genus because *Obelia* is the
archetypal hydrozoan used to illustrate the hydrozoan
life cycle and the alternation of generations. But it's an
odd choice, since *Obelia* is, in fact, a highly aberrant
hydrozoan. Most hydromedusae have a hemispherical
body with long, flexible tentacles, but *Obelia* species have
a stiff, flat body with short, stiff tentacles that radiate
out. In fact, they don't look much like a hydromedusa at
all! The polyp colonies grow in large, tumbleweed-like
bushes, and they are especially common on and around
aquaculture installations. Here, the medusae
bloom in dense swarms and can be dangerous
to fish because they sting their gills.

SIZE: Bell diameter to ¹⁄₁₆ inch (2 mm)

Sticking Jelly
Cladonema radiatum

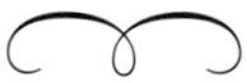

Cladonema radiatum is one of the most delightful
of all the micromedusae, for it often shows up uninvited
in home aquaria. Usually, aquarium enthusiasts see what
looks like tiny, transparent beads bearing numerous
threads attached to the insides of the glass walls. The
tentacles of *C. radiatum* are branched, with the lower
stubby branches sticking to objects like rocks and algae
(and aquarium walls), while the upper branches are
longer and more flexible, waving in the current to
fish for food particles. In their natural habitat, these
jellyfish spend most of their time clinging to one spot,
but they may occasionally change place by swimming.
They possess black or deep-red ocelli, or eye spots,
which are presumably able to detect shadows.

SIZE: Bell height to ⅛ inch (3 mm)

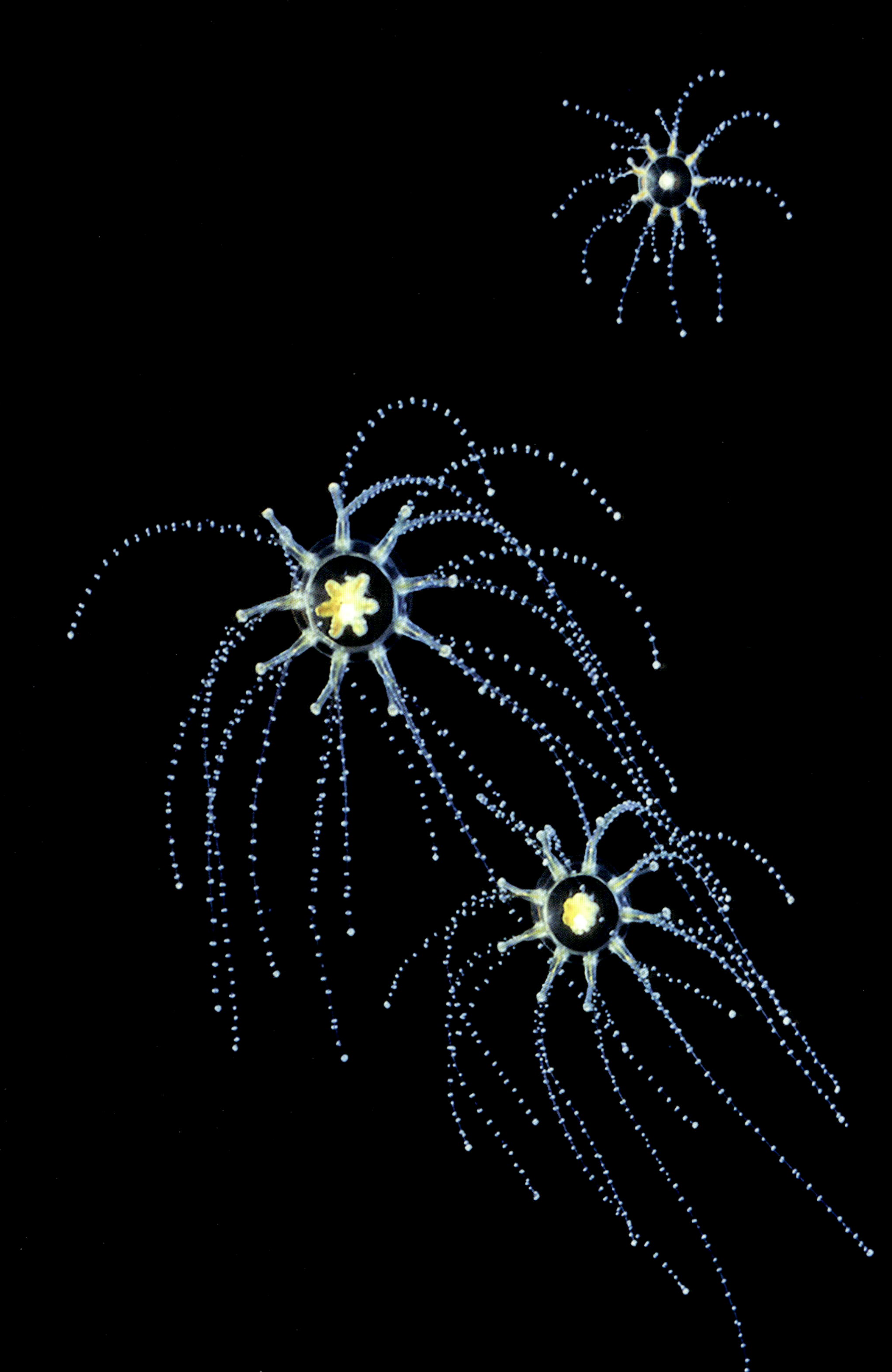

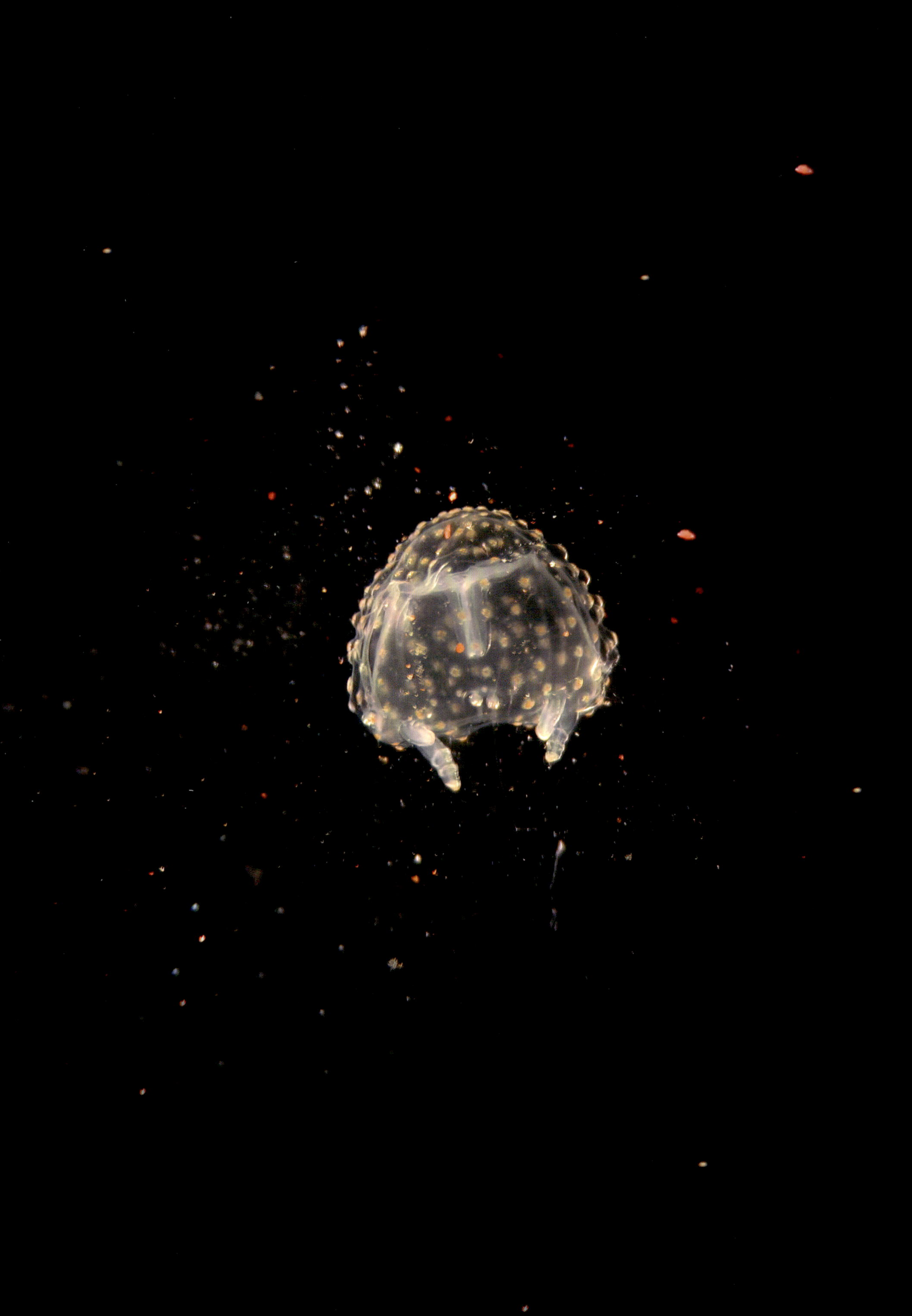

Baby Irukandji

Carukia barnesi

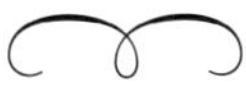

Irukandjis are among the most venomous creatures on Earth. But unlike snakes, where the juveniles are the most dangerous, it appears that young Irukandjis are harmless. As with many types of jellies, Irukandjis are produced through a clonal process, whereby tiny polyps bud off tiny medusae. Each nearly microscopic "newborn," when first budded off from its polyp parent, resembles a miniature strawberry with four stubby tentacles. Their bodies are densely covered in warts studded with stinging cells, and the red body coloration may signal to would-be predators, "Don't Touch!" These baby jellies grow rapidly and become highly toxic in just a matter of days. But beware, they travel in mixed swarms, meaning that dangerous adults will be present too.

SIZE: Bell height to ⅛ inch (3 mm)

Grape Jelly

Nanomia

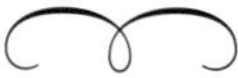

Members of the *Nanomia* genus are a delight
to behold: the arranged rows of swimming bells pulsate
out of unison, acting like a multi-jet swimming machine
with forward and backward thrusters, while a shiny,
gas-filled float leads the way and the long stem is towed
behind. The colony members that do the stinging, eating,
and reproducing are arranged at intervals along the
stem. The stem can relax to be very long when the colony
is fishing for food, but it will retract and become quite
compact with the least provocation. Don't let your guard
down, however, because like many of its relatives
known as siphonophores, or free-swimming,
multipart, colonial hydrozoans, *Nanomia* can
deliver quite a painful sting.

SIZE: Colony length ⅛–8 inches (3 mm–20 cm)

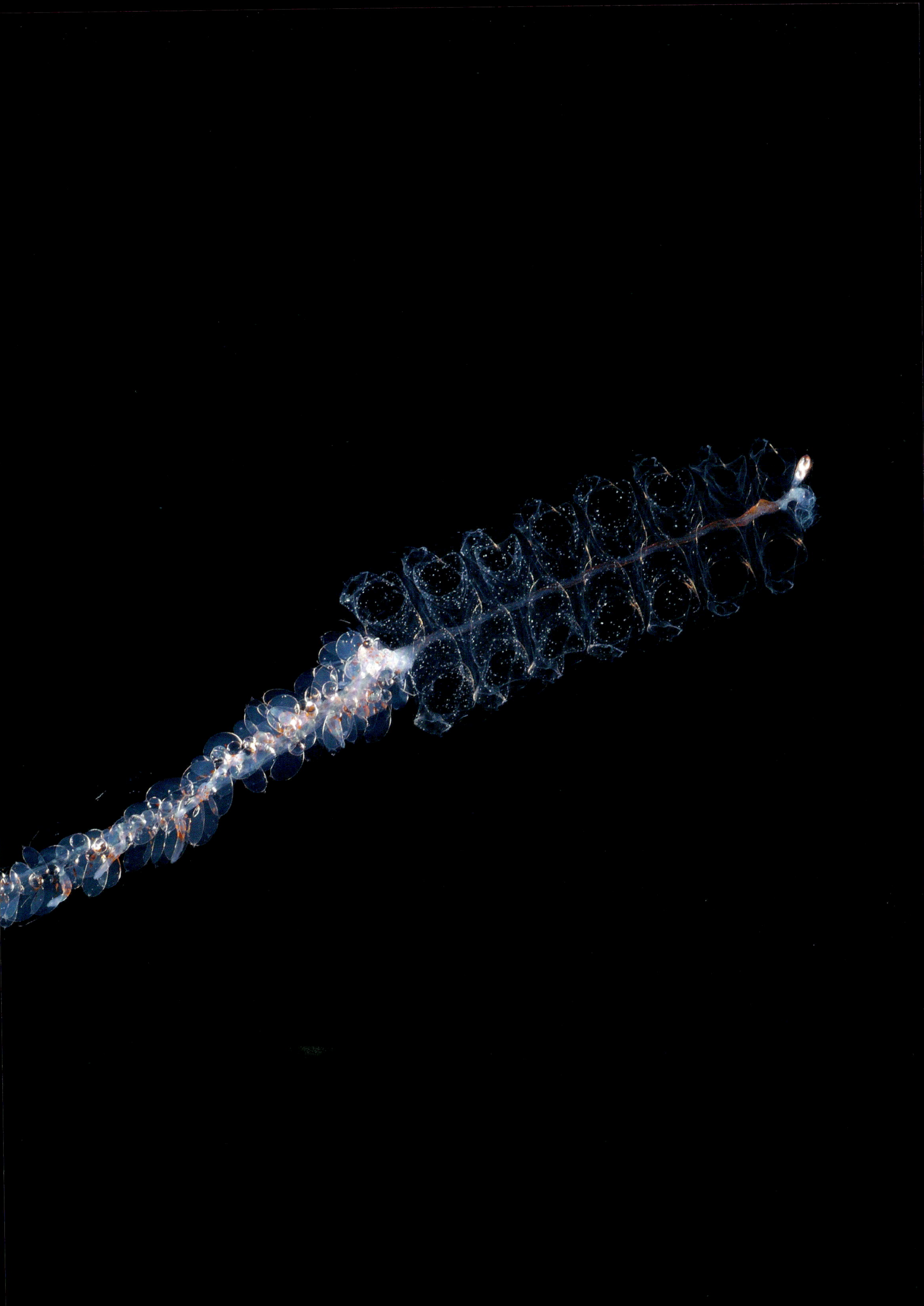

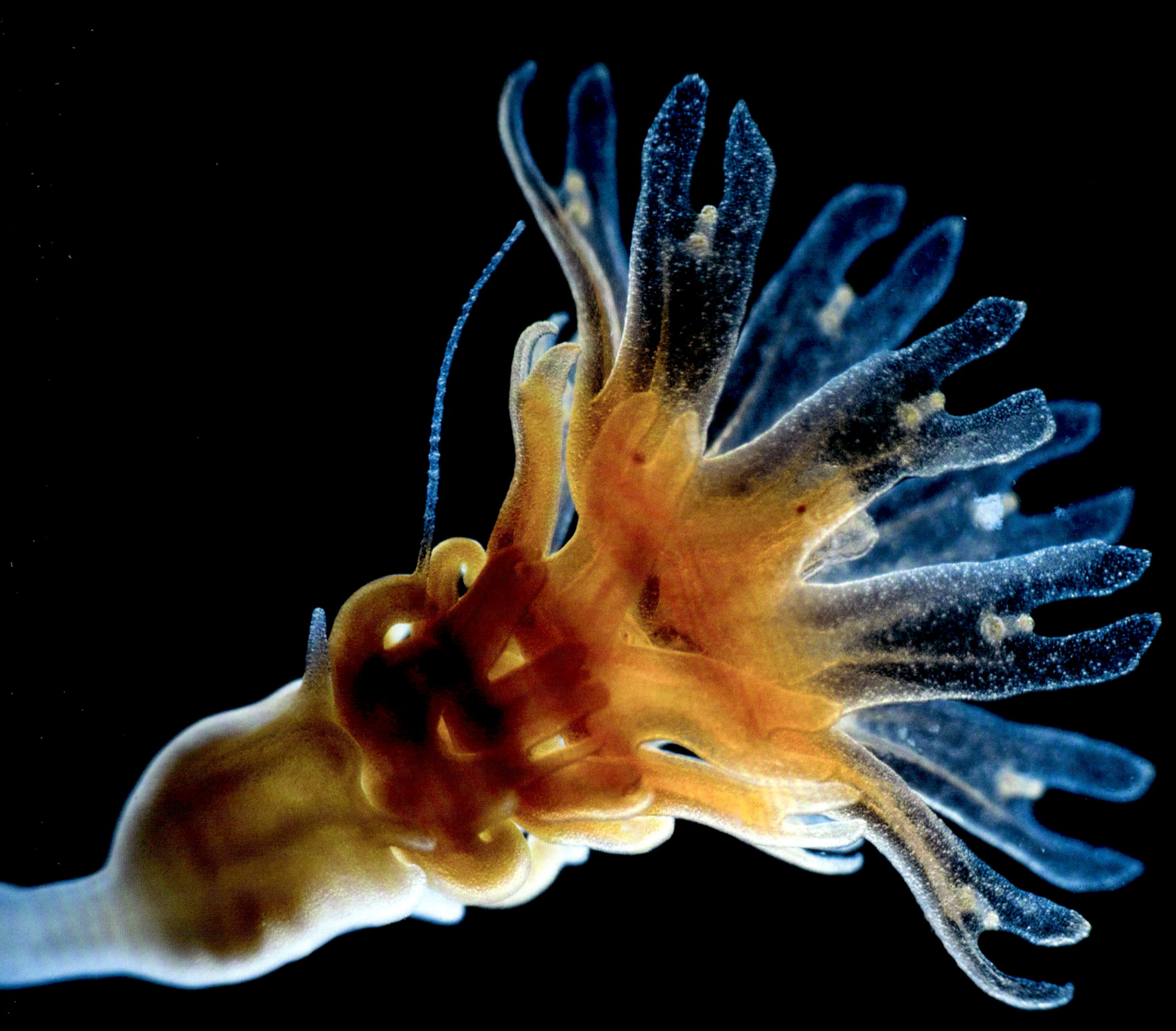

Larval Jellyfish

Ephyra

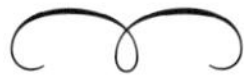

Today, we know that these whimsical little, star- or daisy-shaped, pulsing beings are the youngest life stage of some types of jellyfish. But it wasn't always this way. In the scientific paradigm of the 1820s and 1830s, *Ephyra* was considered a separate genus of jellyfish, along with *Scyphistoma* and *Strobila*. These names are used to refer to the various juvenile life-cycle stages today. The scyphistoma, or polyp, is the primary clonal stage of jellyfish. Under certain conditions, the scyphistoma elongates and differentiates into a stack of star-like discs called ephyrae (plural). This process is called strobilation. And the polyp undergoing strobilation is called a strobila. The image to the left is a strobila bearing five ephyrae in different stages of development.

SIZE: Body diameter to 1/16 inch (2 mm)

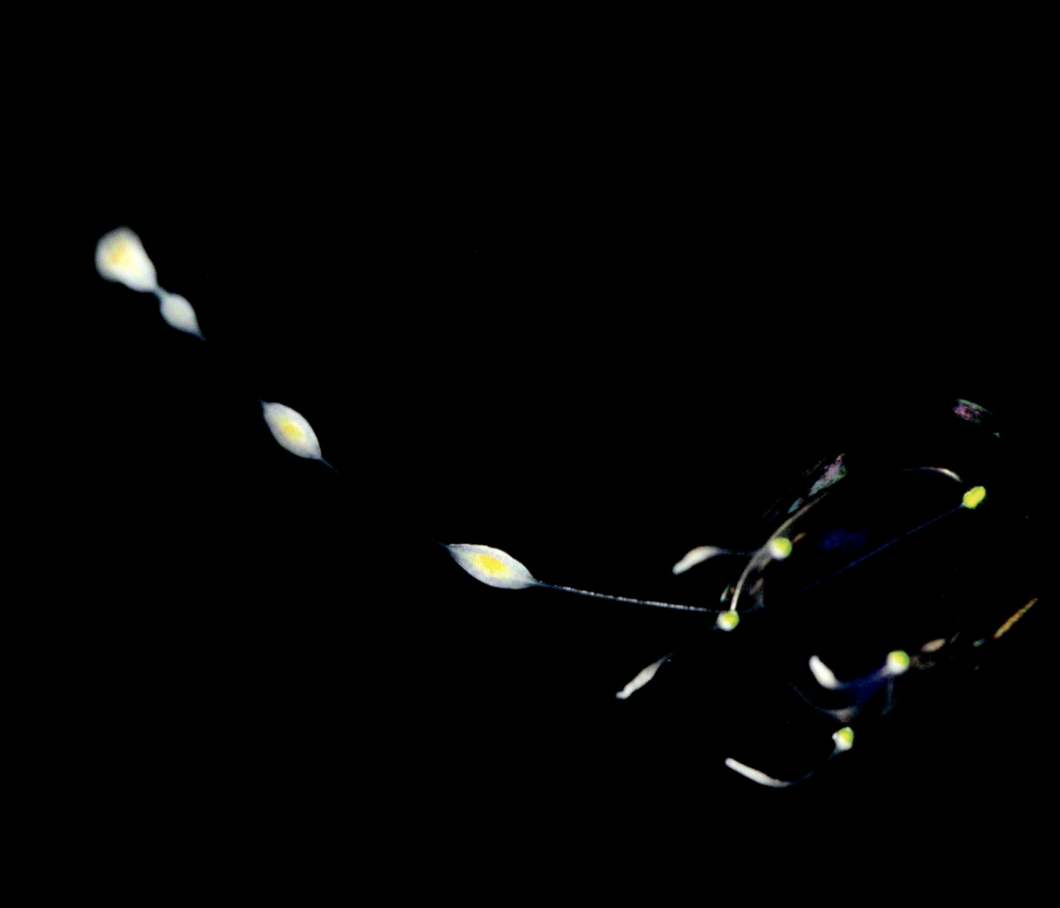

Graceful Jelly

Slabberia

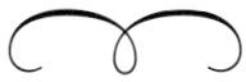

Species of *Slabberia* are among the most exquisite of all micromedusae, trailing their long appendages as they swim. At first glance, they may be confused with *Sarsia* (see page 212). Like *Sarsia*, the bell is simple and unadorned, as are the four fine tentacles. But in *Slabberia*, the manubrium, or throat, is enormously elongated, and in some cases may be many times the body length. The manubrium is encircled by multiple thickenings of reproductive organs. The sexes are separate and may be easily distinguished in mature individuals under a low-power microscope or hand lens. For more than a century, these common medusae were known by a different genus, *Dipurena*, but have recently been revised. By any name, however, they are elegant and beautiful.

SIZE: Bell height to ⅛ inch (3 mm)

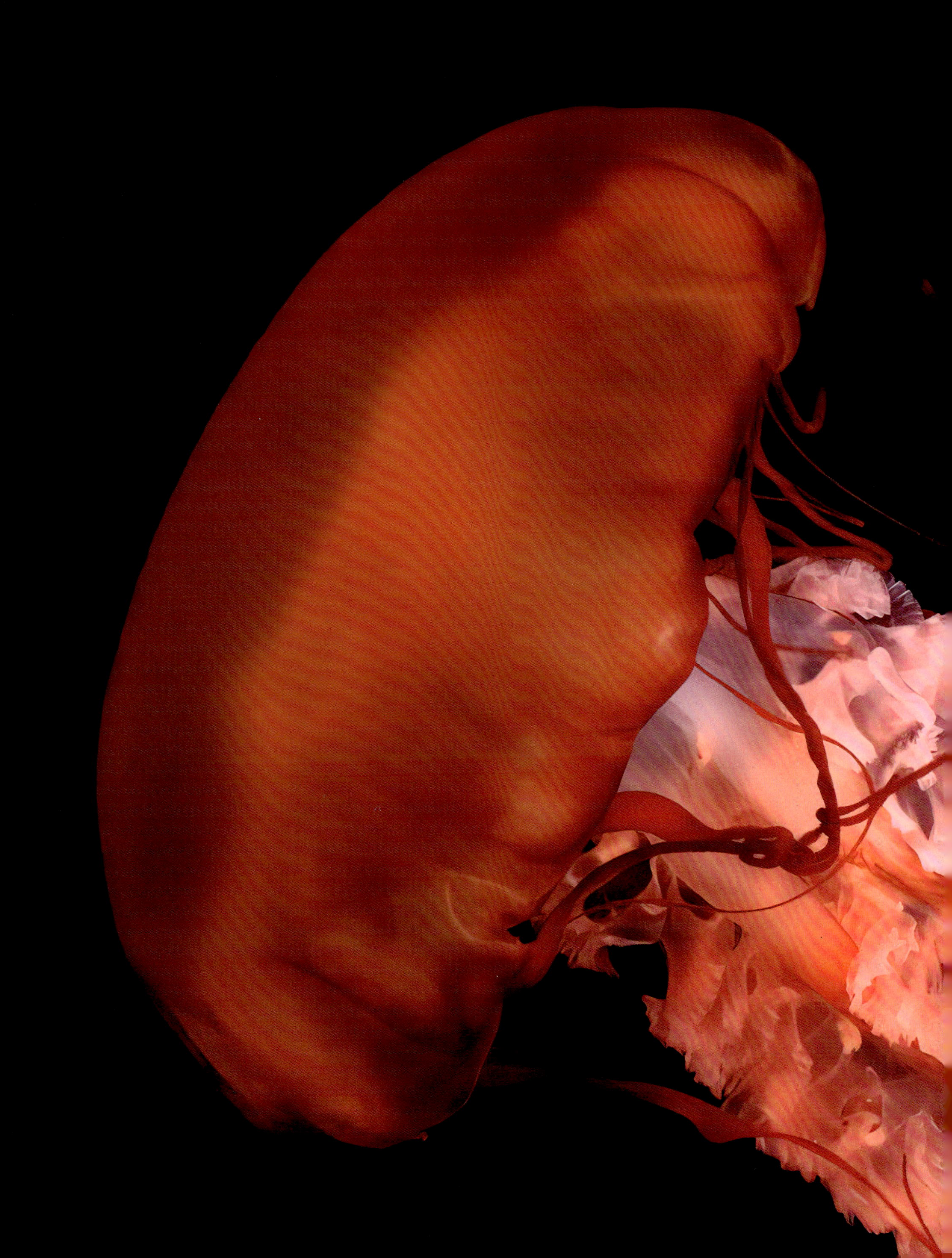

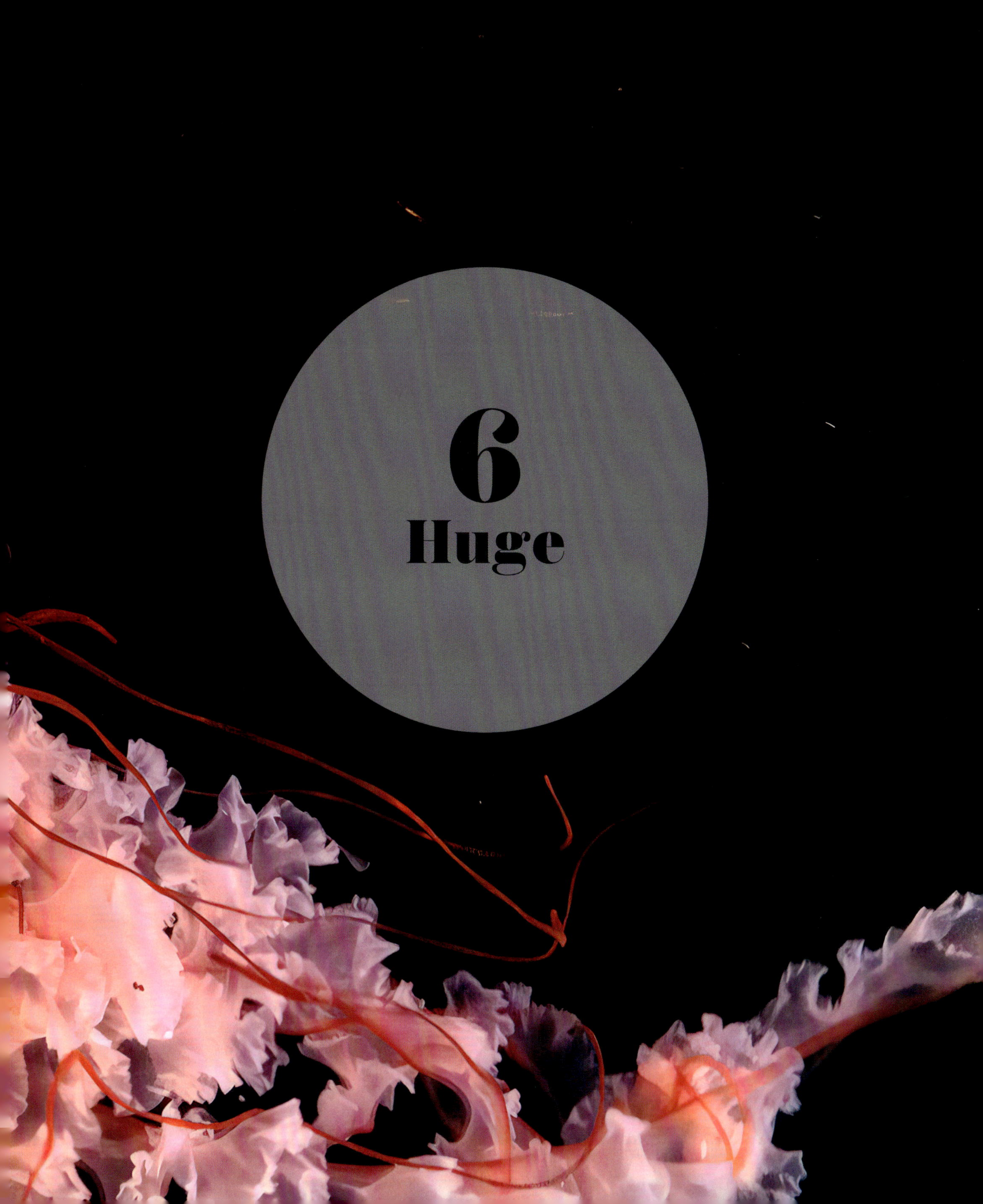
6
Huge

It might be tempting to think that all species on Earth are known, but nothing could be further from the truth. In fact, current estimates suggest that only around 10 percent of species are identified. We might also assume that all the big ones must be known: this too is false. In this chapter, we turn our attention to some species that really challenge these preconceptions. For example, the largest invertebrate discovered in the twentieth century was a jellyfish, *Chrysaora achlyos*, and it wasn't obscure at all; in fact, it had featured repeatedly in books and even in *National Geographic* magazine. But it was misidentified every time.

Another good example is one of the largest known jellyfishes of all time, a still-unnamed fossil from hundreds of millions of years ago. Not all large jellies are new species, of course. Many have been known for a while. For example, the barrel jellyfish (*Rhizostoma pulmo*, see page 154), which seasonally terrorizes swimmers along European coastlines, was classified in 1778. With a bell the size of a trashcan lid and as long as a human is tall, this painful stinger carries a formidable warning: Do Not Touch! Another good example is the bitey whitey (*Lobonema smithii*, see page 160), which commanded attention when its severe sting proved fatal at the beginning of the twentieth century.

It's not just medusae that grow to great sizes. For example, strange, free-swimming, colonial sea squirts called pyrosomes look like windsocks. One species that has been known for hundreds of years around the world may grow so large in the Tasman Sea between Tasmania and New Zealand that a person can swim through it as if it were a tunnel. And on the other side of Australia in the Indian Ocean, an extremely long colonial hydrozoan called a siphonophore was recently discovered during deep sea exploration. This is just a sample of the biggest jellies, of course.

One interesting aspect of giant jellies is that all their harmful effects may be magnified. For example, if they are toxic, they have more tentacles with more stinging cells, so you may sustain a nastier sting, simply through a higher venom load. Similarly, if a species has a voracious appetite for plankton, bigger species will eat more, so their impact may be greater, putting pressure on the food sources of other organisms.

The sea is full of many weird and wonderful jellies, and these shapeshifters become even more intriguing when they are huge.

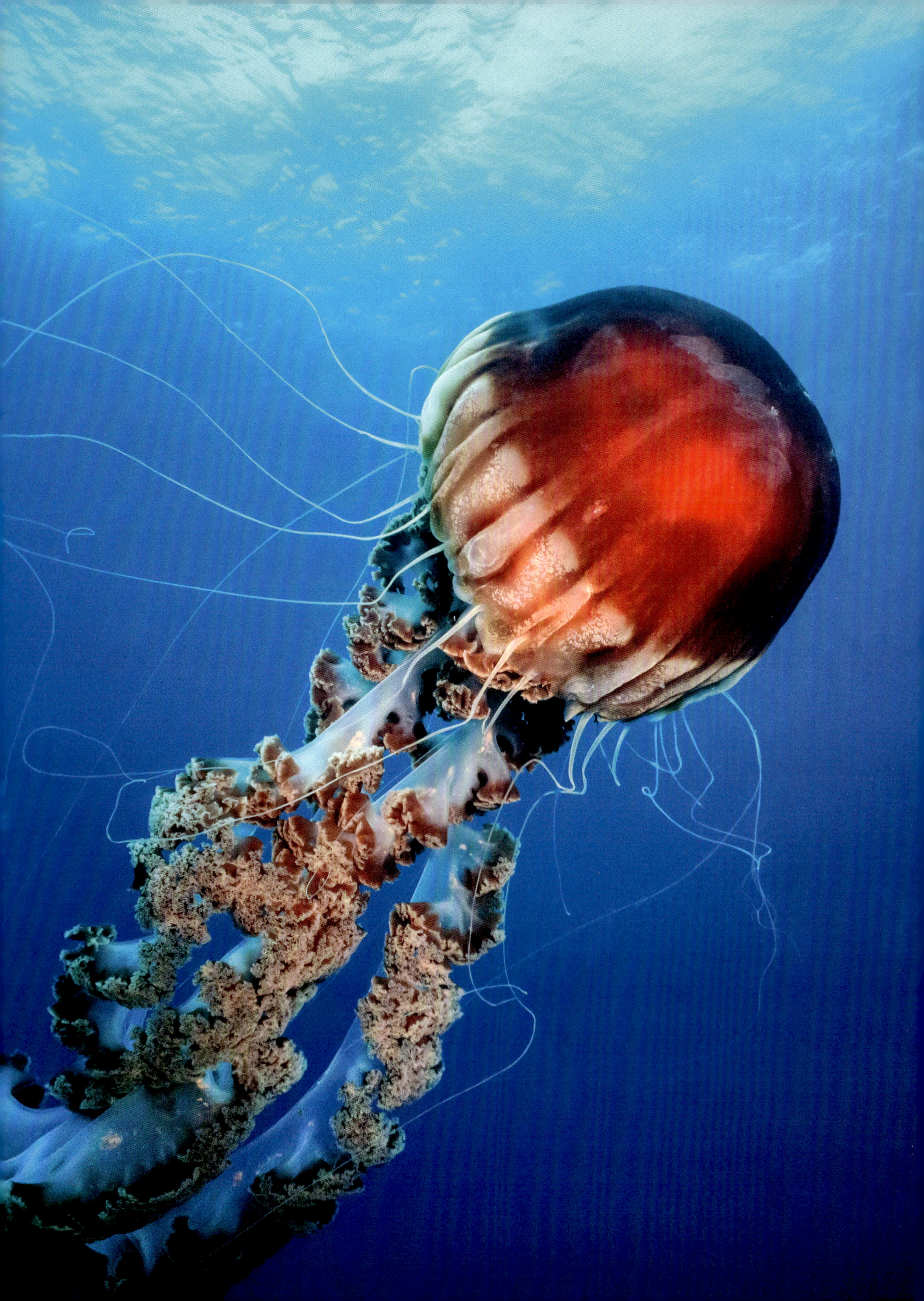

Black Sea Nettle

Chrysaora achlyos

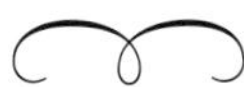

The black sea nettle was only named and classified
in 1997 based on specimens washed up on a beach in
Los Angeles. It is not actually black, but more the color
of a fine burgundy wine—it appears black underwater
because of the optical effect that water has on color.
These facts would normally be enough to make a species
noteworthy. But there is nothing normal about *Chrysaora
achlyos*. With a body bigger than a large trashcan lid and
pleated oral arms that extend longer than the height
of a two-story house, it should come as no surprise
that it was designated as the largest invertebrate
discovered in the twentieth century.

SIZE: Bell diameter to 3 feet (1 m)

Barrel Jellyfish

Rhizostoma pulmo

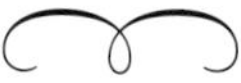

In general, Europe isn't known for having
very many dangerous species, and most of the large,
scary ones have long been hunted out, fished out, or
otherwise died out due to climatic and land-use changes.
So, a moderately venomous jellyfish the size of a human
and weighing up to 55 pounds (25 kg) is noteworthy. The
barrel jellyfish is found throughout Europe's Atlantic
coasts, the Mediterranean, and the inland seas. At first
glance, it is rather beautiful, given its striking, white-
with-purple trim color pattern. Its sting is painful and
may cause ulcers or dermatitis; the fact that it is not
known to be life-threatening, however, is of little
comfort to people just wanting to enjoy the beach.

SIZE: Bell diameter to 5 feet (1.5 m)

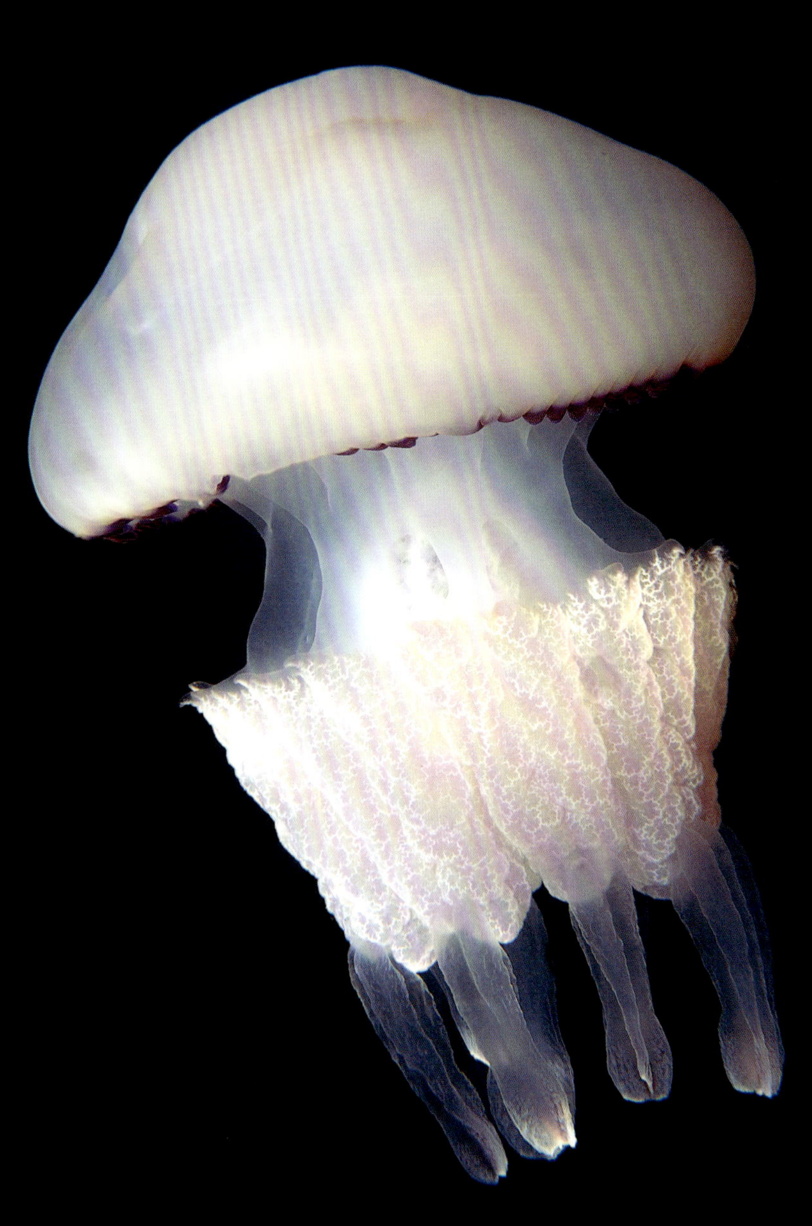

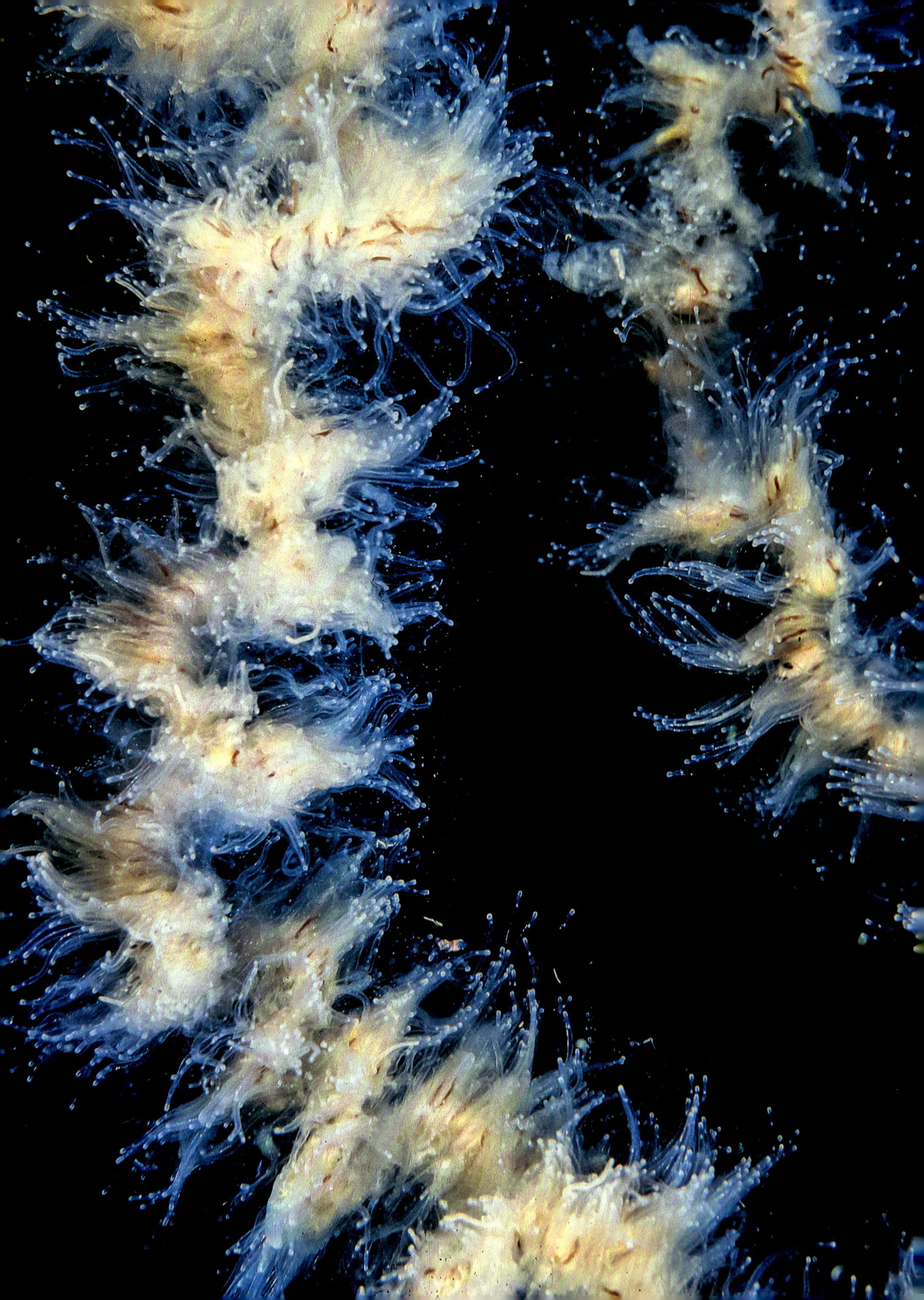

Feather Boa Jelly

Apolemia

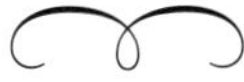

Siphonophores are strange colonial organisms
that are essentially repeating groups of functionally
distinct zooids, or living units, or, in the jargon of
siphonophore scientists, persons. Each "person" has
a different function: food-capture persons, digestive
persons, defensive persons, reproductive persons,
and so on. These persons occur together in groups,
such that they essentially make up a whole being, and
many of these groups are stuck together on a common
stalk, making up one colony. This repeating growth
form allows them to grow very large. An *Apolemia*
siphonophore found off the West Australian coast in 2020
was the longest animal ever found. It may even be
a new species, previously unknown to science!

SIZE: Colony length to 154 feet (47 m)

Unnamed Jellyfish Fossil

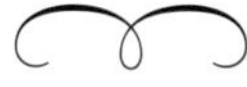

Around 500 million years ago, a bloom of countless
jellyfish became stranded on a tropical beach in what
is now central Wisconsin. These jellyfish somehow
fossilized. Even more remarkable, at least seven different
fossilization events of jellyfish blooms occurred at this
beach, separated by perhaps millions of years, and are
now stacked on top of each other in layers of rock like the
pages in a history book. It is thought that these stranded
jellyfish, struggling in vain to return to the ocean,
excavated the sediments with their pulsations, leaving
the impressions we see today. While any jellyfish fossil is
remarkable, this species, which remains unclassified,
is the largest of all known fossil jellyfish.

SIZE: Bell diameter to 3 feet (1 m)

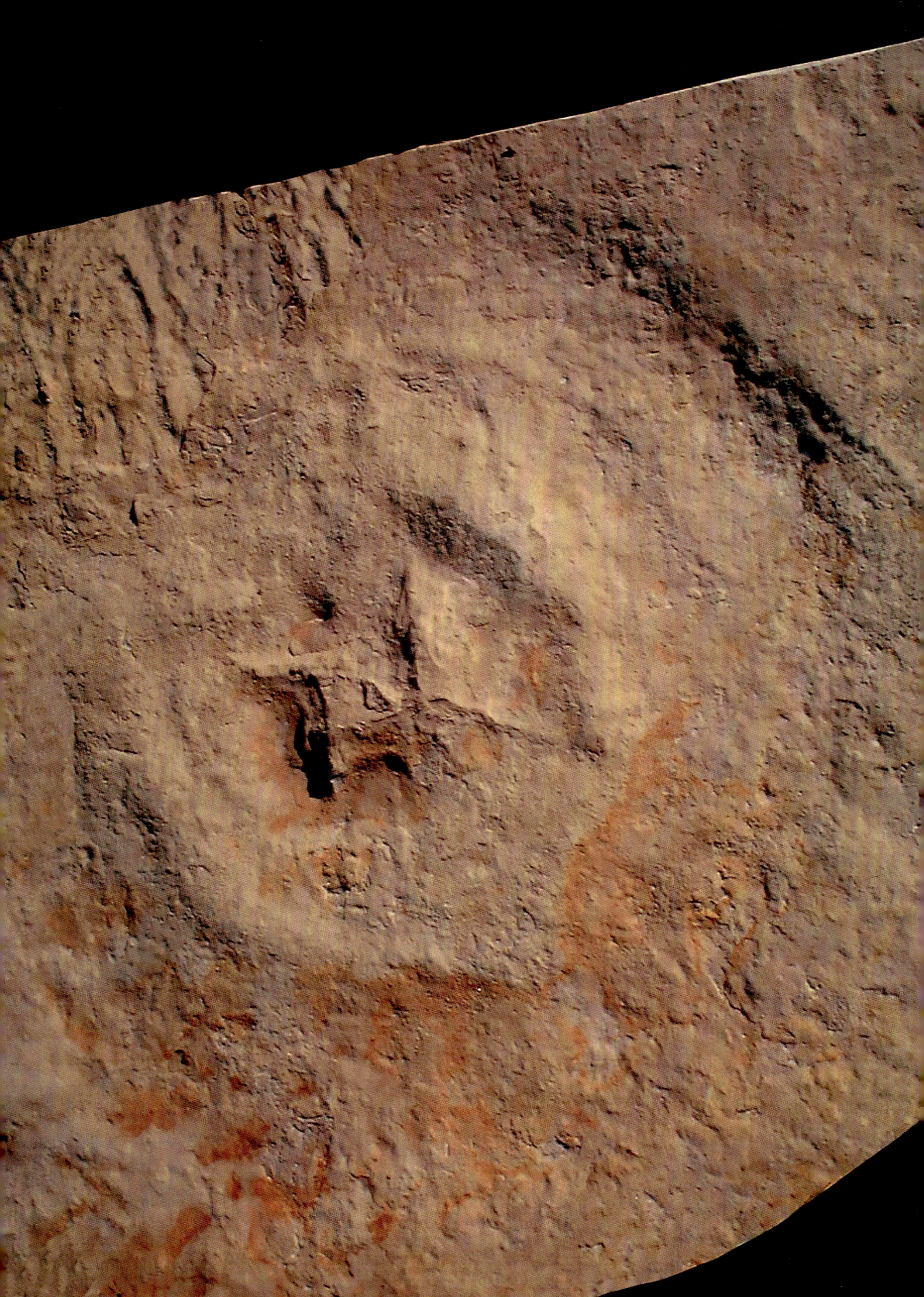

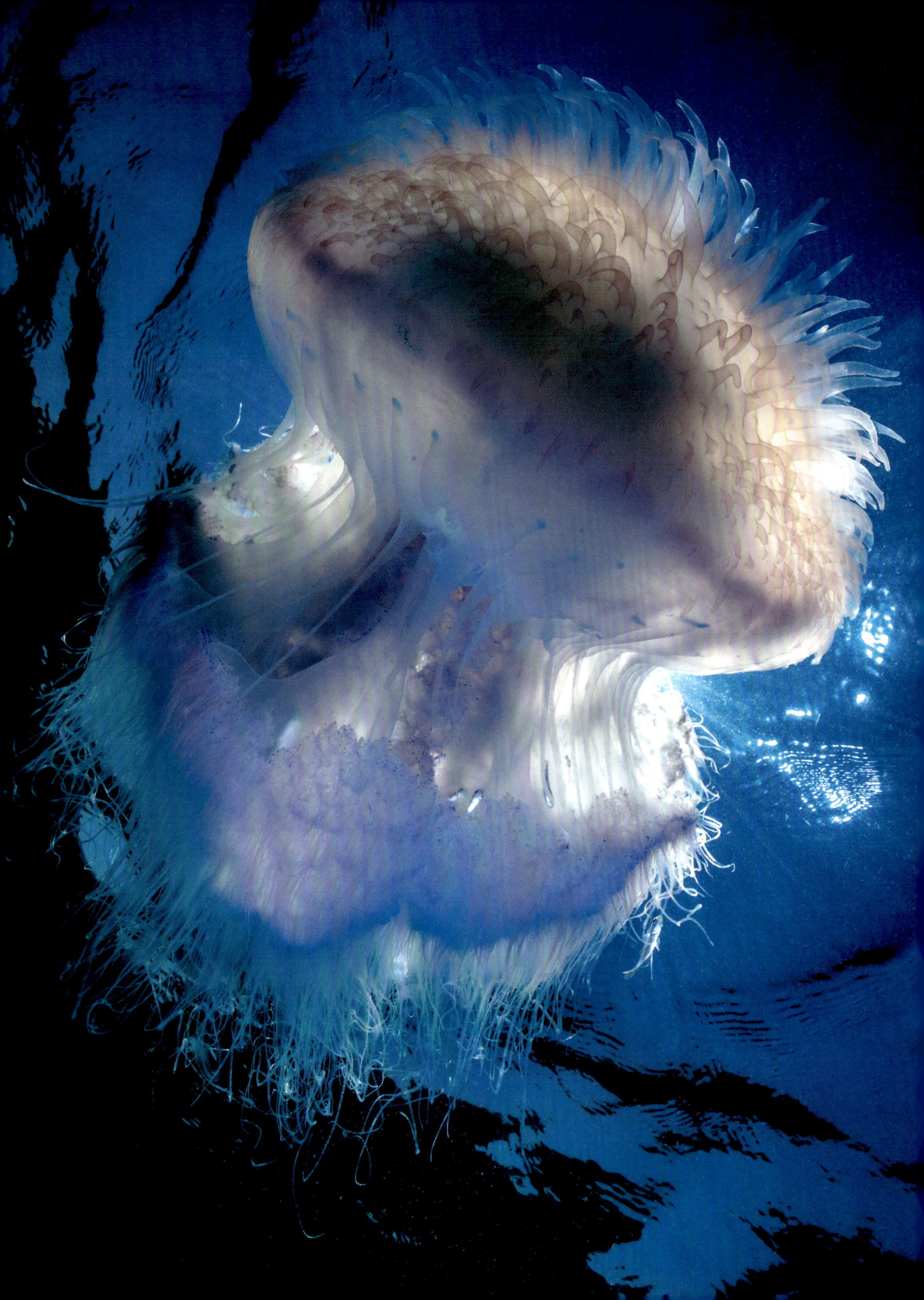

Bitey Whitey

Lobonema smithii

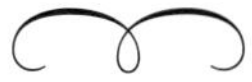

Blubber jellies in general tend to have massive, blubbery bodies and thick, solid oral arms, with no tentacles. But *Lobonema smithii* is a bit of an outlier in these respects. Uniquely, in *L. smithii* the margin of the bell is drawn out into false, tentacle-like extensions. Its body is massive, but more flat than thick, and densely covered in long papillae. Its oral arms are quite lacy or feathery, and often infested with brittle stars, snatching a free ride and feeding as they go; when these hitchhikers become too big or numerous, they weigh the jelly down, enabling them to disembark at their new location.
L. smithii has a nasty sting and several human fatalities have been blamed on this jellyfish.

SIZE: Bell diameter to 3 feet (1 m)

Fire Body

Pyrosoma

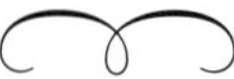

Pyrosomes are among the most unusual of all jellies. They are free-swimming colonial tunicates, or sea squirts. Each gelatinous tube is a separate colony, embedded with hundreds of small zooids, or individuals, which are all clones of each other. These barrel-shaped zooids are oriented in the wall of the tube such that they intake water from the outside and expel water to the inside, which provides jet propulsion for the colony. All species of *Pyrosoma*, which is Latin for "fire body," are highly bioluminescent. A slight disturbance results in ripples of light, just like a pebble thrown into a pond except in three dimensions. One species found in the Tasman Sea between Australia and New Zealand grows so large that a person can swim through it.

SIZE: Body length to 59 feet (18 m); more typically to 3 feet (1 m)

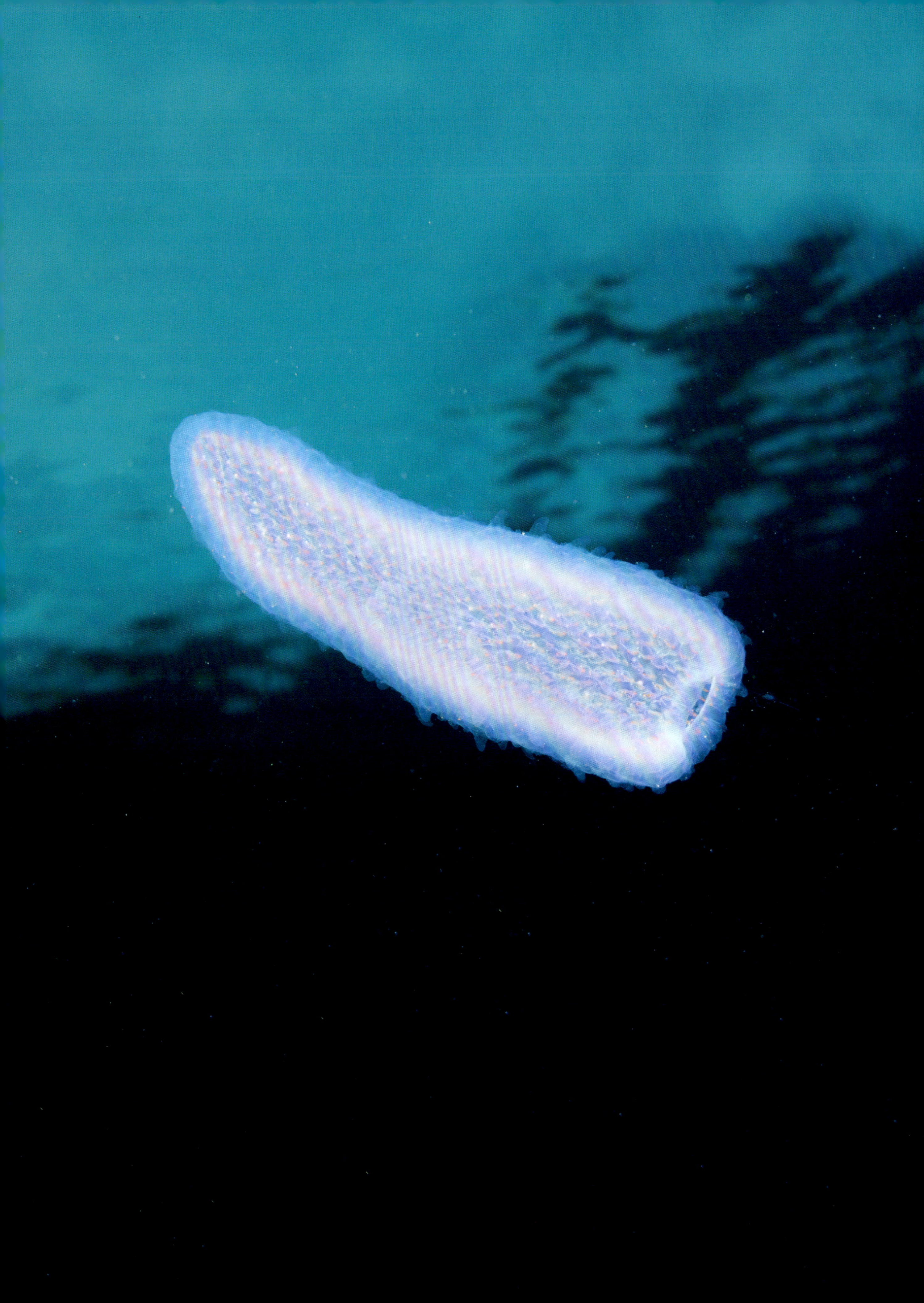

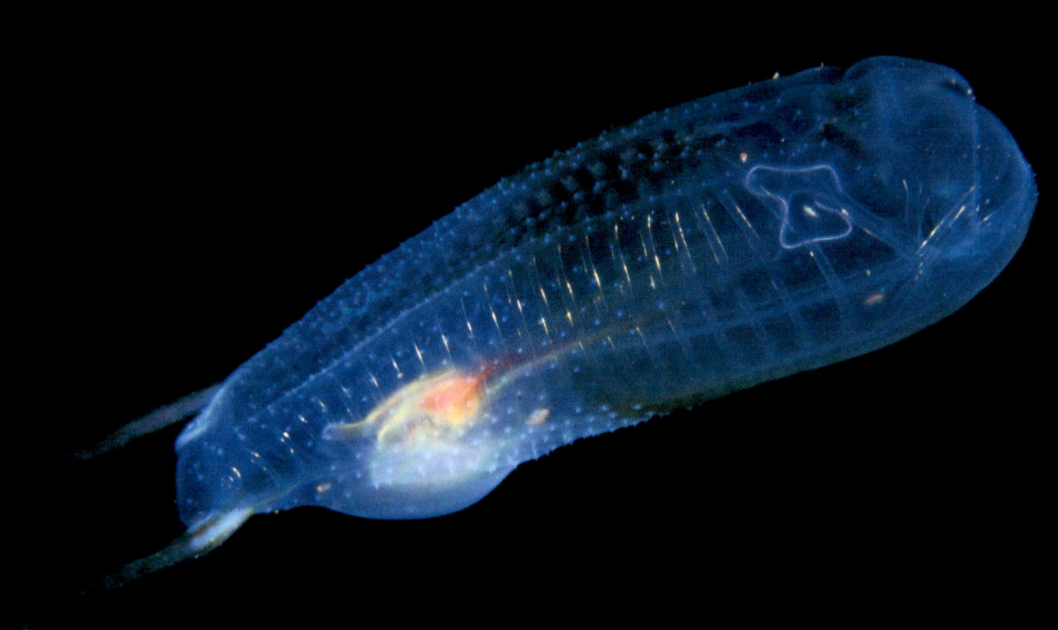

Twin-Sailed Salp

Thetys vagina

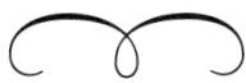

These days, inventors and entrepreneurs
are searching for ways to store carbon in an effort to
remove carbon dioxide from the atmosphere. But,
perhaps not surprisingly, nature worked this out a long,
long time ago. Organisms that photosynthesize use
carbon dioxide in this process and store the carbon in
their tissues as body mass. On land, trees are highly
efficient carbon storage devices, while in the ocean, the
poop pellets from salps are the top performers. Salps eat
vast quantities of photosynthetic phytoplankton, or plant
plankton. Thus, salp poop is very rich in carbon and
sinks very fast, so the carbon is rapidly transferred
to the seafloor. And *Thetys vagina*, the largest of all the
salps, poops the biggest, fastest-sinking pellets.

SIZE: Body length to 13 inches (33 cm)

White Cross Jelly

Staurostoma falklandica

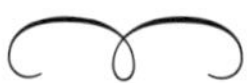

Hydromedusae, or water jellies, are generally
remarkable for being unremarkable—that is, as a rule
they are typically small and fairly plain. But *Staurostoma
falklandica* is anything but small and plain. It is by far
the largest of all the hydromedusae, reaching the size
of a dinner plate. Its most obvious feature, other than
its size, is a conspicuous cross spanning the entire bell.
Most hydromedusae have a cross formed by radial canals
(internal vessels) and the reproductive organs, with their
mouth at the intersection, but in *S. falklandica* the whole
cross is formed into a giant mouth. Originally from the
Falkland Islands, *S. falklandica* is now an invasive species
throughout southern Australia, poised to terrorize
the local salmon farming industry.

SIZE: Bell diameter to 14 inches (35 cm)

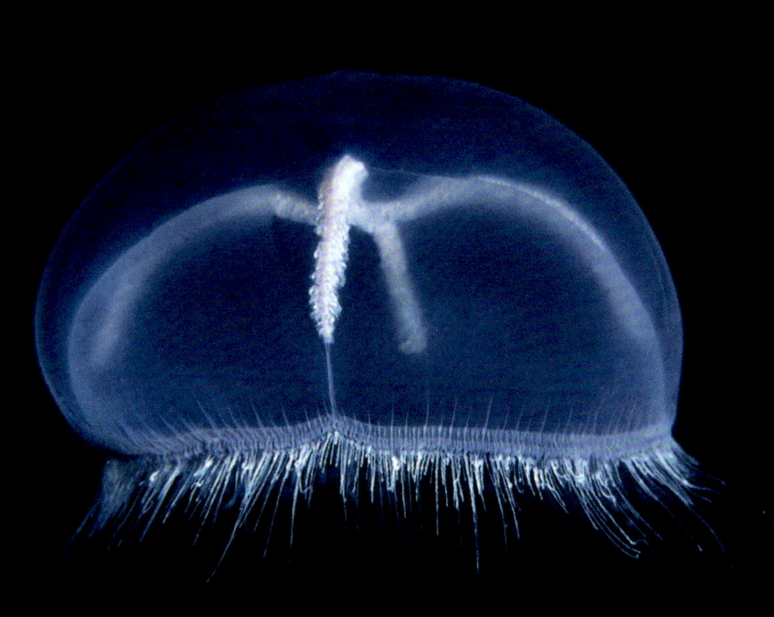

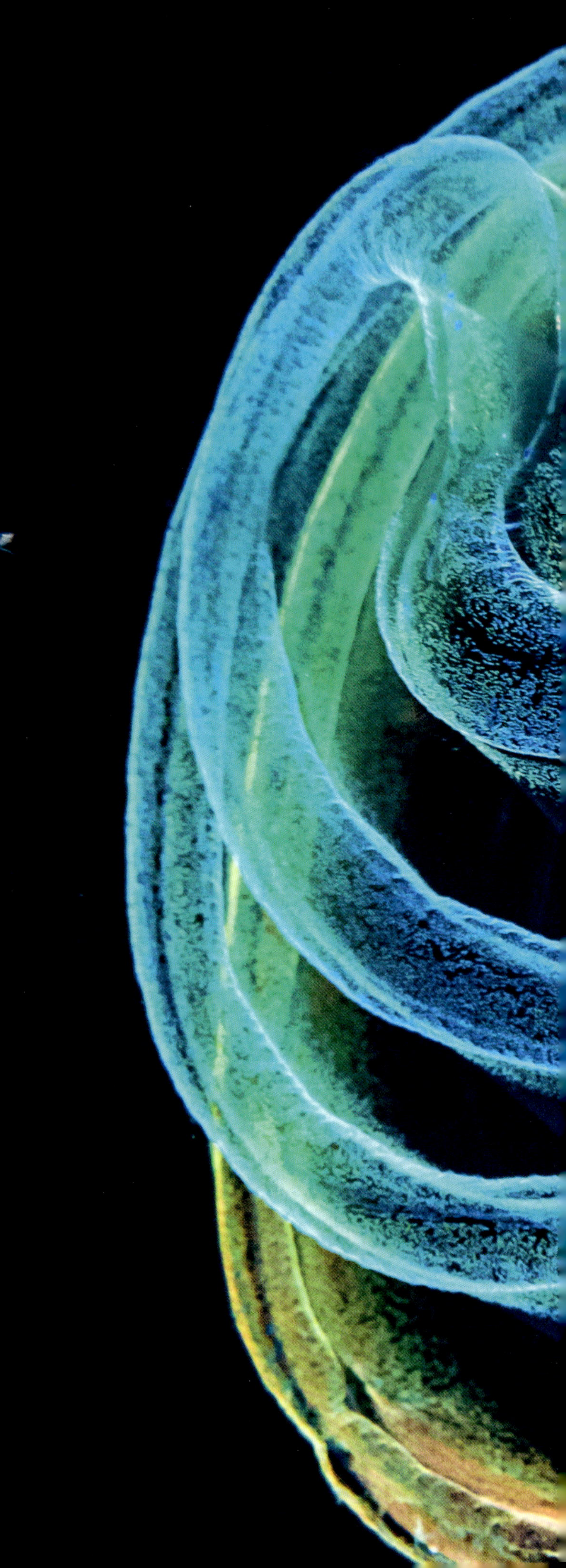

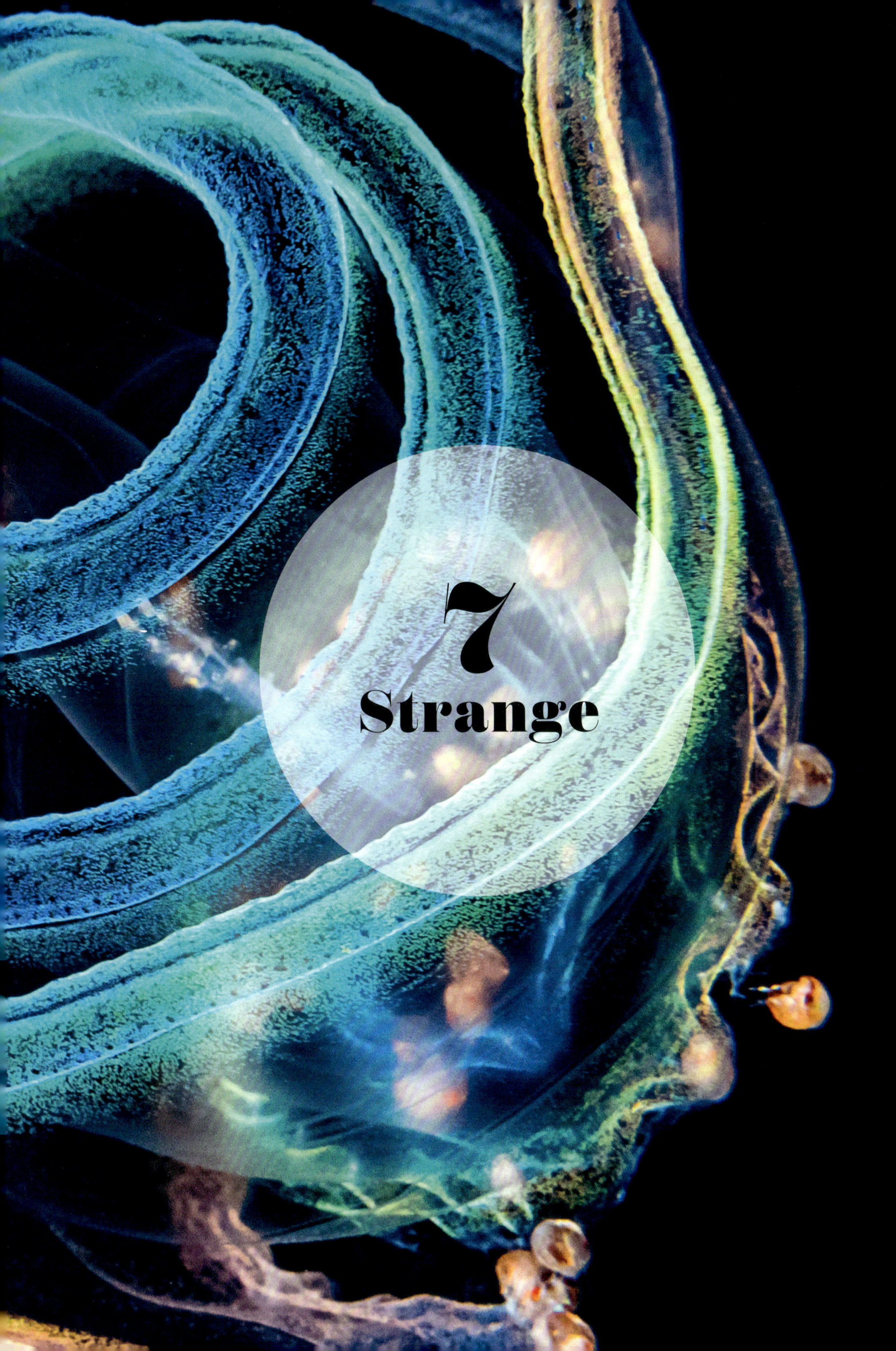

7
Strange

W e now turn our attention to some of the strangest organisms in the animal kingdom. Most of the jelly groups date back half a billion years, giving them plenty of time to evolve some particularly weird features and habits. The medusae, strange as they are compared to the more familiar vertebrates and insects, generally don't make it to the top of the "weird" list. The more fringe groups, like the siphonophores (colonial medusae), salps (free-swimming colonial sea squirts), and ctenophores (comb jellies), however, dominate any list of strange species.

Siphonophores have the attributes of both an individual and a colony. Each siphonophore is comprised of genetically identical clones that don't look the same or function in the same way. The components are as different from each other as our mouth is from our feet, and they are arranged in repeating groups.

Salps are barrel-shaped organisms that clone chains of offspring. Although they look very much like jellyfish, they are, in fact, more closely related to humans than to other types of jellies. They even have a heart, a brain, and a rudimentary spine.

Ctenophores, however, are the weirdest of the bunch. For one thing, their proto-brain-like neural center is located between two anal pores. As well, the whole group has a strong propensity toward bioluminescence, with only a few species unable to flash. And whereas other jellies pulsate their bodies for locomotion, ctenophores instead swim by means of the coordinated beating of eight rows of cilia.

While salps may be larger or smaller, or broader or more stretched, they are all variations on the barrel-shaped body plan. Salps are always either an individual with a chain of young, or a member of a chain. But comb jellies are always individuals. Though they may reproduce by cloning, they do not occur stuck together in colonies. However, different species may be so radically different as to resemble things as diverse as a belt or a marble or a plastic bag or the Batman logo.

Siphonophores are wildly different at all levels of organization. Colonies may resemble a cube or an arrowhead, or what can only be described as a long stingy stringy thingy. But within each colony, the clonal components may look as different as a pot sticker and a tentacle, a fleshy leaf and a milk bottle, or a witch's hat and a garden trowel.

No matter where one looks in the world of the jellies, you are guaranteed to find something strange.

Venus's Girdle

Cestum veneris

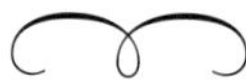

Two of nature's weirdest species are the
Venus's girdle, *Cestum veneris*, and its diminutive cousin
Velamen parallelum. The two differ in size and some minor
internal and external features, but both are shaped like a
belt, being long and strap-like. It might seem logical that
they would move in a similar manner to snakes and eels,
that is, forward in the head-to-tail sense. But the "head"
of *C. veneris* is in the middle of one of the fine edges.
Thus, it moves through the water more like a bird, using
its two long lobes as wings that flap like a seesaw
(one up, one down, then reverse). Its swimming creates
small ripples of water, which disturbs its prey and
allows it to home in for the kill.

SIZE: Body length to 3 feet (1 m)

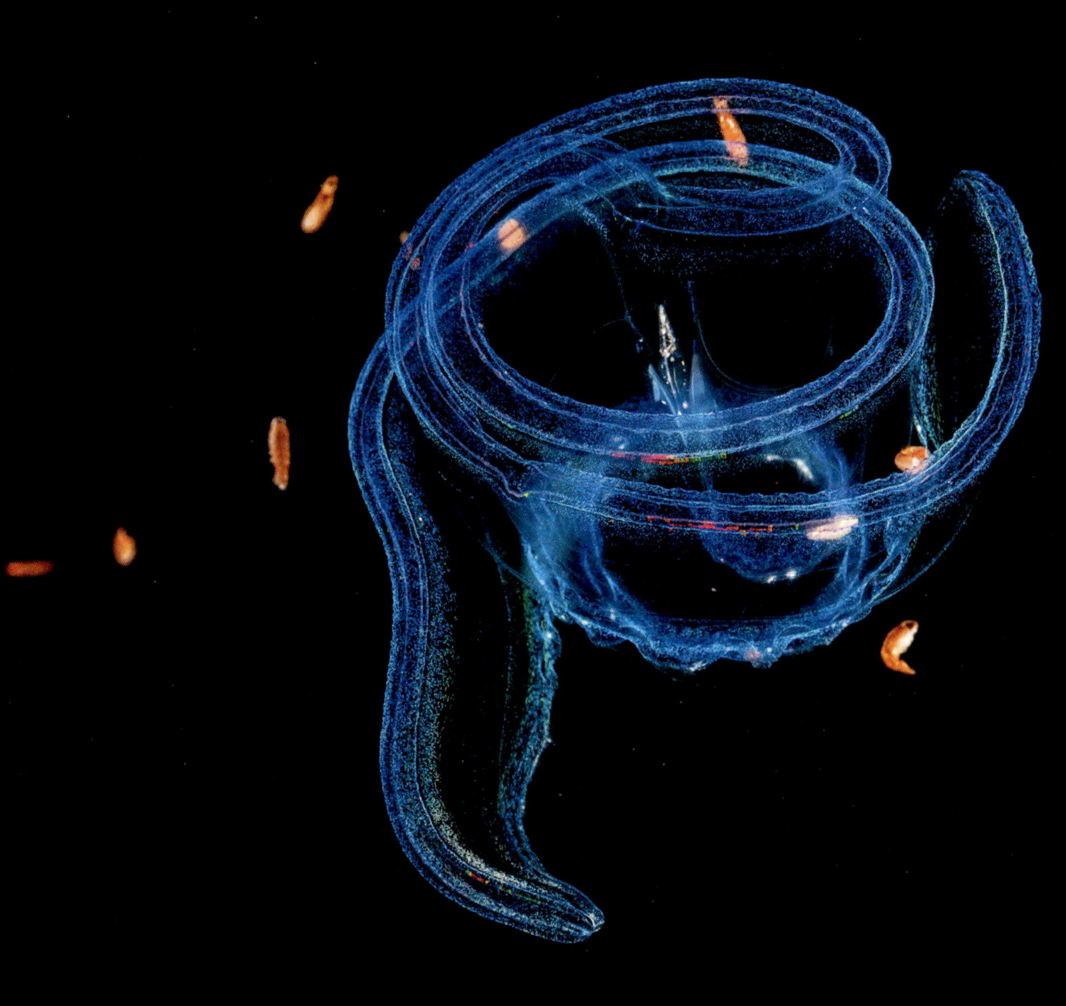

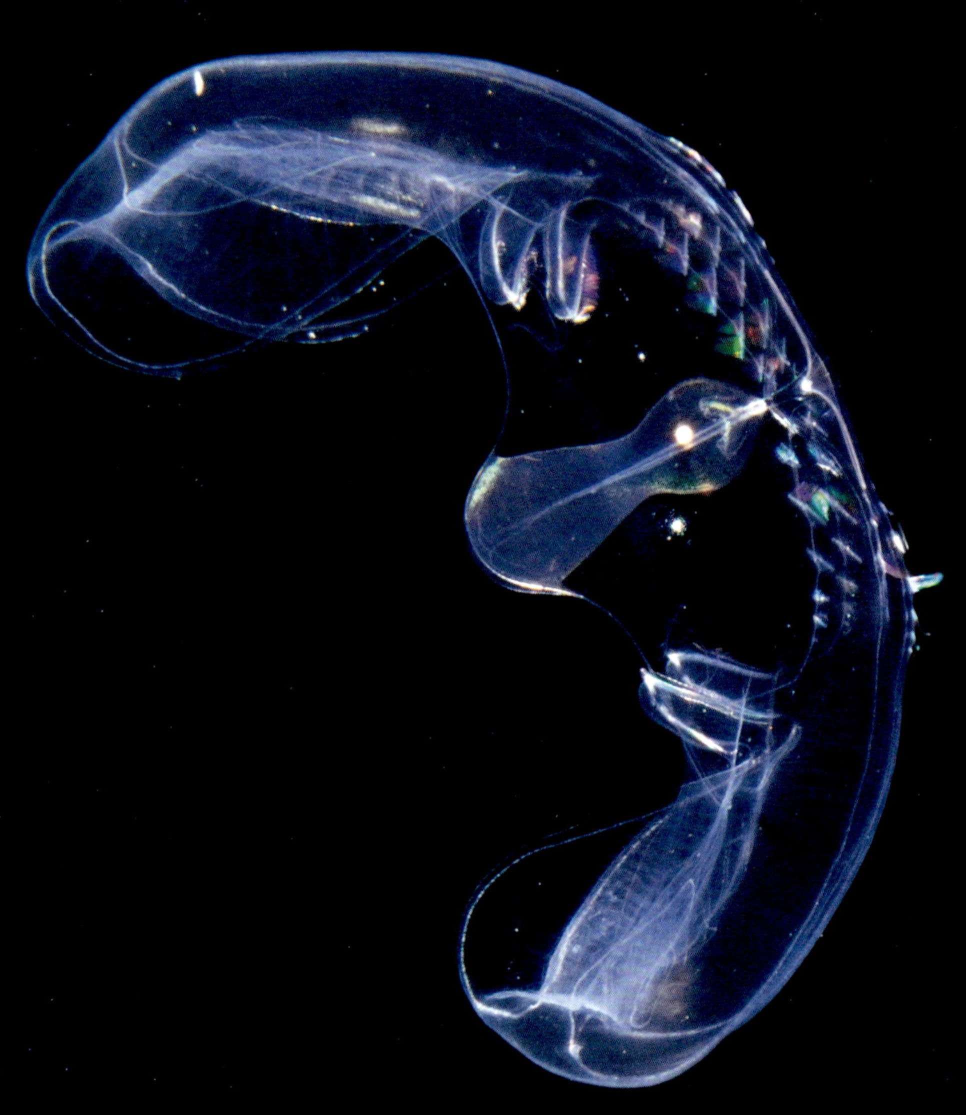

Clapper Jelly
Ocyropsis

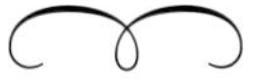

Ctenophores, or comb jellies, are strange as a rule, and members of the *Ocyropsis* genus do not disappoint. Camouflaging in plain sight, their almost completely transparent body makes them virtually invisible to prey and predators alike. Most of the time, *Ocyropsis* move in the normal ctenophore way, that is, stealthily by means of the coordinated beating of eight rows of cilia. But they can also pulsate their body like other types of non-ctenophoran jellies. When disturbed, they begin wildly clapping their two massive lobes together. This flapping motion serves two important purposes. Firstly, it rapidly extricates the comb jelly from danger and, secondly, it no doubt startles any would-be predator. *Ocyropsis* is quite common in the shallow depths of tropical seas around the world.

SIZE: Body length to 4 inches (10 cm)

Common Salp

Thalia democratica

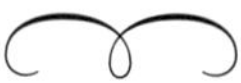

Anyone would be forgiven for wondering where
vast blooms of this incredibly common salp come from,
as they seem to appear overnight. But the answer is
simply amazing—they don't "come from" anywhere.
Its multiple life stages enable *Thalia democratica* to
bloom into superabundance right in front of our
eyes, growing in both individual and population size
almost unimaginably fast. In ideal conditions—that is,
with ample phytoplankton food—it can grow up to 10
percent of its body length *per hour* and go through two
generations in *a day*. In other words, an individual born
at midnight is having babies by noon and becomes a
grandparent by the next midnight. Experiencing
these swarms feels like swimming in bubble tea.

SIZE: Body length to ⅜ in (10 mm)

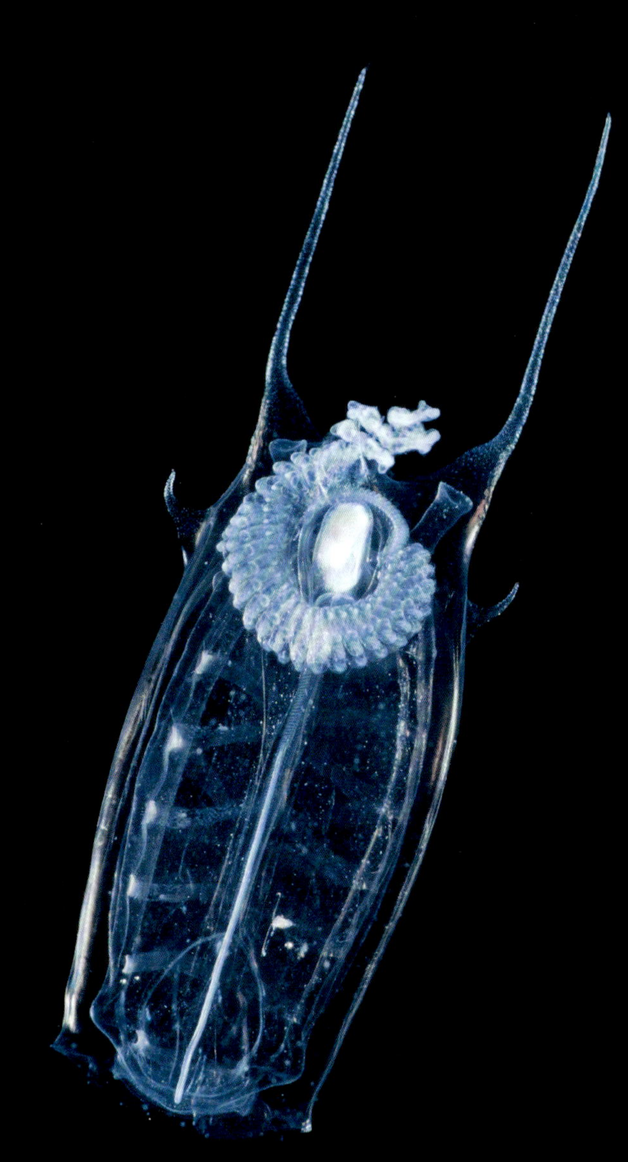

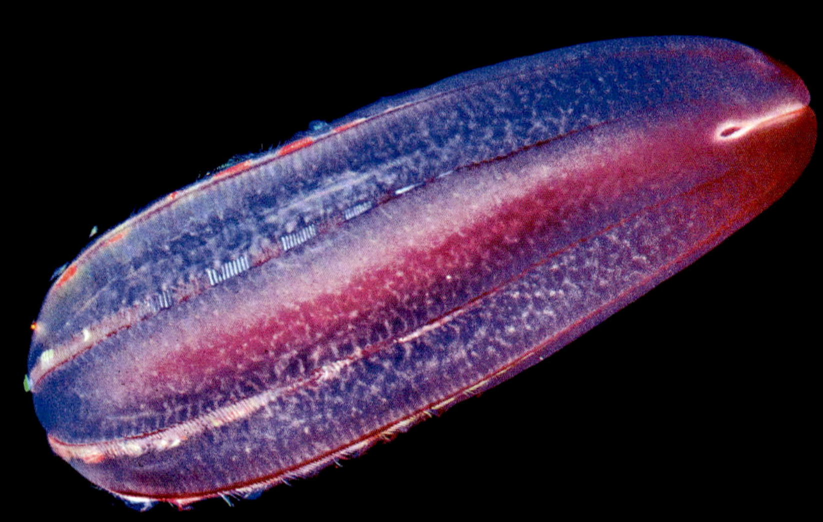

Jellies with Jaws

Beroe

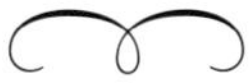

Species in the *Beroe* genus may well be the inspiration for the next Hollywood sci-fi blockbuster. They look so harmless, essentially just a swimming pocket of meltingly soft tissue. They move through the water by stealth, using a rhythmic coordinated beating of eight longitudinal rows of tiny cilia. Members of the *Beroe* genus don't have stinging cells, or even tentacles to look menacing, but they have teeth. Yes, *teeth*! These gelatinous versions of *Jaws* home in on their prey, bump into it, circle it, then lunge for the kill. *Beroe* engulf small prey whole or use their teeth to bite chunks off hapless larger victims. Many species of *Beroe* have been identified, collectively occupying all the oceans and seas of the world.

SIZE: Body length to around 6 inches (15 cm)

Rainbow Jellyfish

Leucothea filmersankeyi

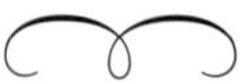

Members of the *Leucothea* genus are often called rainbow jellyfish because of the flashes of color emitted from their cilia as they swim, although all comb jellies do this. *Leucothea* species are, in fact, far stranger than they are beautiful. Their bodies are dominated by two huge lobes; viewed head-on, they look like a sci-fi alien attack vessel. Two long tentacles snaking hypnotically just add to their otherworldliness. The body is covered in sensory papillae, which respond by bending over in unison toward any stimulus. When disturbed, they curl in their lobes, which resemble a clear spiky potato. Despite their large size, the gossamer bodies of *Leucothea* will simply explode into lifeless ribbons at the slightest swish of water.

SIZE: Body length to 12 inches (30 cm)

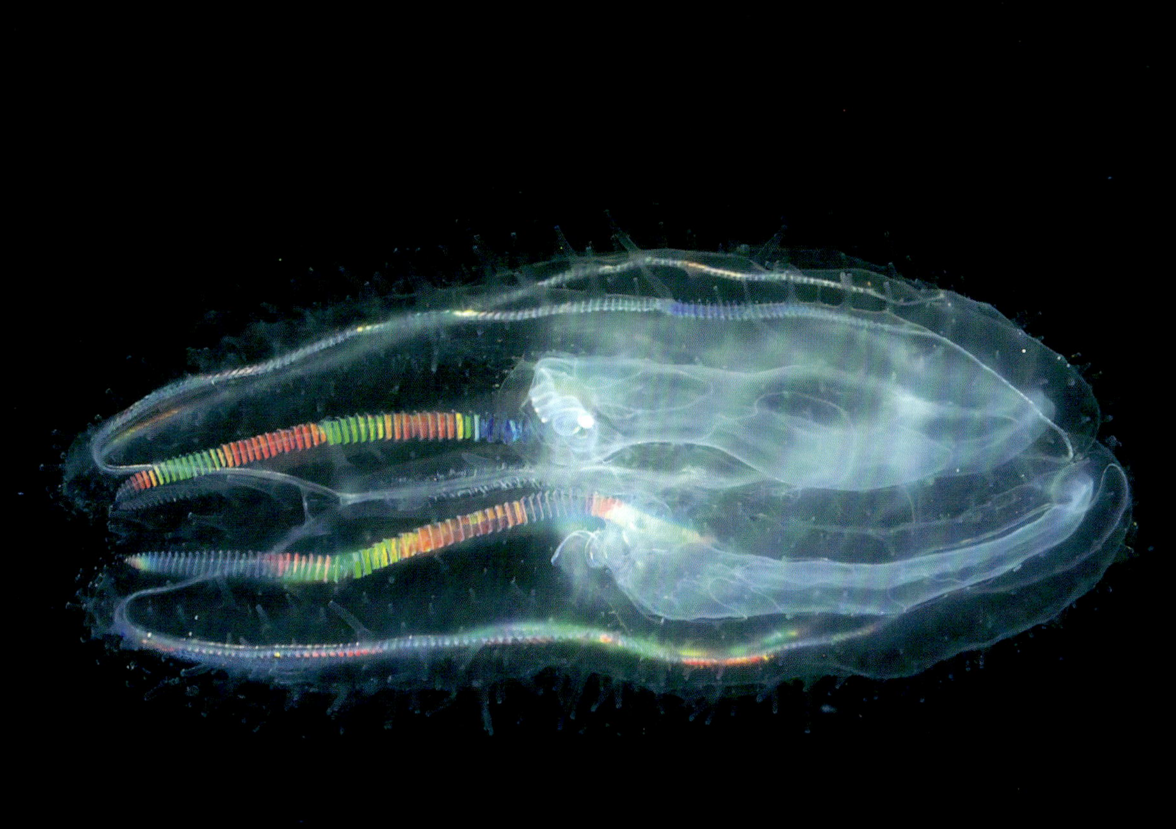

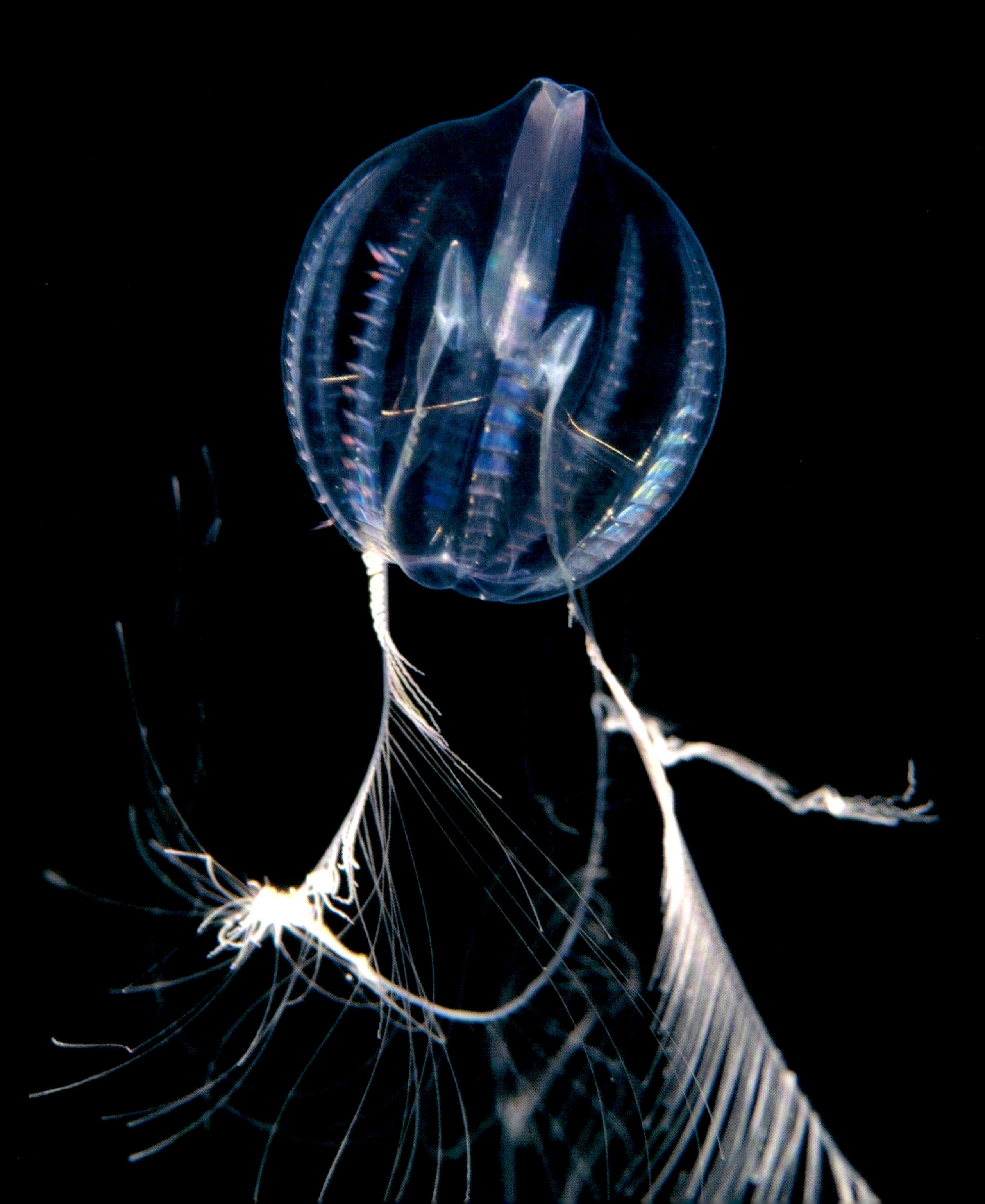

Sea Gooseberry

Pleurobrachia

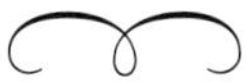

The ever-delightful sea gooseberries are unmistakable due to their transparent spherical body, zooming through the water by means of eight rows of rainbow-emitting locomotory cilia. But when they stop, magic happens. Emerging through two sheaths pointing backward in the body, two long tentacles expand and unfurl into marvelous feathery structures, which may appear whimsical to us humans but are actually a killing field for small plankton. Each tentillum, or side branch of the tentacles, is studded with thousands of microscopic, spring-loaded sticky cells, which *Pleurobrachia* use to ensnare their prey. But the tentacles face away from the mouth, making food transfer difficult. *Pleurobrachia* solve this dilemma by somersaulting until the tentacle carrying the prey swipes across the mouth.

SIZE: Body length to 1 inch (2.5 cm)

Fringey

Manokia stiasnyi

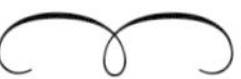

This rare type of cubozoan, or box jellyfish,
seems at first glance to have fringed tentacles. But
closer examination reveals a marvelous secret—they are
polyps! Like most medusae, cubozoans have a colonial
benthic stage. This is a life stage in which clonal groups
of polyps grow on the seabed. But it appears that *Manokia
stiasnyi* has no need of the seabed since it carries its
polyps with it in rows along its tentacles. Whether these
hundreds of polyps perform a digestive function or a
reproductive one, or both, is not yet known. *Manokia
stiasnyi* has been found only a couple of times in Papua
New Guinea and Australia, so we have no idea
where it normally calls home.

SIZE: Bell height to 1¼ inches (3 cm)

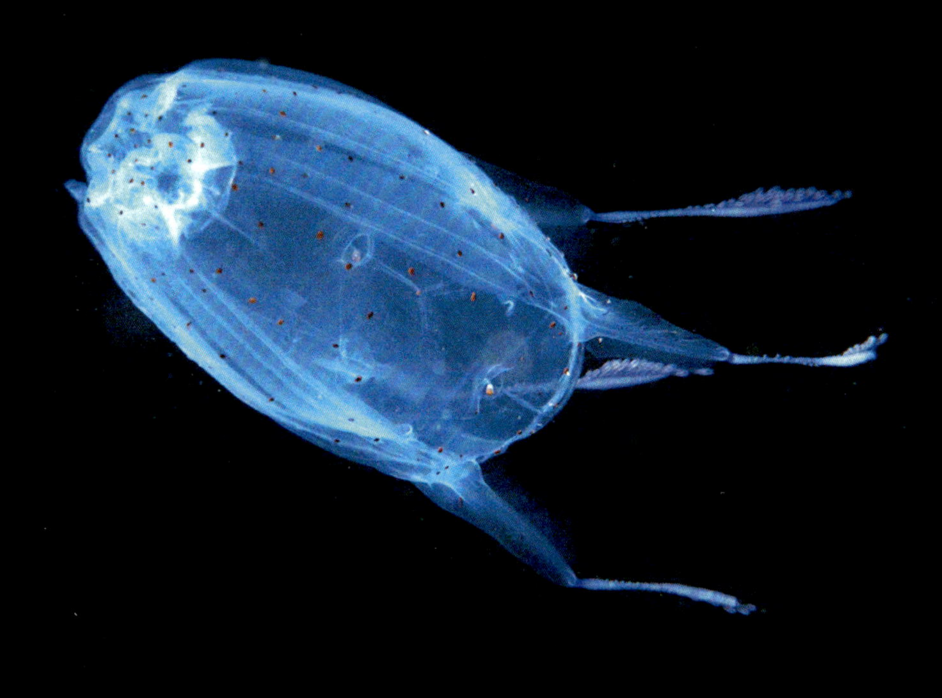

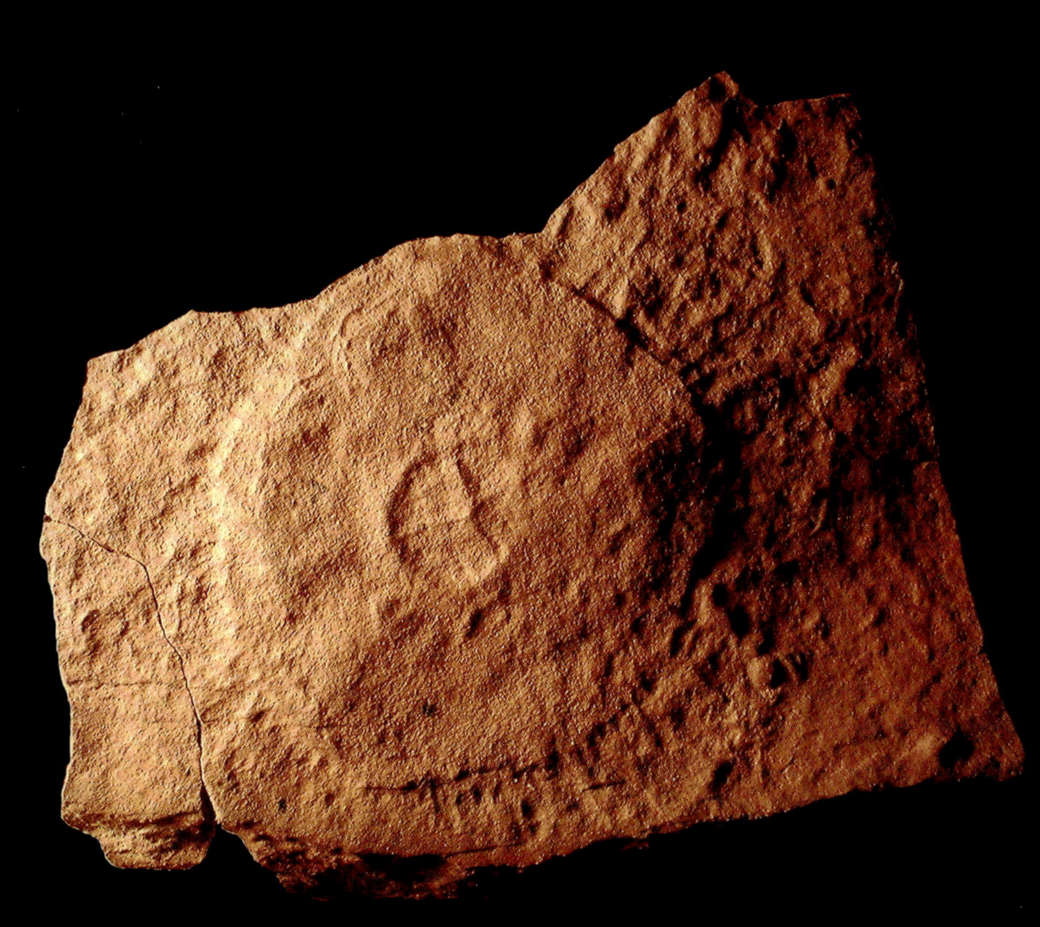

Confusing Sponge Jelly Fossil
Palaeophragmodictya reticulata

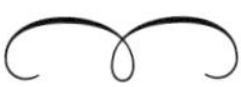

While it may be hard to imagine soft, squishy
jellyfish fossilizing, indeed they can and sometimes do.
But instead of the three-dimensional mineralization
left by big, meaty dinosaur bones, jellies leave mere
impressions, like a footprint or perhaps little more
than a shadow. So imagine the delight of those who
study jellyfish fossils to see *Palaeophragmodictya*, which,
in a parallel circumstance would have been the most
perfectly preserved jellyfish known. The fossil suggests
the bell and tentacles and even the four-parted symmetry
so characteristic of jellyfish. But alas, it was classified
as a sponge instead, despite lacking sponges' key
characters, demonstrating the difficulties inherent
to understanding mere glimpses of life long ago.

SIZE: Bell diameter to 4 inches (10 cm)

Garden Trowel Jelly

Ceratocymba sagittata

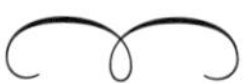

There is arguably no stranger organism on the planet than *Ceratocymba sagittata*. Like all siphonophores, which blur the separation between an individual and a colony, *C. sagittata* comprises numerous functional parts that all live together as one super-organism. One such part looks like a witches' hat, while another looks like a garden trowel. The witches' hat is called a nectophore, or swimming bell; this functions as a means of locomotion for the colony. The garden trowel is called a bract; this functions as a protective shield for the mature reproductive stage, known as a gonophore, in which the sexes are mirror images of each other. Regardless of all the weird terminology, this fella is strange!

SIZE: Body length to ¾ inch (20 mm)

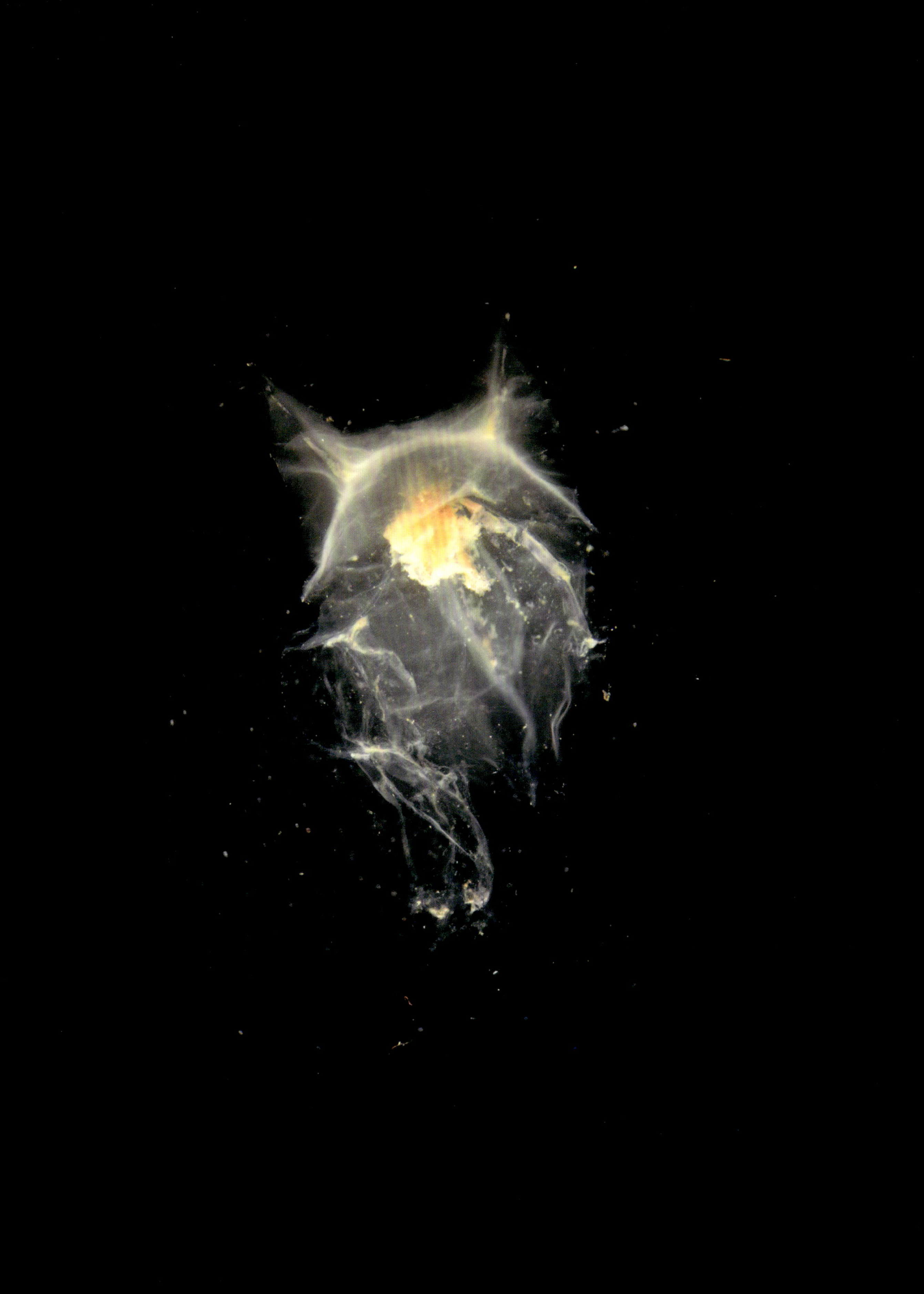

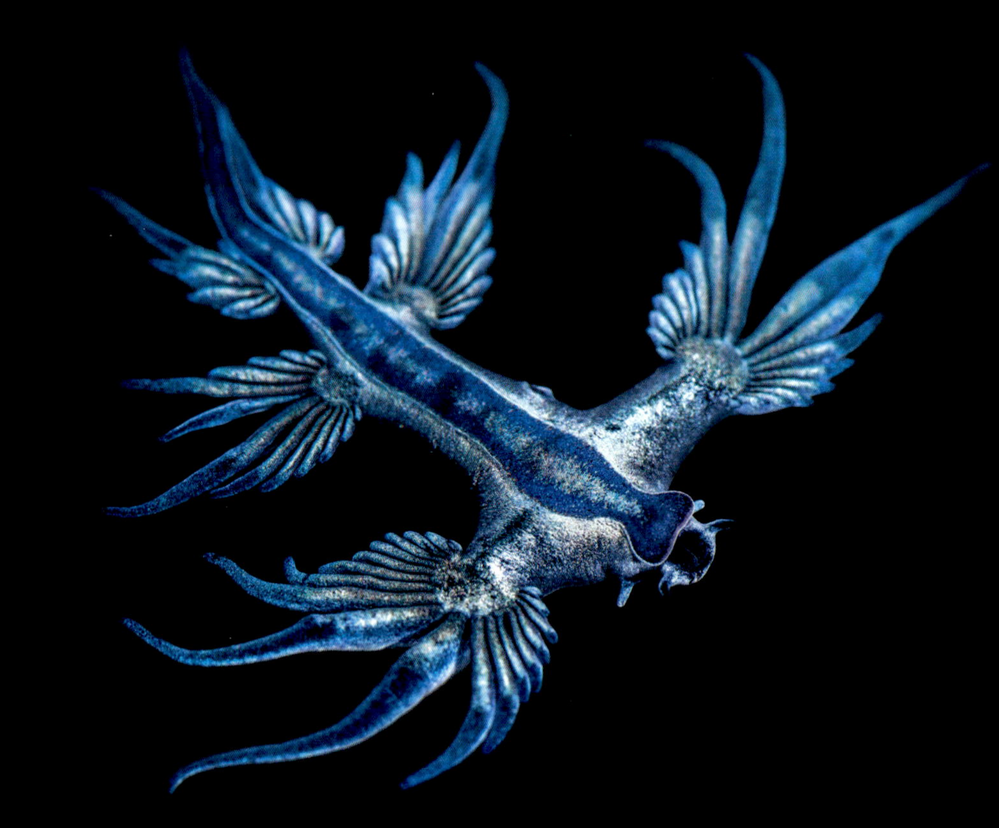

Sea Lizard

Glaucus atlanticus

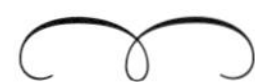

The sea lizard is neither a reptile nor a jellyfish, but it is certainly the next best thing—it is a sea slug (shell-less sea snail) that preys on jellyfish and consumes their stinging cells without triggering them to discharge, then deploys these weapons for its own defense. *Glaucus atlanticus* lives at the air-water interface, where it gulps mouthfuls of air to help it keep afloat. Fascinatingly, it uses its muscular foot to glide along the underside of the air. It is found at subtropical beaches around the world when bluebottles and Portuguese men-of-war are driven ashore on stormy tides; savvy beachcombers who know to look between the bluebottles are rewarded with sightings of this stunning minibeast.

SIZE: Body length to 1¼ inches (3 cm)

Creeping Comb Jelly

Coeloplana

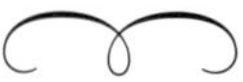

While we generally think of jellyfish as drifting
or free-swimming, a few different groups have adapted
to a benthic (sedentary) lifestyle, sticking to the seabed.
Comb jellies are weird by any definition, but among
the strangest are the coeloplanas, which look more like
flatworms than jellyfish. Coeloplanas are a mere film
of tissue that glides or creeps over algae, corals, or even
the spines of sea urchins—each species is commensal
with a specific host. When not gliding, their body
spontaneously texturizes, rising into two volcano-shaped
structures, each bearing a long, gossamer-fine, feathery
tentacle, along with numerous wart-like papillae.
The papillae may be respiratory or sensory, as they
respond to stimulation by vanishing.

SIZE: Body length to around 2½ inches (6 cm)

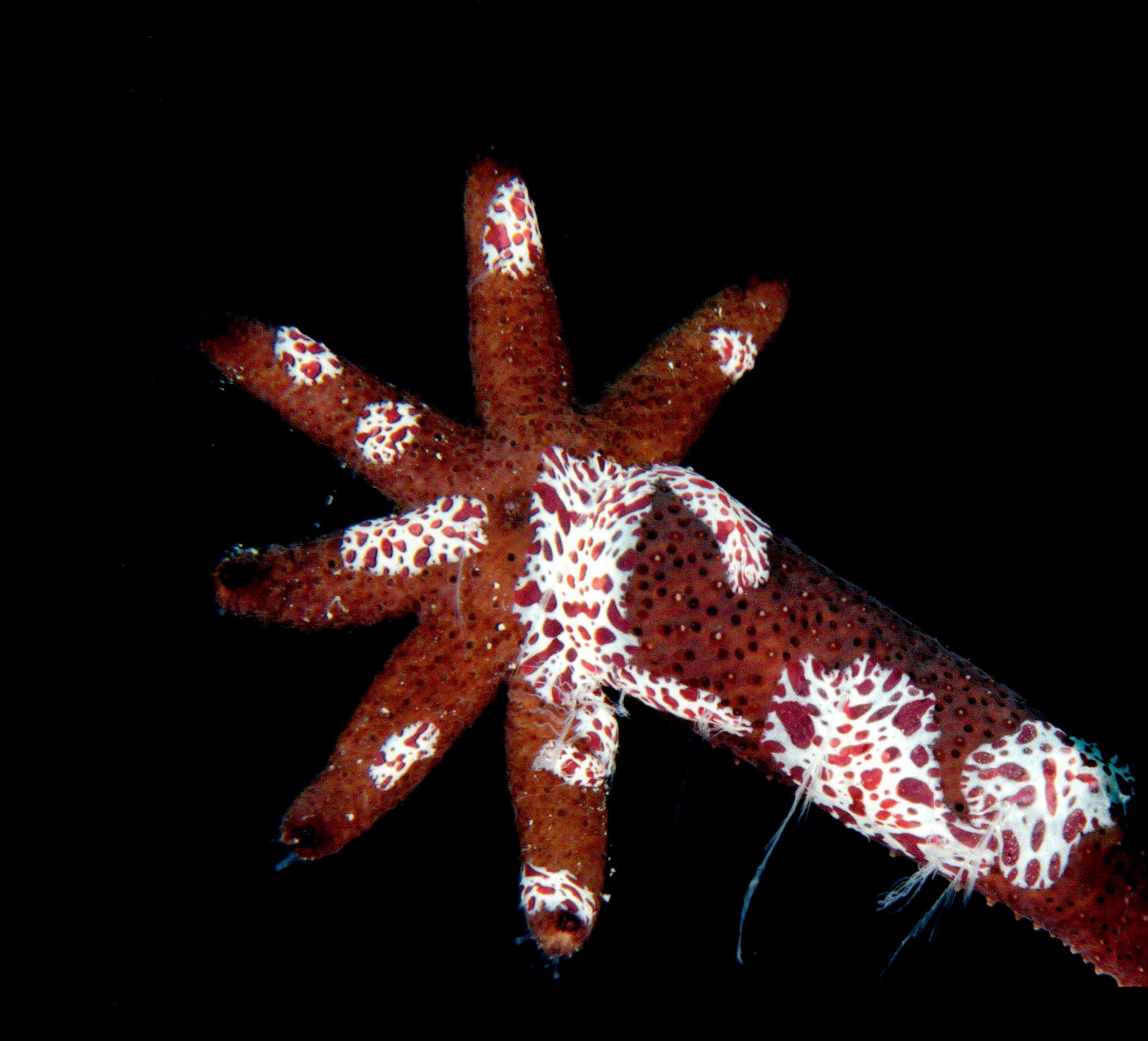

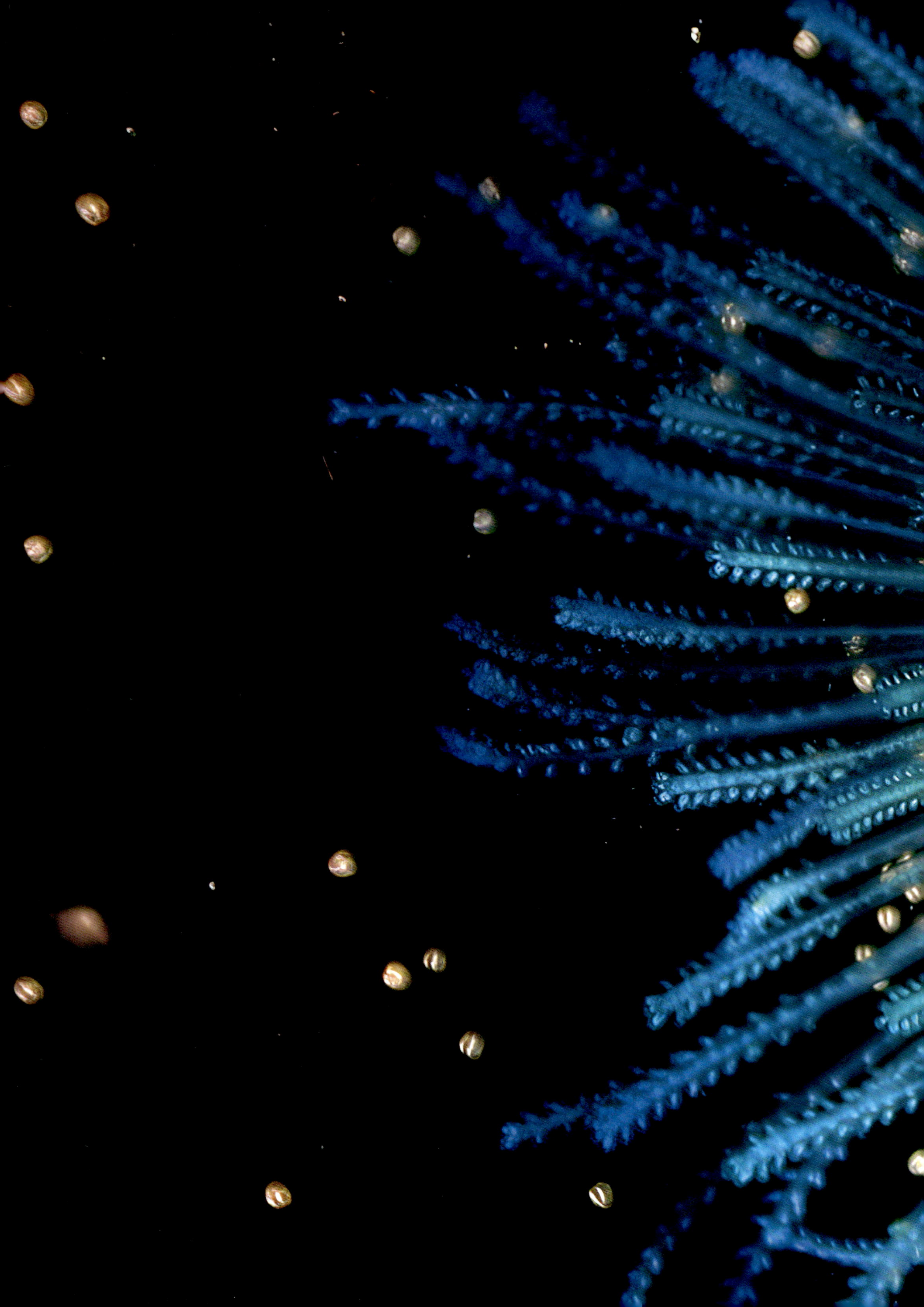

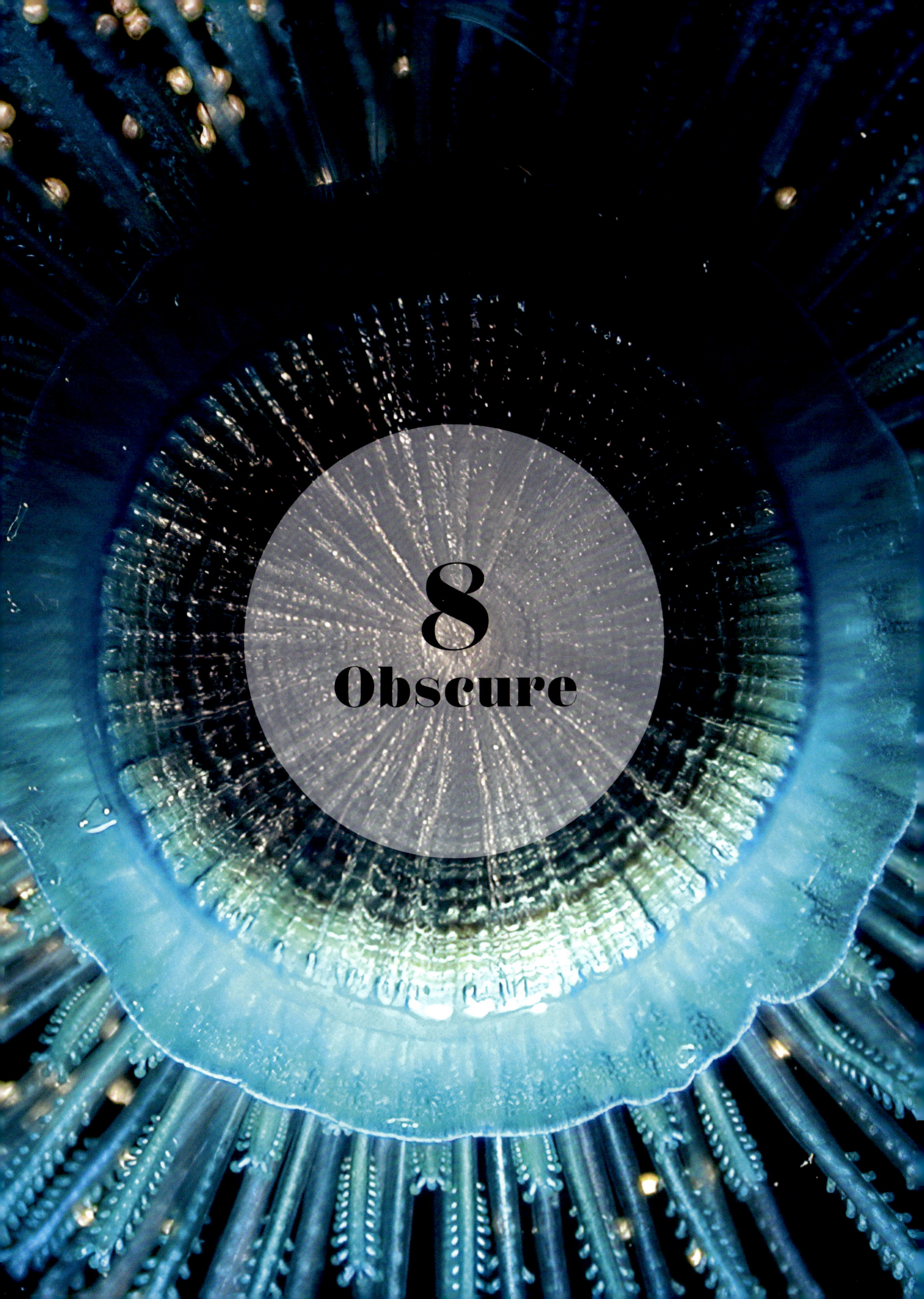
8
Obscure

Four-Leaf Jelly

Liriope tetraphylla

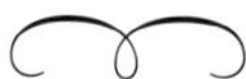

This delightful, umbrella-shaped medusa makes its
home in the open ocean, although it is occasionally
pushed ashore by winds and storms. For this reason,
Liriope tetraphylla is considered an indicator species of an
offshore water mass. The long journey it undertakes to
arrive at accessible coastlines belies its delicate nature.
The bell is an almost perfect hemispherical bowl, its sides
housing the broad, leaf-shaped reproductive organs. The
dangly bit in the middle is a solid gelatinous structure
called a peduncle, similar to a museum plinth holding a
precious artifact, but in this case, it bears the creature's
tiny stomach and ruffly mouth at its very end. Its four
long and four short tentacles simply enhance its beauty.

SIZE: Bell diameter to 1¼ inches (3 cm)

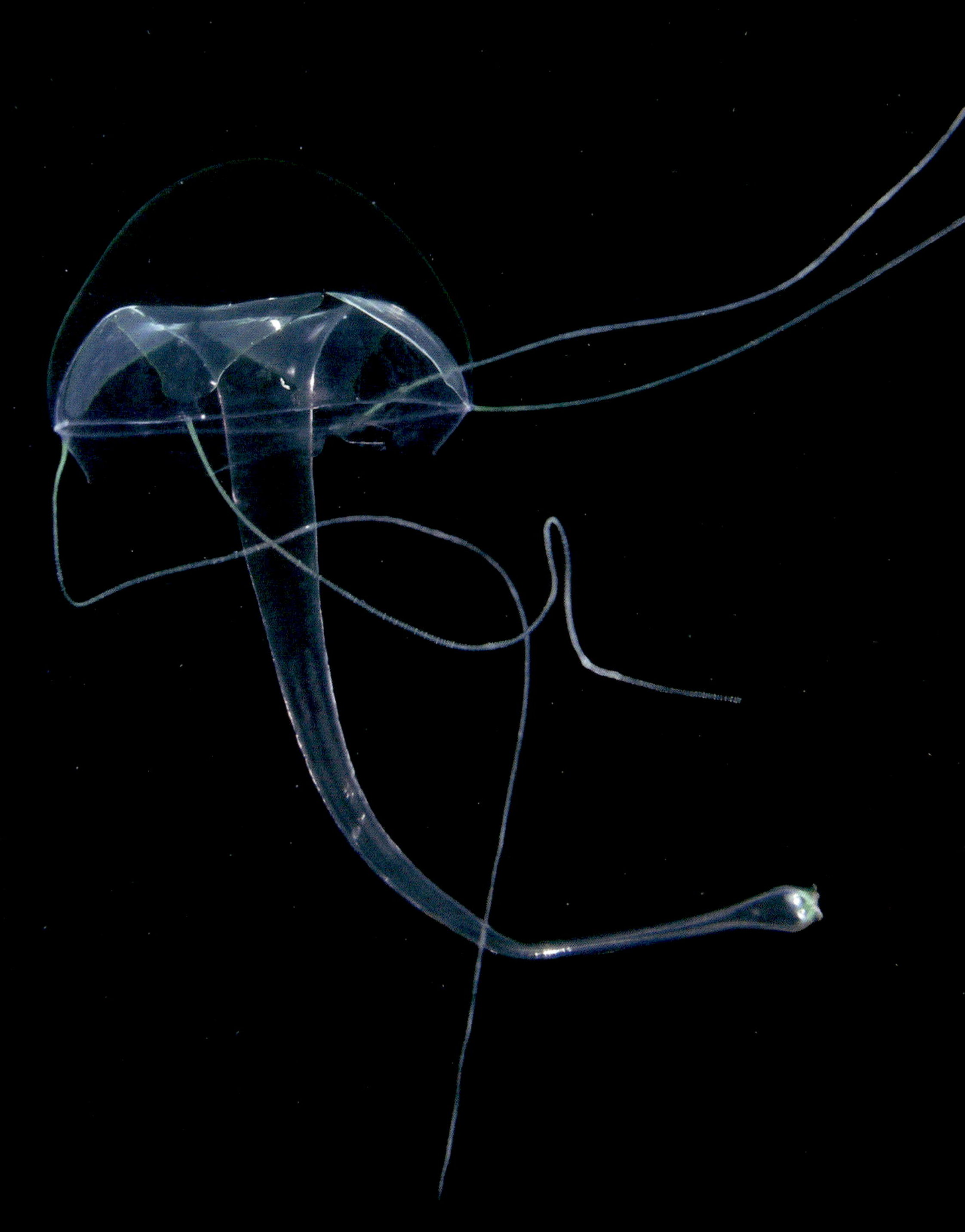

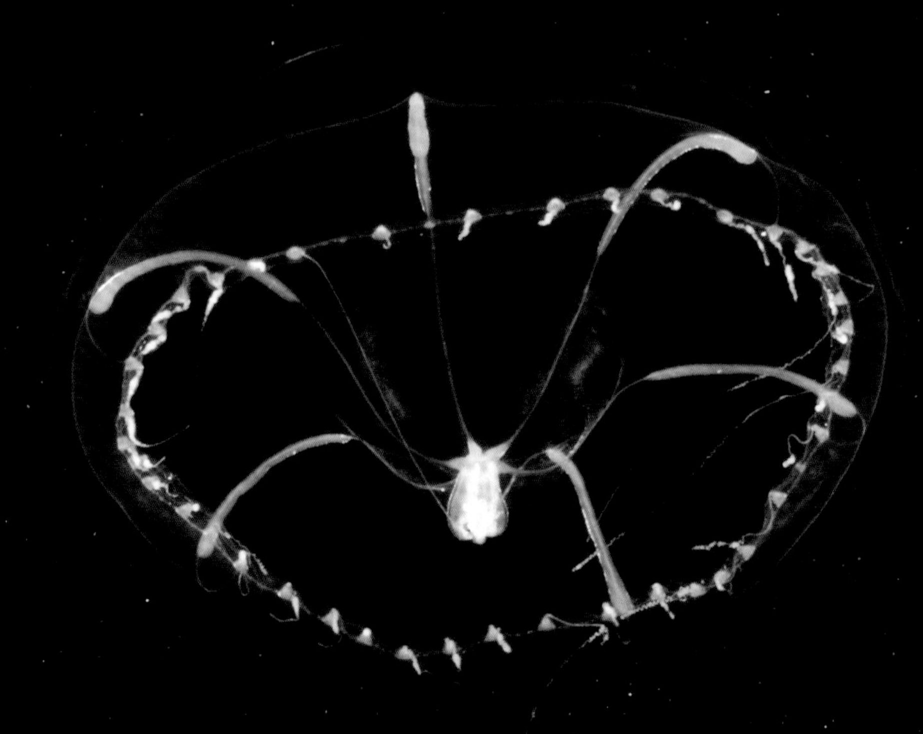

Jelly Buttons

Eirene hexanemalis

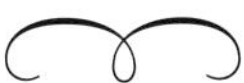

This small, simple species is one of the most
common of the hydromedusae in Australian waters,
but is obscure through its invisibility. It is no larger than
a lima bean and completely transparent in water. But
in certain conditions *Eirene hexanemalis* occurs in such
tremendous numbers as to limit underwater visibility
and can rapidly clog a plankton net. Its body is a small,
firm, dome-shaped button of jelly, with six equally
spaced lines of reproductive organs radiating from the
tiny central mouth to the margin. It also has numerous
long tentacles that are as fine as cobwebs. Most people
never get to see *E. hexanemalis* like this, since they are
usually cast up on the beach at the waterline in their
thousands, looking like large drops of water.

SIZE: Bell diameter to ¾ inch (20 mm)

Beaded Lantern Jelly

Corymorphid medusae

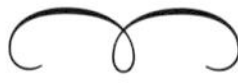

Some of the world's smallest jellyfish are the most
wondrous, but because of their minute size, they remain
obscure to all but the most ardent enthusiasts. These
medusae are as beautiful and as delicate as a Fabergé
egg, speckled in gold, or red, or purple, or with a long,
pointy hat or no hat at all, and bearing but a single, long,
lopsided tentacle studded like a string of beads. Gazing
through a microscope at these tiny creatures, they seem
more like jewels than jellies. Different species are found
in different areas, collectively spanning the gamut of
colors and shapes. It would be difficult not to fall in love
with jellies after seeing these little beings.

SIZE: Bell height to ³⁄₁₆ inch (5 mm)

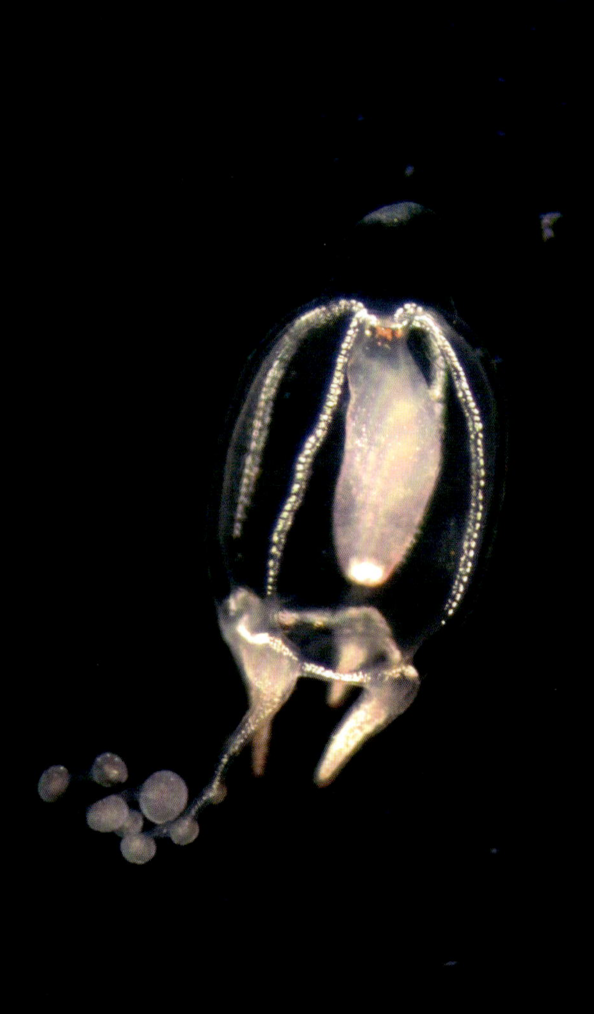

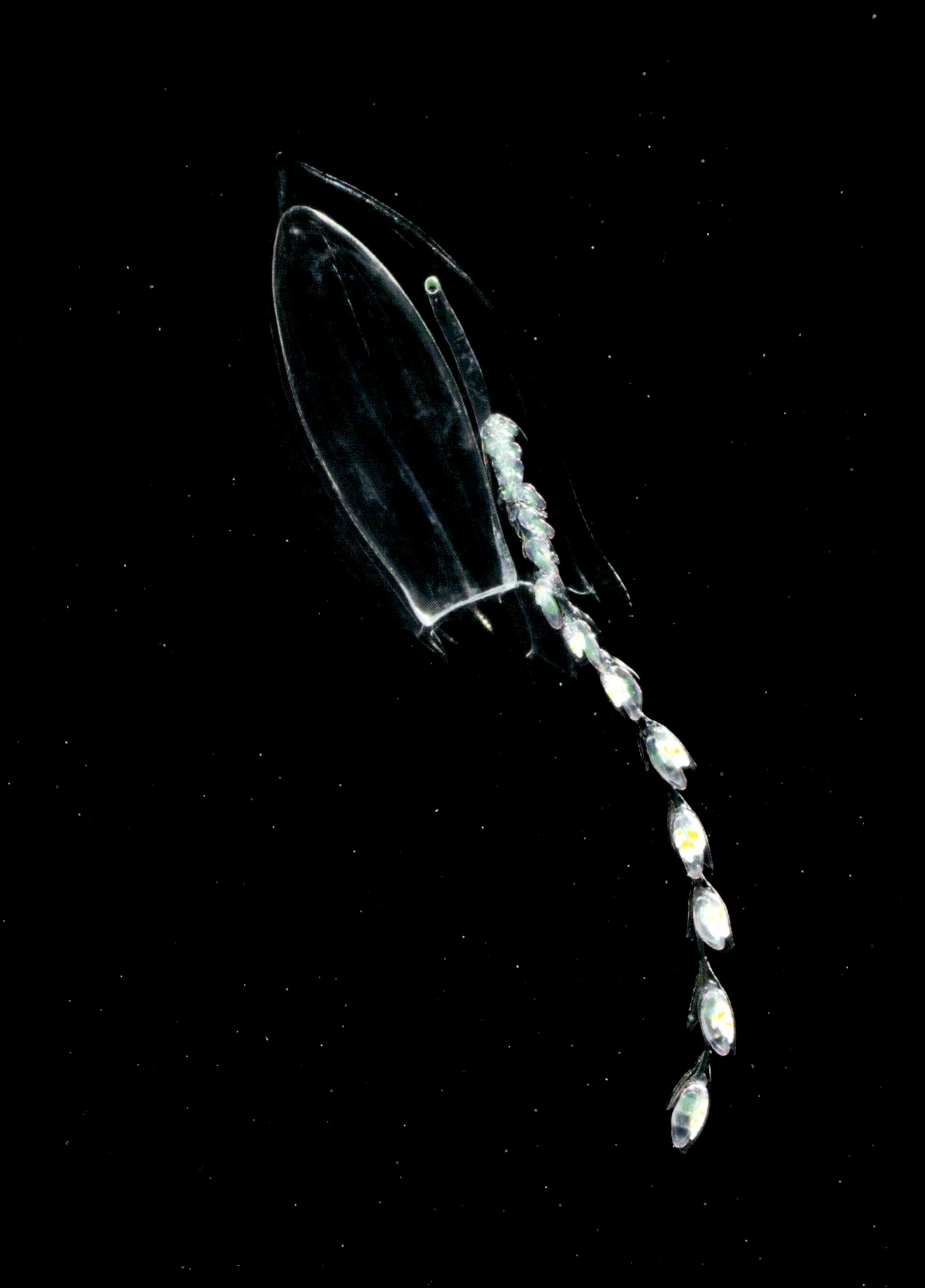

Bullet Jelly

Muggiaea atlantica

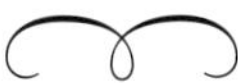

Muggiaea atlantica is a funny little fella. At first
glance, if you are lucky enough to see one at all, it gives
the impression of a transparent, ridged bullet. And
indeed, it uses its bullet shape to shoot around its watery
domain. But closer examination reveals so much more.
Most of its ridged body is occupied by an enormous
cavity; each pulsation of the body forces water out,
providing a strong jet propulsion. At the posterior end
of its body, on one side lies a small gelatinous extension
with a small pocket; nestled inside this small concavity is
the entire colony—all the feeding, breeding, and stinging
members arranged on a long tentacle when unfurled.

SIZE: Body length to ¼ inch (6 mm)

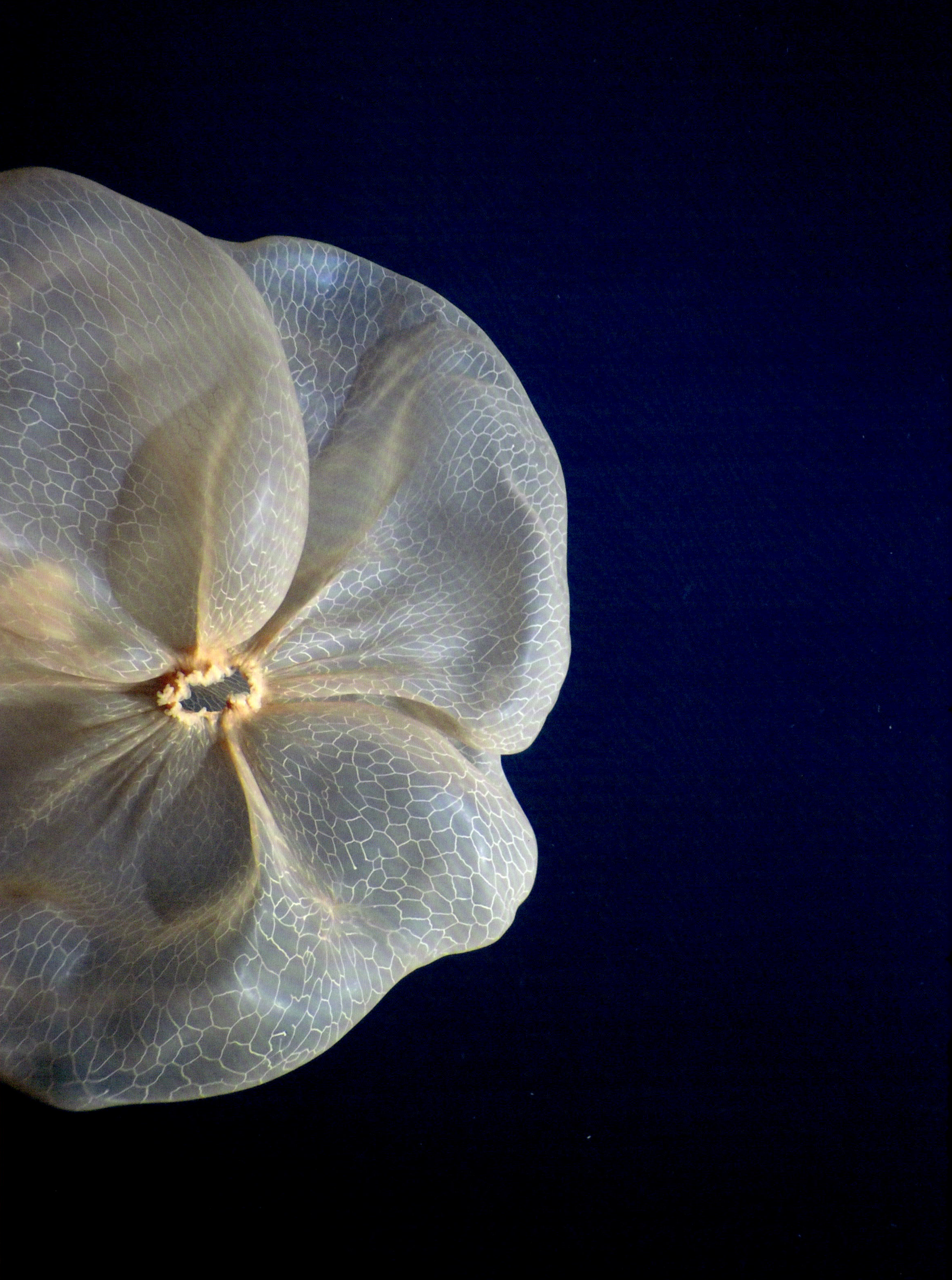

Undulating Jellyfish

Deepstaria enigmatica

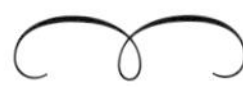

As its name suggests, *Deepstaria enigmatica* was an enigma for a long time, known only from fragments found in plankton nets that had sampled the ocean's depths. It wasn't until submersibles came into frequent use that this species was finally observed *in situ*, or in its natural habitat. This incredibly diaphanous species is almost as delicate as a ribbon of smoke rising from a candle. To catch food, its huge body forms a tent around its tiny prey such as a copepod, pursing the opening shut, and then it waits. When the copepod jumps to get away, it usually flicks itself into the "wall" of the "tent." Stinging cells spear the prey and ciliary currents convey it to the mouth of the jellyfish.

SIZE: Bell diameter to 2 feet (60 cm)

Medusae of the Blue Button

Porpita porpita

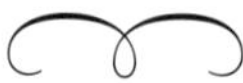

While the blue button (*Porpita porpita*, see page 70) colony is unmistakable and definitely not obscure with its floating chitinous disc and whimsical, blue, studded tentacles, its tiny medusa is one of the most obscure of all species. Each medusa is incredibly tiny and simple, with no mouth or tentacles. And it is incredibly short-lived, with but a single aim during its few hours of existence— to breed. They are essentially just a microscopic dispersal system for sperm and eggs. At the right angle, they look like tiny golden stars, but more often they could easily be mistaken for grains of sand. It is the perfect camouflage for the medusae released by beached colonies.

SIZE: Bell height less than $\frac{1}{16}$ inch (1 mm)

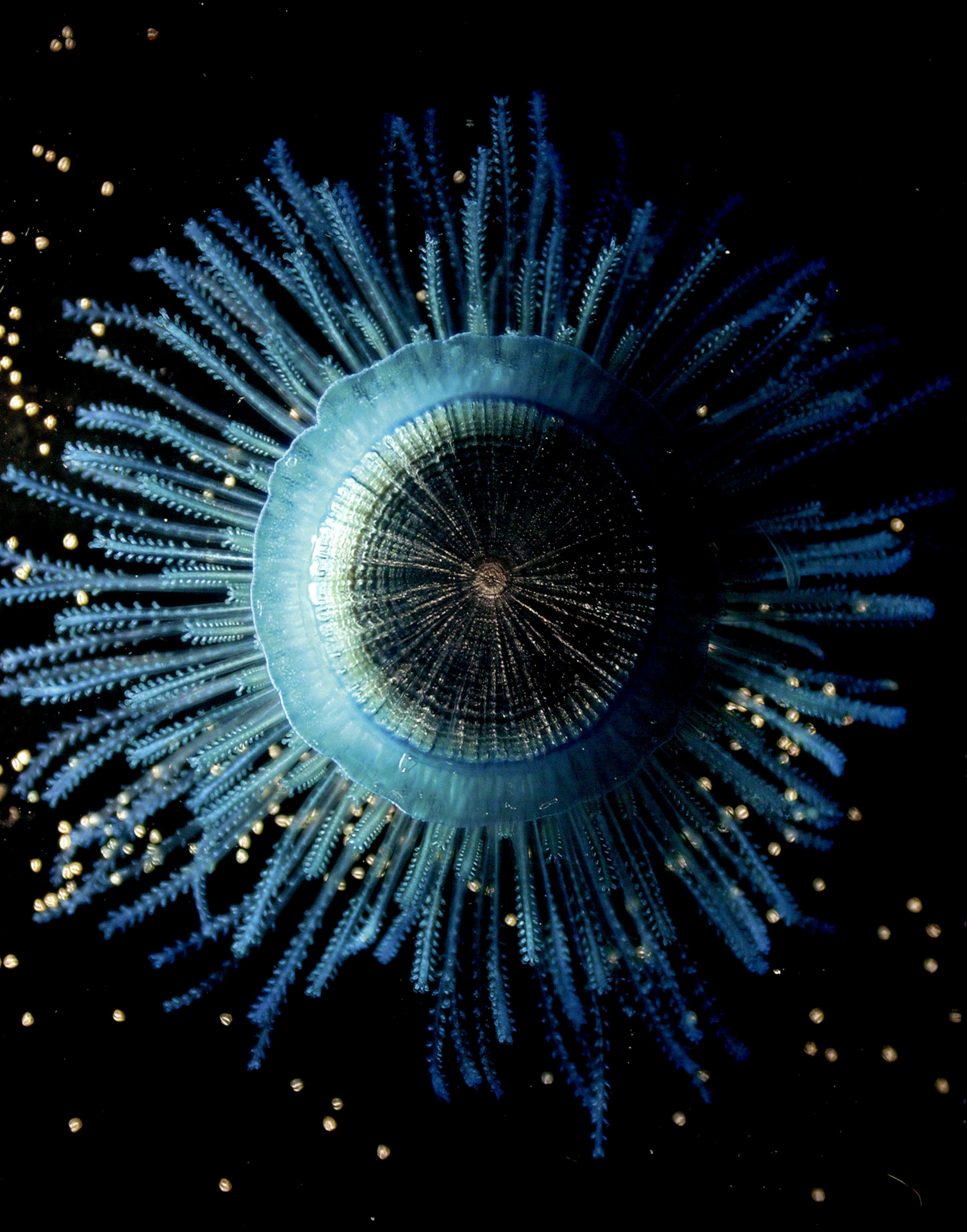

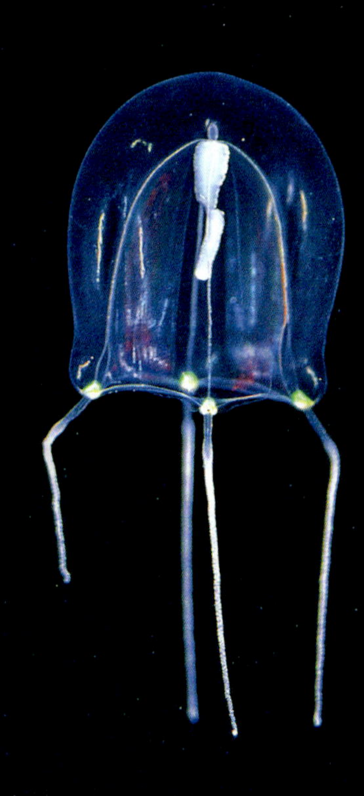

Elegant Medusa

Sarsia

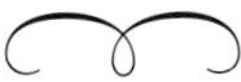

Members of the *Sarsia* genus are among the most
common of hydromedusae. They are as elegant as they
are simple. The body is tall and slender, and when fully
relaxed, the stomach is very long and often observed
protruding from the bell margin. Their hydroids are
among the most distinctive, with each polyp long and
slender like a tiny baseball bat studded with tentacles
and each capped with a ball of stinging cells. Despite
their elegance and the fact that they are so common, they
remain obscure to most people. One of the underdogs of
the jellyfish world, they are near impossible to see in
the water, too small to make good display species, and
would be easily overlooked if washed up on a beach.

SIZE: Bell height typically around ³⁄₁₆ inch (5 mm)

Ghostly Veil

Bathocyroe fosteri

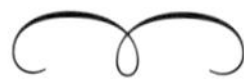

Few species are more obscure than those hidden
away in the depths of the oceans. But even by deep-
sea standards, the comb jelly *Bathocyroe fosteri* is one
of the most obscure. It is so delicate that its filmy body
explodes on contact with a sampling net, so it can never
be collected by standard methods. Researchers exploring
the ocean with submersibles in the 1970s were able to
collect specimens using specially designed slurp guns,
which gently suck the jellyfish into canisters with little
disturbance. That way, the animals remain intact long
enough to be observed. Even then, they are impossible
to preserve as museum specimens because
they also explode on contact with chemicals
such as alcohol or formaldehyde.

SIZE: Body width to 1½ inches (4 cm)

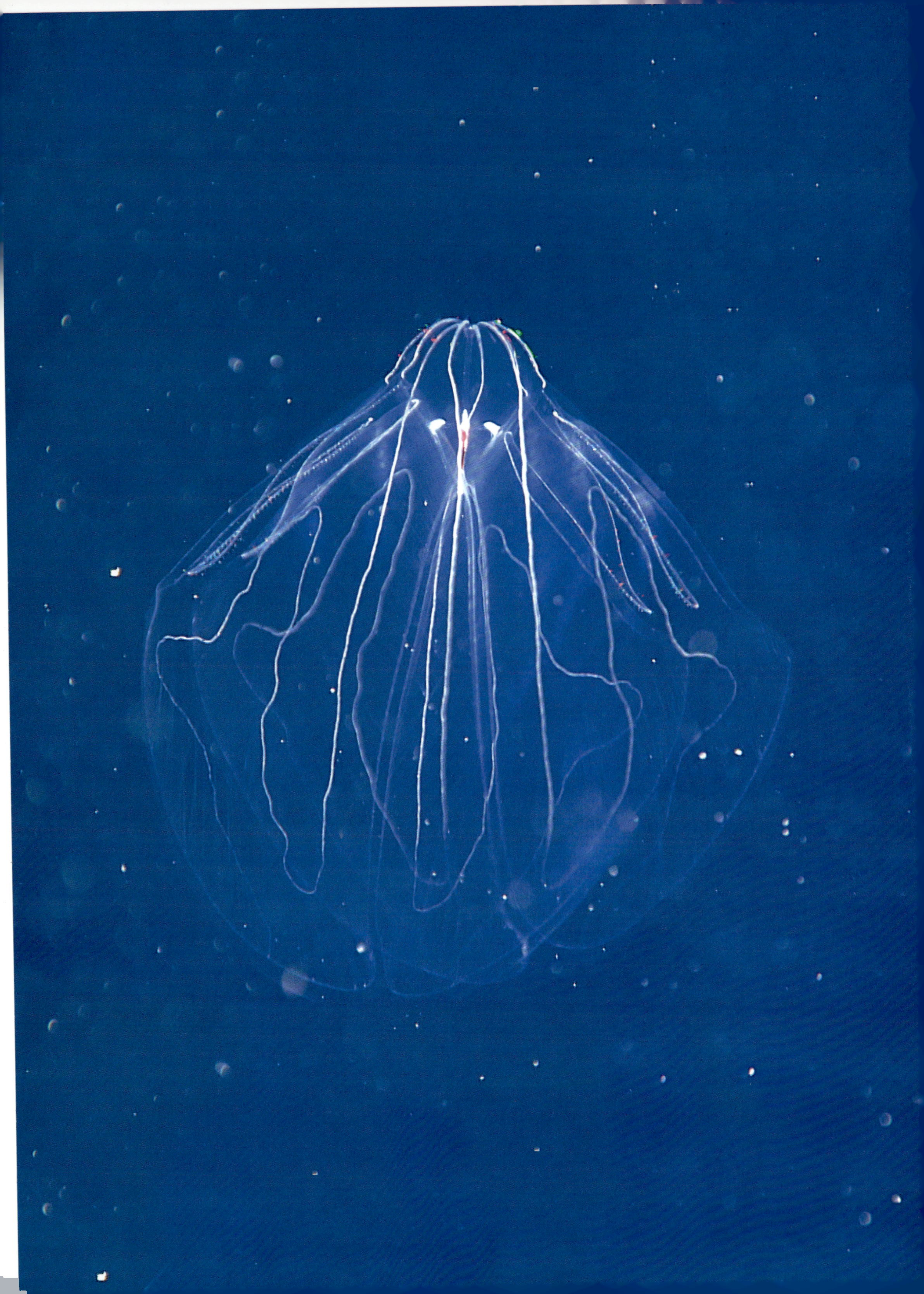

Painted Box Jellyfish

Chirodectes

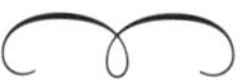

Box jellies are generally almost invisible in water.
Instead, the Painted Box Jellies' striking markings
help them camouflage in their variegated coral reef
habitat. Two species of *Chirodectes* are known. The first,
C. maculatus, was identified in the 1990s when a single
specimen was found at the Great Barrier Reef after a
cyclone. Decades passed and no new specimens were
discovered, with still no clue as to its origin. Then,
unexpectedly, in 2022, much larger similar specimens
were filmed by scuba divers at Kavieng Island, off Papua
New Guinea. The original was hand-sized and covered
in spots, while these were the size of soccer balls with
beautiful ring markings—and new to science. Sometimes,
even the most dazzling species can be obscure!

SIZE: Bell diameter to 12 inches (30 cm)

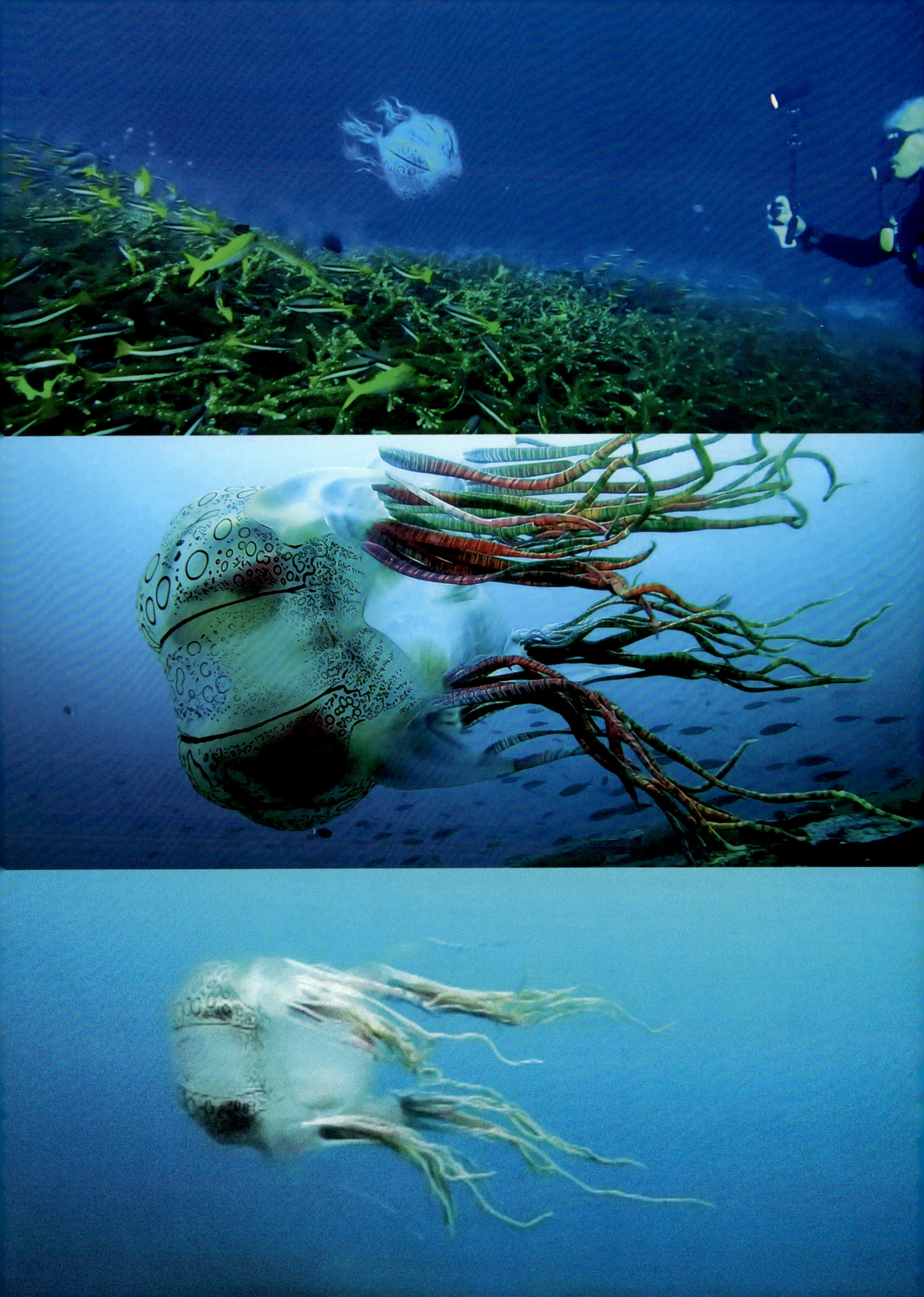

Index

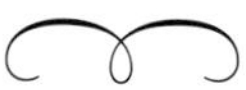

Picture credits

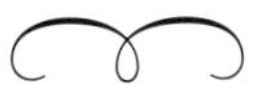

Every effort has been made to trace the copyright holders, but if any have been inadvertently overlooked, UniPress would be pleased to make the necessary arrangements at the first opportunity.

Page 2 Norbert Wu / Minden Pictures / Nature in Stock; **7** Wellcome Images; **8–9** Phillip Colla / BluePlanetArchive; **13** © Bob Hartwick; **14** © Lisa-ann Gershwin; **17** Sergio Hanquet / Nature Picture Library; **18** © Matty Smith; **21** Alexander Semenov / Science Photo Library; **22** Mark Kirkland / VWPics / BluePlanetArchive; **25** © Manuel Martínez Chacón; **26** Ethan Daniels / BluePlanetArchive; **29** Norbert Wu / Minden Pictures / Nature in Stock; **30** David Wrobel / BluePlanetArchive; **33** Franco Banfi / BluePlanetArchive; **34** © Denis Riek, www.roboastra.com; **36–37** © Lisa-ann Gershwin; **41** Elephotos / Shutterstock; **42** Nobuo Kitagawa / e-Photo / BluePlanetArchive; **45** © Justin Gilligan / OceanwideImages.com; **46** Peter Scoones / Science Photo Library; **49** Hiroya Minakuchi / Minden Pictures / Nature in Stock; **50** WaterFrame / Alamy Stock Photo; **53** Roberto Machado Noa / LightRocket via Getty Images; **54** © Callum Evans, Cape Town; **57** © Ivan Fiala/ Institute of Parasitology, Biology Centre of the Czech Academy of Sciences; **58** Alexander Semenov / Science Photo Library; **61** Jess Hadden Photo, Exmouth, WA; **62** Kondratuk Aleksei / Shutterstock; **64–65** Alexander Semenov / Science Photo Library; **69** David Wrobel / BluePlanetArchive; **70** © Matty Smith, Cardiff Heights, NSW; **73** © Denis Riek, www.roboastra.com; **74** Brandon Cole / Nature Picture Library; **77** Dray van Beeck / Shutterstock; **78** Magnus Lundgren / Nature Picture Library; **81** Marc Chamberlain / BluePlanetArchive; **82** © Smitty411 / Dreamstime.com; **85** Jeff Mondragon / BluePlanetArchive; **86** David Wrobel / BluePlanetArchive; **89** David Wrobel / BluePlanetArchive; **90** George Stoyle / Nature in Stock; **93** Tim & Alistair Lionel / Science Photo Library; **94–95** Masa Ushioda / BluePlanetArchive; **99** Alvaro E. Migotto / BluePlanetArchive; **100** SunflowerMomma / Shutterstock; **103** Top Photo Corporation / Alamy Stock Photo; **104** © Merrick Ekins; **107** Emmanuel Lattes / Alamy Stock Photo; **108** David Fleetham / Alamy Stock Photo; **111** Norbert Wu / Minden Pictures / Nature in Stock; **112** David Shale / Nature Picture Library; **115** © Steve Parish / Sealife Fine Art Photography, www.steveparish-natureconnect.com. au; **116** © Lisa-ann Gershwin; **119** © Lisa-ann Gershwin; **120–121** David Shale / Nature Picture Library; **125** © Denis Riek, www.roboastra.com; **126** © Lisa-ann Gershwin; **129** © Lisa-ann Gershwin; **130** Ferdinando Boero/University of Naples Federico II/CoNISMa / CNR-IAS/Fondazione Dohrn; **133** © Tina L Walters/Skidaway Institute of Oceanography, University of Georgia; **134** Lennart Nilsson, TT / Science Photo Library; **137** David Wrobel / BluePlanetArchive; **138** © Lisa-ann Gershwin; **141** David Shale / Nature Picture Library; **142** Ruben Duro / Science Photo Library; **145** © Denis Riek, www.roboastra.com; **146** © Gustav Paulay/ Florida Museum of Natural History; **148–149** © Lisa-ann Gershwin; **153** Mark Conlin / BluePlanetArchive; **155** Hans Leijnse / Nature in Stock; **156** David Wrobel / BluePlanetArchive; **159** © Lisa-ann Gershwin; **160** Pete Atkinson / Media Bakery; **163** Richard Herrmann / Minden Pictures / Nature in Stock; **164** Brandon Cole / Nature Picture Library; **167** Jim Greenfield / imagequestmarine. com; **168–169** Doug Perrine / BluePlanetArchive; **173** Doug Perrine / BluePlanetArchive; **174** Hiroya Minakuchi / Minden Pictures / Nature in Stock; **177** Albert Lleal / Minden Pictures / Nature in Stock; **178** David Wrobel / BluePlanetArchive; **181** © Lisa-ann Gershwin and M George; **182** Andrey Nekrasov / ImageBroker / AdobeStock; **185** Suzan Meldonian / Nite Flight Photographics; **186** © Lisa-ann Gershwin; **189** © Lisa-ann Gershwin; **190** Fabien Michenet / Biosphoto / Alamy Stock Photo; **193** Colin Marshall / Biosphoto / Alamy Stock Photo; **194–195** © Lisa-ann Gershwin; **199** © Denis Riek, www.roboastra.com; **200** © Denis Riek, www. roboastra.com; **203** © Lisa-ann Gershwin; **204** © Denis Riek, www.roboastra.com; **207** Dr. D.P. Wilson / Science Photo Library; **208** Megan Lubetkin & Dan Fornari /© Woods Hole Oceanographic Institution, WHOI-MISO; **211** © Lisa-ann Gershwin; **212** David Wrobel / BluePlanetArchive; **215** NOAA / Ocean Explorer; **216** © Peter Schuchert , Muséum d'histoire naturelle, Geneva; **219** Dorian Borcherds Scuba Ventures, Kavieng, Papua New Guinea and Alexandre Gorski, Kryivi Rih, Ukraine; **224** © Lisa-ann Gershwin.

Endpapers © Lisa-ann Gershwin

Acknowledgments

I am humbly grateful to each and every photographer whose images grace these pages and which are a celebration of the wonder and awe of jellyfish! I also owe a debt of gratitude to my editorial and production team at Unipress—Ruth Patrick, Julia Ruxton, Alex Coco, Lesley Henderson, and Kate Shanahan—for creating a work of art of which I am so blushingly proud. And I heartily thank a few close friends who reviewed text, bounced ideas back at me, and held my hand through the angsty moments (in alphabetical order): Phil and Ann Alderslade, Dain Bolwell, Peter Davie, Austra Maddox, Tom and Tina McGlynn, Pam Powell, Ben Richardson, Maria Riedl, and Pat Sankey. I love you guys to bits!

This book was conceived, designed, and produced by
UniPress Books Limited

Publisher: Nigel Browning
Commissioning editor: Kate Shanahan
Project manager: Ruth Patrick
Editor: Caroline West
Designer: Alexandre Coco
Picture researcher: Julia Ruxton
Proofreader: Robin Pridy

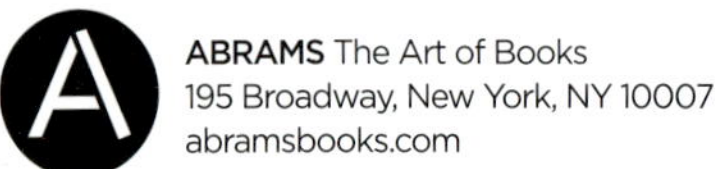

ABRAMS The Art of Books
195 Broadway, New York, NY 10007
abramsbooks.com

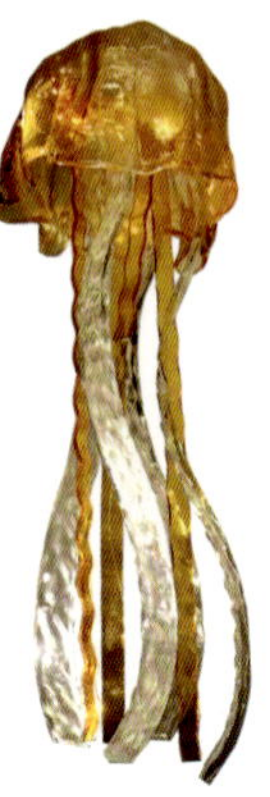

Windchime Jellies *Chironex glasseri*
The world's most venomous animal, the deadly box jellyfish (*Chironex fleckeri,* see page 12), is notorious for the number of deaths it has caused. *Chironex glasseri*, perhaps the world's glassiest animal, started as a whimsical play on words and is now known for the smiles it provokes. This slumped glass windchime was named and classified in the spoof scientific publication, the *Journal of Irreproducible Results*, thus becoming only the second fake animal species to be formally described, the first being the Loch Ness Monster. Nessie, as the monster is affectionately called, was named *Nessiteras rhombopteryx* in 1975 for conservation purposes. It was later noted that the scientific name is an anagram of "Monster hoax by Sir Peter S."

Front Cover
Ethan Daniels / Blue PlanetArchive

Back Cover
Fabien Michenet / Biosphoto / Alamy Stock Photo

Title page
Chrysaora achlyos, the so-called black sea nettle (see also page 152), was named the largest invertebrate discovered in the twentieth century and was also the first of many new species discovered by the author.